The

WOMEN'S
INFORMATION
EXCHANGE
NATIONAL
DIRECTORY

Compiled by

Deborah Brecher and Jill Lippitt

Produced by the Philip Lief Group, Inc.

AVON BOOKS ◆ NEW YORK

Every effort has been made to provide the most current mailing addresses, phone numbers, and other information about the organizations in this book. However, these facts do change and neither publisher, producer, nor compilers can be held responsible for returned mail or misdirected calls.

THE WOMEN'S INFORMATION EXCHANGE NATIONAL DIRECTORY is an original publication of Avon Books. This work has never before appeared in book form.

AVON BOOKS
A division of
The Hearst Corporation
1350 Avenue of the Americas
New York, New York 10019

Copyright © 1994 by The Philip Lief Group, Inc.
Published by arrangement with The Philip Lief Group, Inc.
Library of Congress Catalog Card Number: 93-41914
ISBN: 0-380-77570-0

Library of Congress Cataloging in Publication Data:

The Women's information exchange national directory / compiled by
   Deborah Brecher and Jill Lippitt.
      p. cm.
      1. Women—Services for—United States—Directories. 2. Women—United States—Information services—Directories. 3. Women—United States—Societies and clubs—Directories. 4. Social work with women—United States—Directories. I. Brecher, Deborah L. II. Lippitt, Jill.
HV1443.N38 1994   93-41914
362.83′8′02573—dc20   CIP

First Avon Books Trade Printing: May 1994

AVON TRADEMARK REG. U.S. PAT. OFF. AND IN OTHER COUNTRIES, MARCA REGISTRADA, HECHO EN U.S.A.

Printed in the U.S.A.

OPM   10 9 8 7 6 5 4 3 2 1

Acknowledgments

We couldn't have done this book, or our lives, without the continuous support we get from our work partner Jean Taylor Evans, who takes up our slack with good humor and the equanimity of a Buddha.

Carol Seajay of the Feminist Bookstore News was gracious enough to review our list of bookstores and women's presses, and to help us get them in order. She toils long and hard to build the feminist bookstore/print movement, and the contribution of her valuable time is deeply appreciated.

While we can't acknowledge all the groups that responded to our postcard appeal by sending us information for inclusion in the book, we do want particularly to thank the Federation of Feminist Health Centers and the National Network of Women's Funds, who provided us with the lists of their member associations so that those chapters of our book would be comprehensive.

To those groups who responded to our postcard appeal, and are not included in the book, please know that we appreciate your efforts, and even though space did not permit us to list you all, your updated information is now part of our National Women's Mailing List, and will bring you greater visibility as individuals and groups use our lists to communicate with organizations such as yours.

Our thanks also to Judy Linden, who conceived this project, convinced us to do it, then shepherded us—sometimes nipping at our heels—to its completion.

And lastly to Claudia, Addie, and Elsa—the kids who we neglected at times in order to meet our deadlines, we appreciate your capacity to fill us with joy, and promise not to take on too many more projects like this that interfere with our precious time with you.

Table of Contents

Introduction

With all the attention the media has paid to the "Year of the Woman," it's easy to conclude that there is a new surge of interest in the women's movement. This is not quite the case. Admittedly, events like the Clarence Thomas Senate confirmation hearings and Hillary Rodham Clinton's shattering of the First Lady stereotype by becoming the first president's wife to head a national health care campaign (and pump iron in the White House) have placed women in the public eye. But mainstream media's sudden spotlighting of female movers and shakers does not accurately reflect the progress of the movement, which has been marked by silent, steady expansion. A more reliable charting of the feminine crusade is mirrored in the words uttered by Ruth Bader Ginsburg, upon accepting nomination to the United States Supreme Court: "I owe this opportunity to the struggles of suffragists like Susan B. Anthony ... I stand on the shoulders of these bold women." It is only after decades of determined, collaborative effort that American women have won unprecedented positions of professional, political, and personal power.

Such a vigorous ascent to prestige can be attributed at least in part to the growing number of networks that women have created of themselves, by themselves, and for themselves. One such network is the Women's Information Exchange (WIE), a non-profit feminist organization, which we founded in 1981. Today, our mission is to reach out to women from every background, color, occupation, life-style, physical ability, political and sexual orientation, and geographical location to facilitate, through resource-sharing and communication, their empowerment in every sphere of life. To that end our first project was to create the National Women's Mailing List (NWML), a completely voluntary listing of over seventy thousand individuals and twelve thousand women's groups across the country. This book is comprised of those organizations.

How This Book Is Different From Others

The Women's Information Exchange National Directory is a comprehensive yet practical women's resource guide. We have taken care to bolster its appeal to women from every social, political, ethnic, age, economic, and occupational classification nationwide. Choosing the organizations contained in this book from our twelve-thousand-strong mailing list was no easy task, so we formulated a criteria. To be included, an organization has to be either a national organization that functions on a national level, a local organization that works on local issues of national importance, or a local group that could serve as a model for other groups in terms of service, delivery, or orientation of issues. While the bulk of organizations we've chosen operate from a feminist perspective, all entries in this book seek to reach out to a wider audience of individuals.

While embroiled in the selection process, we sought to incorporate organizations and associations that reflect the broad diversity of women's concerns. The resulting areas of interest include women's sports groups (Run, Jane, Run—Women in Sports in Indianapolis, IN), professional networks (International Women Pilots Association in Oklahoma City, OK), women's art and media groups (Women Make Movies in New York, NY), associations serving women of color (Women of Color Resource Center in Berkeley, CA), mental health services (Depression After Delivery National Self-Help Support in Morrisville, PA), and lesbian groups (Custody Action for Lesbian Mothers (CALM) in Narberth, PA), to name just a few.

Additionally, we've tailored this guide to cater to scores of specific needs and interests, including environmental groups, social events, services for the physically challenged or economically disadvantaged, older women's services, and foundations and funding sources. The net result is a book encyclopedic in scope; one that blends highly visible national organizations with less familiar but strong and viable grassroots groups from coast to coast.

How to Use This Book

When searching for information on a specific topic of interest, first check the Table of Contents, where subject categories are listed in alphabetical order. We've included subcategories in some of the broader sections (Health Organizations, for example) to help speed up your search. Within each category and subcategory you will find several organizations listed that should be able to respond to your need. When it came to large national women's organizations (like the Young Women's Christian Association, the American Association of University Women, and Planned Parenthood), we listed the national headquarters rather than their individual locations (which in the case of the YWCA totalled about four thousand). However, we did choose to list certain local programs individually because they're particularly noteworthy (like the Displaced Homemakers' Programs of certain YWCAs). Some of the entries are cross-referenced to help you locate other relevant sources expeditiously. Each entry contains the group's name and mailing address. We tried to include phone numbers whenever possible. Many times no phone number appears. In that case you'll need to write to the particular women's organization for more information. Some grass-roots local women's groups don't have offices and therefore use post office boxes. If you have a specific association in mind, check the index located at the back of the book. Here you'll find an alphabetical listing of all the organizations.

We hope you find *The Women's Information Exchange National Directory* to be an all-encompassing volume of unprecedented breadth and diversity, one that spans the spectrum of need and want, one that will, for instance, place fledgling entrepreneurs in touch with appropriate legal and economic corporations or provide women thinking of pursuing second careers with access to seminars, workshops, and financing groups, as well as contacts in their fields of interest. Ultimately, we hope this book will provide a multitude of opportunities for communication among women all over the country.

On a closing note, we wish to impress upon our readers that this guide is by no means exhaustive. We welcome any suggestions for future additional entries—our way of actively encouraging our readers to expand the already thriving community of women's networks.

Happy hunting!

JILL LIPPITT & DEBORAH BRECHER

❑ Art and Media

ART ASSOCIATIONS, SPONSORS, AND PRODUCERS

Artistas Indigenas
48 Shattuck Sq.
Berkeley, CA 94704
(510) 527-1492

Offers activities and services to women artists and art patrons from the American and Pacific islands. Sponsors annual traveling exhibitions. See also Organizations Representing Women of Color.

Central Wisconsin Women's Caucus for Art
P. O. Box 7441
Madison, WI 53707-7441

An organization of Wisconsin women artists and art patrons. Sponsors activities to promote and exhibit art and offers general art education and appreciation activities to the public.

Coalition of Women's Art Organizations
123 E Beutel Rd.
Port Washington, WI 53074-1103
(414) 284-4458

A national network of art professionals and organizations that lobbies to advance women in the arts. Calls for the complete equality of women and seeks to reject or accept legislation on both state and national levels to meet this goal. See also Women's Rights.

International Registry for Religious Women Artists
Liturgical Arts Resource Center
Marylhurst, OR 97036
(503) 697-3097

Sponsors exhibits, festivals, and art education activities. Focuses on art by religious women and women's art with religious themes. See also Religious and Spiritual Groups.

Korean American Women Artists and Writers Association
447 7th Ave., #4
San Francisco, CA 94118-3011

Holds conferences, exhibits, and activities. Works to promote and improve the status of women in these fields. See also Organizations Representing Women of Color.

1

National Association of Women Artists, Incorporated
41 Union Square West, Rm. 906
New York, NY 10003
(212) 675-1616

An art association for women in the fine arts. Seeks exhibition space and provides free cultural and educational programs to the community. See also Educational Services and Organizations.

National Museum of Women in the Arts
Library and Research Center
1250 New York Ave. NW
Washington, D. C. 20036
(202) 783-5000

Offers research activities for those interested in women in arts. Specializes in visual art. See also Educational Services and Organizations.

New Mexico Women in the Arts
Univ. of New Mexico
Dept. of Art and Art History
Albuquerque, NM 87131-1401
(505) 277-0111

Promotes and supports women artists in New Mexico. Offers educational opportunities to artists.

New York Feminist Art Institute
91 Franklin St.
New York, NY 10013
(212) 219-9590

A school and resource center for women in the arts. Offers classes, workshops, events, exhibitions, and

performances. Rents studio space to artists. See also Educational Services and Organizations.

Oregon Committee of the National Museum of Women in the Arts
P. O. Box 855
Portland, OR 97207-0855

Promotes public awareness and appreciation of the arts in Oregon.

Oregon Women's Caucus for Arts
605 SE 18th
Portland, OR 97214-2743

Promotes appreciation of the arts in Oregon. Offers public education and workshops.

Southwestern University Center for Texas Women in the Arts
Georgetown, TX 78626
(512) 863-6511;
Fax: (512) 863-5788

Promotes and supports Texas women in the fields of visual and performing arts.

Through the Flower
P. O. Box 8138
Santa Fe, NM 87504
(505) 982-8112;
Fax: (505) 989-8356

A nonprofit arts organization established to support Judy Chicago's The Dinner Party, *a multimedia work that presents a symbolic history of women in Western civilization. Projects include ceramics, china painting, and needlework created as tributes to women's achievements.*

Women in the Arts
Univ. School of Music
Ann Arbor, MI 48109
(313) 764-0594

An organization of individuals interested in promoting and supporting women's contributions to the arts. Includes fields of music, dance, art, and literature. Presents recitals, panel discussions, and workshops.

Women in the Arts Foundation
1175 York Ave., Apt. 2G
New York, NY 10021
(212) 751-1915

An organization of women artists and women interested in the arts working to overcome discrimination against women artists and to arrange exhibits of the work of women artists. Publishes a newsletter and bulletin. See also Women's Rights.

Women's Art Registry of Minnesota
2402 University Ave. W
St. Paul, MN 55114
(612) 649-0059

Promotes women artists through education, exhibition, mentorship, and networking. Through the arts, seeks to make the presence of women's voice and vision a significant influence in community and society.

Women's Caucus for Art
Moore College for Art
20th and The Parkway
Philadelphia, PA 19103
(215) 854-0922

Works on public education about visual art, develops unbiased approaches to art curricula, and supports and lobbies for women artists. Sponsors conferences, awards ceremonies, exhibitions, and meetings. See also Educational Services and Organizations.

Women's Collective Art Space
2402 University Ave. W, 2nd Fl.
St. Paul, MN 54114
(612) 649-0059

Works to improve the visibility of women artists. Offers public education on the historical and contemporary contributions of women artists. Provides exhibition space, houses a slide registry, and offers educational packages about women artists. See also Women's History.

Women's Interart Center
549 W 52nd St.
New York, NY 10019
(212) 246-1050

A multiart organization that provides a place for women artists to work on art, learn new skills, and offer support to each other. Produces theater, film, video, and exhibition events in New York City galleries.

ARTS AND CRAFTS

Crystal Mist Glass Carving
P. O. Box 186
Guffey, CO 80820
(719) 689-2326

Creates and sells sand-carved and stained glass by women. Glass designs appear on lamps, mugs, glasses, jewelry boxes, and vases. Catalog available.

Enterprising Women
2425 Diamond St.
Sellerville, PA 18960
(215) 822-9208

A designer and distributor of original woodcut editions and poster reproductions of historic, contemporary, and imaginary women. Also carries women's greeting cards.

Jane Iris Designs
P. O. Box 608
Graton, CA 95444
(707) 823-5687;
Fax: (707) 823-8764

Designs and manufactures feminist jewelry. Designs are created to foster personal empowerment and planetary transformation through the use of ancient female imagery.

Lielin-West
P. O. Box 733
Benicia, CA 94510
(707) 745-9000

Creates and sells lesbian and feminist jewelry. Wholesale and retail catalogs available.

Star River Productions, Incorporated
The Great Goddess Collection
P. O. Box 7754
North Brunswick, NJ 08902
(908) 247-9875

Publishes a gift catalog of the Great Goddess Collection. The collection consists of reproductions of ancient art intended to celebrate, nurture, and empower women's lives. The catalog also includes women's books and jewelry.

Willow Moon Designs
P. O. Box 271
Rt. 2 Box 131-G
Elkins, AR 72727

A women's store that sells and makes women's clothing and gifts. Specializes in hand-dyed cotton clothing, silkscreens, and women's notecards.

Wise Women, Incorporated
P. O. Box 356
Kennebunk, ME 04043
(207) 985-2534

A designer and distributor of women's clothing. Specializes in astrological designs and t-shirts.

Womancrafts
376 Commercial
Box 190
Provincetown, MA 02657
(508) 487-2501

A shop and gallery that exhibits and sells art and crafts by women. Mail ordering is available.

Womancrafts West
1007 ½ Valencia St.
San Francisco, CA 94110
(415) 648-2020

A retail gallery and store featuring

the works of several hundred women artists and craftsworkers.

Womanwild: Treasures by Women
5237 N Clark St.
Chicago, IL 60640
(312) 878-8300

A gift store and gallery featuring women's arts and crafts.

FESTIVALS AND EVENTS

Campfest
RR5 Box 185
Franklinville, NJ 08322
(609) 694-2037

An organization that sponsors an annual women's music festival on Memorial Day weekend.

Country Women's Festival
P.O. Box 916
Hopland, CA 95449
(707) 744-1648

An annual weekend camping festival for women. Features women musicians, poets, and comedians, as well as games, spiritual events, and women's rituals.

East Coast Lesbian Festival
279 Lester Ave.
Oakland, CA 94606
(510) 763-9228

A festival of lesbian culture, featuring music, speakers, dance, and more.

Gulf Coast Womyn's Festival and Spirit Fest
1806 Curcor Dr.
Gulfport, MS 39507
(601) 896-3196

Gulf Coast Womyn's Festival is a music, crafts, political, and friendship gathering open to all women. Spirit Fest is a spirituality, music, crafts, and friendship retreat.

Michigan Womyn's Music Festival
P. O. Box 22
Walhalla, MI 49458
(616) 757-4766

A six-day women's camping event and music festival. Annual event draws thousands of women from the United States, Canada, and worldwide.

National Women's Music Festival
P. O. Box 1427
Indianapolis, IN 46206
(317) 923-5574

Annual four-day women's music festival held the weekend after Memorial Day on the campus of Indiana University. Includes concerts, dances, theater presentations, art exhibits, and workshops, lectures, and networking sessions.

New England Women's Musical Retreat
P. O. Box 217
New Haven, CT 06513
(203) 468-8505

An annual festival of women's music and culture.

Northampton Lesbian Festival
160 Main St.
Northampton, MA 01060

An annual festival of lesbian music and culture.

RhythmFest
957 N Highland Ave. NE
Atlanta, GA 30306
(404) 873-1551

A festival featuring women's music, art, comedy, and culture.

Richmond Women's Festival
P. O. Box 7216
Richmond, VA 23221
(804) 379-6422

A festival to affirm lesbians and feminists.

Sisterfire Festival
1475 Harvard St. NW
Washington, DC 20009
(202) 234-9308

An annual festival of multicultural women's music.

Sisterspace Pocono Weekend
351 S 47 St., #B-101
Philadelphia, PA 19143
(215) 476-2424

An opportunity for women to come together to enjoy women's music, comedy, crafts, and community.

Southern Women's Music Festival
West Coast Women's Music Festival
15842 Chase St.
Sepulveda, CA 91343
(818) 893-4075

Annual festival with several thousand participants. Featuring the major performers of women's music and comedy.

Virginia Women's Music Festival
Rte. 2, Box 1096
Kents Stone, VA 23084

Music, comedy, and more.

WIMINFEST
P. O. Box 80204
Albuquerque, NM 87105

A women's production company responsible for producing WIMIN-FEST every year over Memorial Day weekend, in addition to other concert and cultural events for women. WIMINFEST is a three-day music, arts, and performance festival for lesbian women.

**Woman Source,
Annual Gathering**
P. O. Box 335
Ashland, OR 97520
(503) 482-2026

*Annual gathering of about 100
women that usually takes place in
July. A variety of workshops are offered that change from year to year.*

FILM, RADIO, AND TELEVISION

**American Federation of
Television and Radio Artists**
National Women's Division
260 Madison Ave.
New York, NY 10016
(212) 532-0800

*Focuses on issues and concerns of
women in television and radio, including employment and upgrading
the image of women in the media.
See also Professional and Business
Associations and Networks.*

**American Film Institute
Directing Workshop
for Women**
2021 N Western Ave.
P. O. Box 27999
Los Angeles, CA 90027
(213) 856-7722

*An intensive film workshop for
midcareer professional women in
the media arts. Geared for women
who are looking for the opportunity
to direct a narrative film. Final
project is one half-hour video. See
also Work, Union, and Career Services.*

**American Women in Radio and
Television**
1101 Connecticut Ave. NW, Ste. 700
Washington, DC 20036
(202) 429-5102;
Fax: (202) 223-4579

*A professional membership organi-
zation that advances women in elec-
tronic media fields. Sponsors
competitions and award ceremonies
and offers resource listings and publications. Has forty-five chapters.*

Cambridge Documentary Films
P. O. Box 385
Cambridge, MA 02139
(617) 354-3677;
Fax: (617) 492-7653

*Produces alternative media re-
sources for organizations working
for social change. Films challenge
audiences to think and act on social issues. Topics include battered
women, media images of women,
health hazards, rape, and gay and
lesbian issues.*

**Challenging Media
Images of Women.**
See Women's Rights.

Charis Video
P. O. Box 797
Brooklyn, NY 11231
(718) 855-4458

Offers rental of lesbian videos through the mail. Videos include stories, erotica, documentaries, and performance. Also distributes several lesbian humor and lesbian life-style videos to women's and gay bookstores.

Dancing Cane Productions
Box 5540
Berkeley, CA 94705
(510) 547-7544

Produces videos by and for women, especially on health and travel issues.

**Disabled Women's
Theatre Project**
462 Broadway, Ste. 500
New York, NY 10013
(212) 925-0606;
Fax: (212) 925-2052

Offers a videotape of a series of skits and performances by the Disabled Women's Theatre Project. Performances convey the outrageous, absurd, funny, painful, and dramatic moments in disabled women's lives. Also offers a tape featuring profiles of women with disabilities working to overcome discrimination.

**International Women's
Media Project**
2033 M St. NW, Ste. 900
Washington, DC 20036
(202) 233-0030

Works to establish international cross-cultural exchange between women working in print, television, radio, and other communications media. Publishes a quarterly newsletter. See also Global Feminism and World Peace.

Iris Films
Box 5353
Berkeley, CA 94705
(510) 845-5414;
Fax: (510) 658-4783

A nonprofit organization that produces films and videos dedicated to social justice issues. See also Women's Rights.

Ishtar Films
6253 Hollywood Blvd., Ste. 1107
Hollywood, CA 90028
(213) 461-1560

Production and distribution company whose interest is in films, videos, and music about women, women's issues, and history. Focuses on educating women in film and video production and marketing, and offers seminars, concerts, and screenings. See also Women's History.

Mediawatch
P. O. Box 618
Santa Cruz, CA 95061
(408) 423-6355

A nonprofit organization and newsletter dedicated to improving the image of women in the media.

Moonforce Media
P. O. Box 2934
Washington, DC 20013
(301) 585-8886;
Fax: (301) 585-8886

A nonprofit organization that produces videos to fight heterosexism and sexism. Films cover issues such as social justice, gay and lesbian rights, sexual harassment, and homosexuality.

Newist
Cesa *7 Telecommunications
IS1110, Univ. of Wisconsin
Green Bay, WI 54311
(414) 465-2599;
Fax: (414) 465-2576

Produces videos of social concern. Topics include feminism, poverty, adolescent pregnancy, homelessness, divorce, AIDS, drug abuse, alcoholism, and homosexuality.

Screen Actors Guild
National Women's Conference Committee
1515 Broadway, 44th Fl.
New York, NY 10036-8901
(212) 827-1433;
Fax: (212) 944-6774

Seeks equity in all facets of work. Also advocates the positive portrayal of women in videos, film, television, and commercials. Activities are directed toward female members of the guild. See also Professional and Business Associations and Networks.

Stuntwomen's Association of Motion Pictures
202 Vance
Pacific Palisades, CA 90272
(213) 462-1605

An organization of stunt actresses and stunt coordinators. Offers meetings and networking opportunities. See also Professional and Business Associations and Networks.

Tri-Image Productions
P. O. Box 50145
Long Beach, CA 90815
(310) 429-4802;
Fax: (310) 425-6494

A producer and distributor of sensual, erotic, and politically correct lesbian videos. Promotes and cultivates the lives and loves of lesbians.

Wolfe Video
P. O. Box 64
New Almaden, CA 95042
(408) 268-6782;
Fax: (408) 268-9449

A video production and distribution company. Videos are about women's culture, ideas, and talents, with emphasis on lesbian culture.

Women in Film
6464 Sunset Blvd., Ste. 530
Hollywood, CA 90028
(213) 463-6040;
Fax: (213) 463-0963

Supports and networks women in the film and television industry. Sponsors screenings, workshops, lectures, and speakers. Offers financial assistance to women for education, research, and completion of film projects.

Women Make Movies
462 Broadway, Ste. 500
New York, NY 10013
(212) 925-0606;
Fax: (212) 925-2052

National feminist media arts organization that produces, promotes, distributes, and exhibits films and videotapes by and about women. The organization has a collection of more than three hundred titles.

Women of the Motion Picture Industry, International
P. O. Box 900
Beverly Hills, CA 90213
(213) 203-4083

A federation of clubs of women employed in the production, distribution, and exhibition of motion pictures for theaters and television. Presents awards, conducts charitable programs, and holds conferences. See also Professional and Business Associations and Networks.

Women's Independent Film Exchange
50 W 96th St.
New York, NY 10025
(212) 749-1250

An organization of women freelancers in the film industry. Conducts research and disseminates profiles of pioneer women filmmakers. Sponsors screenings in libraries, schools, and museums.

MUSIC

American Musicological Society
Committee on the Status of Women
Dept. of Music
Middlebury College
Middlebury, VT 05753
(802) 388-3711

Holds meetings at the annual conference to discuss concerns of women in musicology. Focuses on issues of career status and development, family, and research.

American Women Composers, Incorporated
1690 36th St. NW, Ste. 409
Washington, DC 20007
(202) 342-8179

Works to support and promote female composers and to network these women. Offers financial support, workshops, and performances. See also Professional and Business Associations and Networks.

Apple Island Productions
849 E. Washington Ave.
Madison, WI 53703
(608) 258-9777

Produces concerts in Madison.

Artemis Singers
Box 578296
Chicago, IL 60657
(312) 764-4465

An organization of lesbians in the Chicago area interested in performing choral music.

Artemis Sisters Production
P. O. Box 337
Morgantown, WV 26507
(304) 599-4623

A production agency that organizes and promotes women musicians, poets, and storytellers. Helps give local artists stage opportunities.

Association of Women's Music and Culture
2124 Kittredge St., #104
Berkeley, CA 94704
(707) 829-4761

A women's organization created to foster, encourage, and empower women's music and culture through networking, education, support, and services. Works to build a diverse, multicultural, and international women's community and cultural network.

Calliope Women's Chorus
3211 35th Ave. S
Minneapolis, MN 55406-2115

An organization of women in Minneapolis who promote and perform choral music.

Carolsdatter Productions
221-C Dodge Ave.
Evanston, IL 60202
(708) 864-0737

Small independent record label that has released five albums of original

songs by Kristin Lewis. Albums include feminist and children's songs.

Harmony Network
P. O. Box 2550
Guerneville, CA 95446
(707) 869-0989

A feminist booking and production company. Also offers classes and individual consultations on promotions and production of feminist and new-age work.

Hurricane Productions
P. O. Box 71268
Milwaukee, WI 53211
(414) 265-4049

Produces women's music events in the Milwaukee region.

Institute for the Musical Arts
P. O. Box 253
Bodega, CA 94922
(707) 876-3004

Promotes and sponsors women's music and cultural events.

International Congress on Women in Music
P. O. Box 12164
La Crescenta, CA 91224-0864
(818) 248-1249

An organization of musicologists, scholars in women's studies, performers, composers, and feminist activists worldwide. Conducts performances, panels, and workshops to encourage women in music. See also Global Feminism and World Peace.

International Council of Tradition Music
Music and Gender Study Group
Hunter College Dept. of Music
695 Park Ave.
New York, NY 10021
(212) 772-5020

Conducts and reports research on women and music worldwide. See also Global Feminism and World Peace; Educational Services and Organizations.

International Institute for the Study of Women in Music
California State Univ.
Music Dept.
Northridge, CA 91330
(818) 885-3015

Focuses on arts, library collections, and women in music.

International League of Women Composers
670 Southshore Rd.
Three Mile Bay, NY 13693
(315) 649-5086

Provides information for and about women composers and promotes opportunities for women composers. Publishes a newsletter and sponsors a contest for student women composers.

Jasmine Journey Records
P. O. Box 86695
Phoenix, AZ 85080
(602) 582-4196

A production and sales organization offering music that affirms women. Promotes records and concerts.

Labrys Productions
P. O. Box 494
Somerville, NJ 08876

Brings cultural events to the lesbian community of New Jersey.

Ladyslipper
P. O. Box 3124
Durham, NC 27715
(919) 683-1570;
Fax: (919) 682-5601

Seeks to increase awareness of women's music. Offers information on recordings by female musicians, writers, and composers. Also offers numerous publications, songbooks, reviews, and the most comprehensive catalog available of women's music recordings.

Lea Lawson Productions
P. O. Box 671
Santa Cruz, CA 95061
(408) 426-7828

Promotes feminist, political, progressive, and lesbian music in Santa Cruz.

Libana: A Woman's Chorus
P. O. Box 530
Cambridge, MA 02140
(401) 247-2168

An a cappella *group singing women's world music. Noted for their rounds, chants, and ritual music. Several cassettes available.*

Los Angeles Women in Music
6030 Wilshire Blvd., Ste. 303
Los Angeles, CA 90048-4194

An organization for women in the music industry. Promotes professional achievement and advancement. See also Professional and Business Associations and Networks.

Los Angeles Women's Community Chorus
11462 Patom Dr.
Culver City, CA 90230-5339

Promotes appreciation and performance of women's choral music in the Los Angeles area.

Moonbear Productions
P. O. Box 135
Sagle, ID 83860
(208) 265-2200

Produces music and cultural events.

Musica Femina
P. O. Box 15121
Portland, OR 97215
(503) 233-1206

A flute-guitar duo that performs classical and contemporary music by women composers and lesbian and gay composers. The duo has toured nationally and has released four tapes.

Olivia Records
4400 Market St.
Oakland, CA 94608
(510) 655-0364

The oldest women's recording company. Features albums, CDs, and cassettes of numerous feminist performers, including Chris Williamson, Teresa Trull, Lucie Blue Trembleay, and more. Write for catalog.

Oregon Symphony Women's Association
711 SW Alder, #210
Portland, OR 97205
(503) 223-8455

Works to promote and support women in the Oregon Symphony.

Peaceful Women
Rte. 1, Box 281
Bayfield, WI 54814
(715) 779-3422

A four-member women's a cappella group. Their music, which includes folk, original, and spiritual songs, reflects a commitment to women, social justice, and the environment.

Pleiades Records
P. O. Box 7217
Berkeley, CA 94707
(510) 527-9610;
Fax: (510) 527-0503

A women- owned and operated recording company that produces and distributes vocal and piano instrumental music.

Portsmouth Women's Chorus
P. O. Box 234
Portsmouth, NH 03802-0234

A group of women interested in vocal music. Presents concerts in southern Maine and coastal areas of New Hampshire.

Rainbow Dancer Productions
P. O. Box 5881
Bellingham, WA 98227
(206) 733-8855

Private production company that has released four albums of feminist songwriter and performer Linda Allen. Her songs celebrate women's history and tell stories of women's realities, parenting, relationships, and social justice.

Redwood Records
P. O. Box 10408
Oakland, CA 94610
(310) 835-1445;
Fax: (310) 835-1459

Produces recordings to help build alliances between socially involved artists, women's organizations, and cultural organizations. Music addresses contemporary social issues and cross-cultural work.

Rosetta Records, Incorporated
115 W 16th St., #267
New York, NY 10011
(212) 243-3583

An independent company that retrieves lost or forgotten women's music. Specializes in blues music.

Sacramento Women's Chorus
P. O. Box 92069
Davis, CA 95617-9010

Performs vocal music.

Seattle Women's Ensemble
P. O. Box 31462
Seattle, WA 98103

Performs women's music in the Seattle area.

Snake & Snake Productions
Rte. 3 Box 165
Durham, NC 27713

Producers of women's music and cultural events in the Durham area.

Stray Cat Productions
846 Westmoreland Ave.
Syracuse, NY 13210
(315) 474-6316

Local producer of women's concerts.

Tongue in Chic Productions
1202 E Pike, #712
Seattle, WA 98122
(206) 325-1920

Produces women's music and cultural events in the Seattle area.

Tsunami Records
P. O. Box 42282
Tucson, AZ 85733
(602) 325-7828

Records and distributes women's music. Carries t-shirts and bumper stickers related to music. Publishes an international guide to periodicals of interest to feminists, lesbians, and gay men and a directory of radio stations that feature women's music.

Whyscrack Records/Making Light Productions
P. O. Box 41
Provincetown, MA 02657
(508) 487-0301

Feminist comedy recordings by Kate Clinton, outrageous lesbian humorist.

Wild Iris Productions, Incorporated
P. O. Box 17
West Buxton, ME 04093
(207) 247-3461;
Fax: (207) 929-3407

Organizes, promotes, and produces women's music concerts, dances, and other events.

Womansource
P. O. Box 335
Ashland, OR 97520
(503) 482-2026

A feminist organization that sponsors and supports women performers. The organization holds monthly performances and sponsors an annual weekend gathering in the mountains for one hundred and fifty women.

Women Band Directors National Association
345 Overlook Dr.
West Lafayette, IN 47906
(317) 463-1738

Works to improve music education and provide opportunities for women band directors to exchange ideas, methods, and information. Publishes a quarterly newsletter.

See also Professional and Business Associations and Networks.

Women's Jazz Festival
P. O. Box 22321
Kansas City, MO 64113
(913) 631-9511

Promotes and supports women jazz artists and creates a general interest in jazz. Conducts workshops, sponsors Jazz Month, sponsors jam sessions, and holds a lecture and film series. See also Art and Media: Festivals and Events.

Women's Music Archives
208 Wildflower Ln.
Fairfield, CT 06430
(203) 255-1348

Gathers, preserves, and shares women's music memorabilia. Collections include records and tapes, reference books, concert programs, photographs, and so on. See also Women's History.

Women's Philharmonic
330 Townsend, #218
San Francisco, CA 94107
(415) 543-2297;
Fax: (415) 543-3244

A professional orchestra dedicated to the promotion of women composers, conductors, and performers. Also offers a National Women Composers Resource Center.

THEATER

Association for Theatre in Higher Education
Women and Theatre Program
Bowling Green State Univ.
Bowling Green, OH 43403
(419) 372-6831

Promotes the study of women in theater, as well as the way women are presented in theatrical productions. Offers programs, awards, and meetings. See also Educational Services and Organizations; Women's Centers.

Professional Older Women's Theatre Project
153 Mercer St., 2nd Fl.
New York, NY 10012

Promotes and supports older women in the theater arts. See also Special Interests: Older Women's Services.

Theater, T♀♀
21 Valley View Dr.
Amherst, MA 01002
(413) 256-8397

A feminist theater group that produces plays by and for women about women's lives. Accepts scripts, usually about lesbian themes, with all-female casts.

Women's One World Cafe
59 E 4th St.
New York, NY 10003
(212) 460-8967

A theater specializing in productions by and for lesbians. Members help with all aspects of production.

Women's Project and Productions
7 W 63rd St.
New York, NY 10023
(212) 873-3040;
Fax: (212) 873-3788

Provides a place for women in theater arts to work, offers mature artists the opportunity to see their work produced, and offers younger artists the chance to develop their craft. Sponsors play readings and play performances.

Word of Mouth Women's Theater
P. O. Box 1175
Austin, TX 78767
(512) 459-0364

A feminist theater group that performs plays with feminist themes.

Wry Crips Disabled Women's Theater
P. O. Box 21474
Oakland, CA 94620
(510) 601-5819

Women with disabilities reading scripts from their own lives.

VISUAL ART, GALLERIES, AND MUSEUMS

A. I. R. Gallery
63 Crosby St.
New York, NY 10012
(212) 966-0799

A nonprofit cooperative gallery for women artists. Publishes exhibition catalogs.

Arc Gallery
1040 W Huron St.
Chicago, IL 60622
(312) 733-2787

A nonprofit women's cooperative art gallery.

ArtTable
301 E 57th St.
New York, NY 10022
(212) 593-6310;
Fax: (212) 715-1507

A national membership organization for women who are leaders in the visual arts. Provides a forum for the exchange of ideas and information, identifies and supports policies and programs that promote the visual arts, and increases access to the field through programs of mentoring and education.

The Collective Gallery
1626 SW Central Park
Topeka, KS 66604
(913) 234-4254

A cooperative art gallery for women.

Front Range/Women in the Visual Arts
400 Brook Cir.
Jamestown Star Rte.
Boulder, CO 80302
(303) 443-6224

Exhibits the work of artists in Boulder. Holds monthly meetings.

Gallery 25
1936 Echo St.
Fresno, CA 93704
(209) 266-6244

A storefront cooperative gallery that sponsors group and solo shows for up to twenty-five women artists.

Hera Women's Cooperative Art Gallery
P. O. Box 336
Wakefield, RI 02880
(401) 789-1488

A professional artists' gallery that encourages and exhibits a culturally diverse range of visual artists, particularly women and new artists.

In Her Image
3208 SE Hawthorne
Portland, OR 97214
(503) 231-3726

Features feminist visual art.

Lesbian Visual Artists
3543 18th St., #5
San Francisco, CA 94110
(415) 821-2975

A multicultural arts organization dedicated to the promotion of and networking among lesbian visual artists. Works for the inclusion of visual artists in the activist dialogue. Houses a member slide registry and produces an annual newsletter, exhibitions, and events. See also Art and Media.

National Museum of Women in the Arts
1250 New York Ave. NW
Washington, DC 20005
(202) 783-5000;
Fax: (202) 393-3235

Exhibits paintings, sculptures, prints, photographs, and book art by women. Also the location of the National Museum of Women in the Arts Library and Research Center.

New Art Center
6925 Willow St. NW
Washington, DC 20016
(202) 291-2999

A women's art center and gallery.

New York Society of Women Artists
450 West End Ave.
New York, NY 10024
(212) 877-1902

Holds annual group exhibition.

San Francisco Women Artists
370 Hayes St.
San Francisco, CA 94102
(415) 552-7392

A nonprofit membership organization dedicated to encouraging and promoting the work of women artists. Gallery features twelve annual exhibitions, including the Emerging Artists Show, an area-wide competition. Also features a rental program, sponsors art lectures, critiques, and studio visits, and publishes a monthly bulletin.

Soho Twenty
469 Broome St.
New York, NY 10013
(212) 226-4167

Provides gallery space to members. Sponsors dance performances, poetry readings, slide shows, and invitational exhibitions.

Webb House Museum
303 Granville St.
Newark, OH 43055
(614) 345-8540

Exhibits a collection of artwork from women of Ohio. Sponsors two annual exhibits.

Women & Their Work
1137 W 6th St.
Austin, TX 78703
(512) 477-1064;
Fax: (512) 477-1090

Promotes women artists in visual art, dance, music, theater, literature, and film. Women & Their Work gallery exhibits women's painting, sculpture, photography, crafts, and works on paper. Sponsors touring exhibitions and education and outreach programs.

❏ Booksellers

Women's bookstores primarily focus on feminist works and carry books by and about women. Most also carry multicultural, alternative, lesbian, and gay titles. In addition to reading materials, many bookstores sell women's jewelry, music, posters, art, and videos. Check local stores to find out about classes, workshops, newsletters, or calendars of events. Also included in this list are general bookstores or gay and lesbian bookstores that have strong feminist sections. These are marked by an asterisk (*).

Abaton Books
2525 Pikes Peak, Ste. C
Colorado Springs, CO 80904
(719) 475-2508

Alaska Women's Bookstore
2440 E Tudor Rd., No. 304
Anchorage, AK 99507
(907) 562-4716

Amazon Bookstore
1612 Harmon Pl.
Minneapolis, MN 55403
(612) 338-6560;
Fax: (612) 371-9233

Antigone Books
600 N 4th Ave.
Tucson, AZ 85705
(805) 965-5477

Aquarius Books
116 N Grant St.
Bloomington, IN 47408
(812) 336-0988

Aradia Bookstore
116 W Cottage
Flagstaff, AZ 86002

Arbor Moon Feminist Bookstore
2017 O St.
Lincoln, NE 68508
(402) 477-5666

Athena's Attic
108 Austin St.
Danton, TX 76201
(817) 565-9755

* Author, Author for the
Serious Reader
89 Broadway Roundout
Kingston, NY 12401
(914) 339-1883

* Barbara's Bookshop
330 N Broadway
Chicago, IL 60657
(312) 477-0411

* Barbara's Bookshop
1110 W Lake St.
Oak Park, IL 60301
(708) 848-9140

Barbara Walzer Books
P. O. Box 2536
Providence, RI 02906
(401) 785-2277

* Barjon's
2718 Third Ave.
Billings, MT 59101
(406) 252-4398

* Bay Bridge Books
901 Broadway
Oakland, CA
(415) 835-5845

* Beebo's Books
925 Spruce St.
Louisville, CO 80027
(303) 666-4914

* Beyond the Closet Bookstore
1501 Belmont Ave.
Seattle, WA 98122
(206) 322-4609

* Black Books Plus
702 Amsterdam Ave.
New York, NY 10025
(212) 749-9632

Bloodroot Restaurant and
Feminist Bookstore
85 Ferris St.
Bridgeport, CT 06605
(203) 576-9168

Blue Earth
8215 SE 13th Ave.
Portland, OR 97202
(503) 234-2224

Bluestocking Books
829 Gervals St.
Columbia, SC 29201
(803) 929-0114

Book Gallery
19 W Mechanic St.
New Hope, PA 18938
(215) 862-5110

Book Garden
2625 E 12th Ave.
Denver, CO 80206
(303) 399-2004

* Booklegger
402 E 2nd St.
Eureka, CA 95501
(707) 445-1344

* Books Etc.
2410 W Ave. N
San Angelo, TX 76904
(915) 942-1544

Book Woman
324 E Sixth St.
Austin, TX 78701
(512) 472-2785

* Borealis Bookstore
113 N Aurora St.
Ithaca, NY 14850
(607) 272-7752

Bread and Roses Books
13812 Ventura Blvd.
Sherman Oaks, CA 91423
(818) 986-5376

* Bright Pink Literature
4637 Paradise Rd.
Las Vegas, NV 89109
(702) 737-7780

Brigit Books
3434 4th St. N, #5
St. Petersburg, FL 33704
(813) 522-5775

* A Brother's Touch
2327 Hennepin
Minneapolis, MN 55405
(612) 377-6279

* Castro Kiosk
554 Castro St.
San Francisco, CA
(415) 431-1003

Category Six Books
1029 E 11th Ave.
Denver, CO 80218
(303) 832-6263

Celebration
108 W 43rd
Austin, TX 78701
(512) 472-2785

Charis Books and More
419 Moreland Ave. NE
Atlanta, GA 30307
(404) 524-0304

* Chelsea Books
2501 E Broadway
Long Beach, CA 90803
(310) 434-2220

Choices Books and Music
913 De La Vina
Santa Barbara, CA 93101
(805) 965-5477

* Chosen Books
120 W 4th St.
Royal Oak, MI 48067
(313) 864-0485

* Circus of Books
4001 Sunset Blvd.
Los Angeles, CA 90029
(213) 656-7199

Clairelight Books
519 Mendocino
Santa Rosa, CA 95401
(707) 575-8879;
Fax: (707) 575-1524

* The Closet
25 N Prince St.
Lancaster, PA 17603
(717) 399-8818

Common Language Bookstore
214 S Fourth Ave.
Ann Arbor, MI 48104
(313) 663-0036

* **Congress Avenue Booksellers**
718 Congress Ave.
Austin, TX 78701
(512) 478-1157

Crazy Ladies Bookstore
4039 Hamilton Ave.
Cincinnati, OH 45223
(513) 541-4198

Crone's Harvest
761 Centre St.
Jamaica Plain, MA 02130
(617) 983-9530

Crossroads Market
3930 Cedar Springs Rd.
Dallas, TX 75219
(214) 521-8919

* **Crystal Works**
301 N St.
Pittsfield, MA 01201
(413) 442-5532

* **Cunningham and Co. Books**
188 State St.
Portland, ME 04102
(207) 775-2246

* **Curious Times**
4008-D Cedar Springs Rd.
Dallas, TX 75219
(214) 528-4087

* **Dangerous Ideas, Inc.**
2416 Wilton Dr.
Ft. Lauderdale, FL 33305
(305) 753-2969

* **Different Drummer Bookshop**
1027 N Coast Hwy., Ste. A
Laguna Beach, CA 92657
(714) 497-6699

* **Different Light**
4014 Santa Monica Blvd.
Hollywood, CA 90029
(213) 668-0629

* **Different Light**
548 Hudson St.
New York, NY 10014
(212) 727-7330

* **Different Light**
489 Castro St.
San Francisco, CA 94114
(415) 550-0827

* **Different Light**
8853 Santa Monica Blvd.
West Hollywood, CA 90069
(213) 854-6601

* **Different World Bookstore**
414 E Grand Ave.
Beloit, WI 53511
(608) 365-1000

* **Dorrwar Bookstore**
312 Wickenden
Providence, RI 02909
(401) 273-9757

* **Downtown Subscription**
376 Garcia St.
Santa Fe, NM 87501
(505) 983-3085

Dreams and Swords
828 E 64th St.
Indianapolis, IN 46220
(317) 253-9966

* **E & J Books & More**
827 Pueblo
El Paso, TX 79903
(915) 564-0524

Ellie's Garden: Women's Books and More
2812 34th St.
Lubbock, TX 79410
(806) 796-0880

* Enchanted Room
808 E University Blvd., Ste. 100
Tucson, AZ 85710
(602) 622-8070

* Everyone's Books
71 Elliott St.
Brattleboro, VT 05301
(802) 254-8160

* Faubourg Marigny Bookstore
600 Frenchmen St.
New Orleans, LA 70116
(504) 943-9875

Food for Thought
314 10th St. N
Fargo, ND 58102
(218) 236-5434

* Food for Thought Books
106 N Pleasant St.
Amherst, MA 01002
(413) 253-5432

Full Circle Books
2205 Silver SE
Albuquerque, NM 87106
(505) 266-0022

* Gables Booksellers
222 Andalusia Ave.
Coral Gables, FL 33134
(305) 446-7215

* GAIA Bookstore and Catalogue Co.
1400 Shattuck Ave., No. 15
Berkeley, CA 94709
(510) 548-4172

* Galisteo News
201 Galisteo St.
Santa Fe, NM 87501
(505) 984-1316

* The Gallery
P. O. Box 94
South Fallsburg, NY 12779
(914) 446-4674

Gertrude Stein Memorial Bookshop
1003 E Carson St.
Pittsburgh, PA 15203
(412) 481-9666

Gifts of Athena
2199 Lee Rd.
Cleveland Heights, OH 44118
(216) 371-1937

Giovanni's Room
345 S 12th St.
Philadelphia, PA 19107
(215) 923-2960

* Glad Day Books
673 Boylston St., 2nd Fl.
Boston, MA 02116
(617) 267-3010

Golden Thread Booksellers: A Feminist Bookstore
915 State St.
New Haven, CT 06511
(202) 777-7807

* Good Vibrations and the Sexuality Library
1210 Valencia St.
San Francisco, CA 94114
(415) 431-1003

* Grailville Art & Bookstore
932 O'Bannonville Rd.
Loveland, OH 45140
(513) 683-0202;
Fax: (513) 683-4752

* Grapevine Books
290 California Ave.
Reno, NV 89509
(702) 786-4869

Grassroots Books
315 S. Gilbert St.
Iowa City, IA 52244
(319) 339-4678

* Groundworks Books
D-023C UCSD Student Center
La Jolla, CA 92093
(619) 452-9625

* Gualala Books
39225 Hwy. One S
Gualala, CA 95445
(707) 884-4255

Heartland Books
P. O. Box 1105—Taplin Hill Road
East Corinth, VT 05040
(800) 535-3755

Heart of the Rose
2726 W Waters
Tampa, FL 33614
(813) 933-9055

Herland Sister Resources, Incorporated
2312 NW 39th St.
Oklahoma City, OK 73112
(405) 521-9696

* Hibiscus Bookstore
P. O. Box 44370
Baton Rouge, LA 70801
(504) 387-4264

* Hidden Room Book Shoppe
7018 W H Ave.
Kalamazoo, MI 49009
(616) 375-9398

House of Sarah Books
225 Hampshire St.
Cambridge, MA 02139
(617) 547-3447

* Huntley Bookstore
175 E 8th
Claremont, CA 91711
(714) 621-8168

* Ibis Books
3301 Governors Dr.
Huntsville, AL 35805
(205) 536-9604

Imprints Bookstore and Gallery
917 N 2nd
Tacoma, WA 98403
(206) 383-6322

Inklings
1846 Richmond
Houston, TX 77090
(713) 521-3369

Iris Books
802 W University
Gainesville, FL 32601
(904) 375-7477

* Isis Bookstore
5701 E Colfax Ave.
Denver, CO 80220
(303) 321-0867

* It's A Scream
4616 Old Harpeth Paytonsville
Thompsons Ste, TN 37179
(615) 244-7346

Jane Addams Books
208 N Neil
Champaign, IL 61820
(217) 356-2555

Judith's Room
681 Washington St.
New York, NY 10014
(212) 727-7330

* Key West Island Books
513 Fleming St.
Key West, FL 33040
(305) 294-2904

* Kindred Spirit Bookshop
1110 N Ben Maddox Way
Visalie, CA 93291
(209) 625-0978

**Lady Iris for Women/
By Women**
10 Ladd St.
Portsmouth, NH 03801
(603) 436-3634

* Lambda Passages
7545 Biscayne Blvd.
Miami, FL 33040
(305) 294-2904

* Lambda Passages Bookstore
3025 Fuller St.
Coconut Grove, FL 33133
(305) 443-6411

* Lambda Rising
39 Baltimore Ave.
Rehoboth, DE 19971
(302) 227-6969

* Lambda Rising
241 W Chase St.
Baltimore, MD 21201
(410) 234-0069

* Lambda Rising 2
1625 Connecticut Ave. NW
Washington, DC 20009
(202) 775-8218

Lammas Women's Bookstore
1426 21st St. NW
Washington, DC 20036
(202) 775-8218

* Lavender Books
Gay/Lesbian Community Center
1213 N Highland Ave.
Long Beach, CA 90038
(213) 464-7400

* Left Bank Books
399 N Euclid Ave.
St. Louis, MO 63108
(314) 367-6731

* Liberty Books
1014-B N Lamar Blvd.
Austin, TX 78703
(512) 495-9737

Lioness Books
2224 J St.
Sacramento, CA 95816
(916) 442-4657

Lodestar Books
2020 11th Ave. S
Birmingham, AL 35205
(205) 939-3356

* Lotus Bookstore
100 Brewery Ln.
Auburn, CA 95603
(916) 885-6685

Lunaria
90 King St.
Northampton, MA 01060
(413) 586-7851

**Mama Bear's Bookstore and
Coffee House**
6536 Telegraph Ave.
Oakland, CA 94609
(510) 428-9684

* MCC Bookstore
5300 Santa Monica Blvd., #304
Los Angeles, CA 90029
(213) 646-5100

* MCC Bookstore
4825 9th Ave. N
St. Petersburg, FL 33713

Meristem
930 S. Cooper St.
Memphis, TN 38104
(901) 276-0282

**Minnesota Women's Press
Bookstore**
771 Raymond
St. Paul, MN 55114
(612) 646-3968

* Modern Times Bookstore
968 Valencia St.
San Francisco, CA 94110
(415) 282-9246

* Mosaic Books
167 Ave. B
New York, NY 10009
(212) 475-8623

Mother Kali's Books
2001 Franklin Blvd., #5
Eugene, OR 97403
(503) 343-4864

My Sister's Words
304 N McBride St.
Syracuse, NY 13203
(315) 428-0227

* New Leaf Books
P. O. Box 159
West Rockport, ME 04865
(207) 596-0040

New Words Bookstore
186 Hampshire St.
Boston, MA 02139
(617) 876-5310

* Now Voyager
357 Commercial St.
Provincetown, MA 02657
(508) 487-3146

Old Wives' Tales Bookstore
1009 Valencia
San Francisco, CA 94110
(415) 821-4676

On the Move: A Mobile Bookstore
P. O. Box 2985
St. Petersburg, FL 33731
(813) 223-9171

* Open Door Bookstore
3434 Allison Way
Louisville, KY 40220
(502) 452-1435

* Opening Books
403 Pratt Ave.
Huntsville, AL 35801
(205) 536-5880

* Oscar Wilde Memorial Bookshop
15 Christopher St.
New York, NY 10014
(212) 255-8097

* Our World Too
11 S Vandeventer
St. Louis, MO 63108
(314) 533-5322

Out of the Dark
530 Randolph Rd.
Newport News, VA 23601
(804) 596-6220

* OutRight Books
485 S Independence Blvd., #110
Virginia Beach, VA 23452
(804) 490-6658

Page One, Books By and For Women
1196 E Walnut St.
Pasadena, CA 91104
(818) 798-8694

Pandora Book Peddlers
885 Belmont Ave.
North Haledon, NJ 07508
(201) 427-5733

Pandora Books for Open Minds
226 Lovell St.
Kalamazoo, MI 49007
(616) 388-5656

Paradigm Women's Bookstore
3343 Adams Ave.
San Diego, CA 92116
(619) 563-1981;
Fax: (619) 563-1832

Pearl's Booksellers
224 Redondo
Long Beach, CA 90803
(310) 438-8875

* People Like Us Books
330 N Broadway
Chicago, IL 60657
(312) 248-6363

* People's Books
1808 N Farwell Ave.
Milwaukee, WI 53202
(414) 272-1232

* Peralandra Books and Music
1016 Willamette St.
Eugene, OR 97403
(503) 485-4848

Phoenix Books
317 Westport Rd.
Kansas City, MO 64111
(816) 931-5794

Platypus Book Shop
606 Dempster St.
Evanston, IL 60202
(708) 866-8040

* Ponder Pocket
125 E 10th St.
Durango, CO 81301
(303) 259-9335

Radzukina's
714 N Broadway
Haverhill, MA 01832
(502) 521-1333

Reader's Feast Bookstore Cafe
529 Farmington Ave.
Hartford, CT 06105
(203) 232-3710

Recovering Hearts
4 Standis St.
Provincetown, MA 02657
(508) 487-4875

* Red and Black Books
432 15th Ave. E
Seattle, WA 98117
(206) 322-7323

* Regulator Bookstore
720 9th St.
Durham, NC 27705
(919) 286-2700

Renaissance Books and Gifts
1337 E Montclair
Springfield, MO 65804
(417) 883-5161

* Rhino Nest
235 W 400 S.
Salt Lake City, UT 84101
(801) 532-1555

Richmond Womensbooks
2132 W Main St.
Richmond, VA 23220
(804) 788-1607

Rising Moon Books
316 E Blvd.
Charlotte, NC 28203
(704) 332-RISE

A Room Of One's Own
317 W Johnson St.
Madison, WI 53703
(608) 257-7888

Room of Our Own
P. O. Box 129
1486 Haslett Rd.
Haslett, MI 48840
(517) 339-0270

Rubyfruit Books
666–4 W Tennessee St.
Tallahassee, FL 32304
(904) 222-2627

* Saint Elmo's
2214 E Carson
Pittsburgh, PA 15203
(412) 431-9100

Silkwood Books
633 Monroe Ave.
Rochester, NY 14607
(716) 473-8110

Silver Chord
10901 Lillian Way
Pensacola, FL 32506
(904) 453-6652

Sisterhood Bookstore
1351 Westwood Blvd.
Los Angeles, CA 90024
(310) 477-7300

* Sisters and Brothers Bookstore
P. O. Box 8768
Albuquerque, NM 87106
(505) 266-0022

Sisterspirit
175 Stockton Ave.
San Jose, CA 95126
(408) 293-9372

* Six Steps Down
1921 W 25th St.
Cleveland, OH 44113
(216) 566-8897

Smedley's Bookshop
307 W State St.
Ithaca, NY 14850
(607) 273-2325

*** Solutions, A Recovery
Bookstore**
532 S Cooper St.
Memphis, TN 38104
(901) 726-6341

* Something Else Books
2805 N Sheffield Ave.
Chicago, IL 60657
(312) 549-0495

* Sons & Daughters
962 Cherry St. SE
Grand Rapids, MI 49506
(616) 459-8877

*** Sons and Daughters
Bookstore**
30715 Southfield Rd.
Southfield, MI 48076
(313) 645-2210

Southern Sisters, Incorporated
411 Morris St.
Durham, NC 27701
(919) 682-0739

Stepping Stones
226 Hamilton Ave.
Palo Alto, CA 94301
(408) 296-7136

* Sunday Women's Bookstore
12450 N Rte. E
Harrisburg, MO 65256
(314) 874-5969

* Sunflower Books, Etc.
1114 Washington St.
LaGrande, OR 97850
(503) 963-5242

Textures Books
5309 McCullough
San Antonio, TX 78212
(210) 805-8398

**31st Street Bookstore
Cooperative**
425 E 31st St.
Baltimore, MD 21218
(710) 243-3131

*** Three Birds Bookstore and
Coffee Room**
1518 7th Ave.
Tampa, FL 33605
(813) 247-7041

* Tomes and Treasures
202 S Howard Ave.
Tampa, FL 33606
(813) 251-9368

* Trade N' Books
5145 Atlanta Hwy.
Montgomery, AL 36109
(205) 277-0778

Two Sisters Bookshop
605 Cambridge Ave.
Menlo Park, CA 94025
(415) 323-4778

* Unicorn Books
1210 Massachusetts Ave.,
Arlington
Boston, MA 02174
(617) 646-3680

* Unicorn Book Store
8940 Santa Monica Blvd.
West Hollywood, CA 90069
(213) 652-6253

Valley Women Books
1118 N Fulton St.
Fresno, CA 93728
(209) 233-3600

Visions and Voices
255 Harris Ave.
Providence, RI 02909
(401) 273-9757

* WelWoman's Books
135 Park Ave.
Merchantville, NJ 08109
(609) 663-3782

* White Rabbit Books
1833 Spring Garden St.
Greensboro, NC 27403
(919) 272-7604

* White Rabbit Books
309 W Martin St.
Raleigh, NC 27601
(919) 956-1429

Wild Seeds Bookstore and Cafe
704 University Ave.
Rochester, NY 14607
(716) 244-9310

Womankind Books
5 Kivy St.
Huntington Station, NY 11746
(516) 427-1289

A Woman's Place Bookstore
1400 Foothill Dr., #240
Salt Lake City, UT 84108
(801) 583-6431;
Fax: (801) 581-9512

**A Woman's Prerogative
Bookstore**
175 W 9 Mile Rd.
Ferndale, MI 48220
(313) 545-5703

Woman's View Bookstore
P. O. Box 28
1001 SW Hurbert St.
Newport, OR 97365
(503) 265-7721

Women & Children First
5233 N Clark St.
Chicago, IL 60640
(312) 769-9299

* Works
4120 N Keystone Ave.
Indianapolis, IN 46205

MAIL-ORDER BOOK DISTRIBUTORS

Below are several distributors that will send books by mail. Where possible, we've included phone numbers. Otherwise, simply write to them directly with your request.

* Book Connections
P. O. Box 9700
Austin, TX 78766

* Booklegger
402 E 2nd St.
Eureka, CA 95501
(707) 445-1344

For Women Only Books
13479 Howard Rd.
Millfield, OH 45761

Heartland Books
P. O. Box 1105
E. Corinth, VT 05040
(800) 535-3755

* Liberation Book Club
P. O. Box 453
South Norwalk, CT 06856
(203) 322-7829

New Herizons Books & Gifts, Incorporated
P. O. Box 405
Lancaster, MA 01523
(508) 365-4340

A national lesbian mail-order company. Offers books, jewelry, music, videos, and notecards intended for lesbians.

* South of the Garden Books
P. O. Box 7725
Durham, NC 27708
(919) 687-0408

Vintage '45 Press
P. O. Box 266
Orinda, CA 94563
(510) 254-7266

Womanvision Books, Incorporated
P. O. Box 387
Springfield, PA 19064
(215) 622-2492

❏ Displaced Homemakers' Services

*D*isplaced homemakers' services and programs offer women returning to or entering the job market support, information, and training in career development, self-employment, and job skills. Following is a sampling of the displaced homemakers' services nationwide. Also check the Work, Union, and Career Services chapters for other job training programs.

Adult Learning Center
Displaced Homemakers Program
911 Cottonwood
Grand Forks, ND 58201
(701) 746-2425

Adult Vocational Training
Program
Single Parent/Homemaker
Program
531 W Plata
Tucson, AZ 85705
(602) 884-8686

Albany Displaced Homemakers
Center
315 Hamilton St.
Albany, NY 12210
(518) 434-3103

Arizona Women's Education and
Employment
1111 N First St.
Phoenix, AZ 85004
(602) 258-0864

Asian Resources Center
Displaced Homemaker Program
2251 Florin Rd., Ste. E
Sacramento, CA 95822
(916) 452-3601

Assignment House of Chicago
Single Parent/Displaced
Homemaker Building
Opportunity Project
1116 N Kedzie Ave.
Chicago, IL 60647
(312) 486-4489

**Atlanta Area Vocational
Technical School
New Connections Program**
1560 Stewart Ave. SW
Atlanta, GA 30310
(404) 758-9451

**Austin Community College
Displaced Homemaker/Single
Parent Program**
P. O. Box 2285
Austin, TX 78768
(512) 832-4726

**Bangor Hall, University College
Transitions: A Displaced
Homemaker Program**
355 Maine Ave.
Bangor, ME 04401
(217) 581-6132

**Bessemer State Technical College
Displaced Homemakers Program**
P. O. Box 308
Bessemer, AL 35021
(205) 428-6391

**Boone County Career Center
Single Parent/Displaced
Homemaker Program**
Box 50B
Danville, WV 25053
(304) 345-1298

**Boulder County YWCA
Displaced Homemaker Program**
16000 E CentreTech Pkwy.,
Rm. A102
Boulder, CO 80011
(303) 360-4790

**Bronx Community College
Displaced Homemakers Program**
Bould Hall, Rm. 509
University Ave. and West 181 St.
Bronx, NY 10453
(718) 220-6395

**Brookdale Community College
Displaced Homemaker Program**
213 Broadway
Long Beach, NJ 07740
(201) 229-8440

**Broward Community College
Project You**
1000 Coconut Creek Blvd.
Ft. Lauderdale, FL 33066
(305) 973-2232

**Career Development Consultants,
Incorporated
TAP for Single Heads of
Households/Displaced
Homemakers**
245 Newman Ave.
Harrisburg, VA 22801
(703) 434-8579

**Career Learning Center
Single Parent/Homemaker
Program**
514 Mt. Rushmore Rd.
Rapid City, SD 57701
(605) 394-5120

**Career Training Institute
Displaced Homemakers Program**
17½ S Last Chance Gulch
Helena, MT 59601
(406) 752-6565

**Career Works Associates,
Limited**
1033 Quarrier St.
Charlestown, WV 25301
(304) 344-2273

**Casper College Project for Single
Parents and Homemakers in
Transition**
125 College Dr.
Casper, WY 82601
(307) 268-2696

**Center for Displaced
Homemakers**
7393 Florida Blvd.
Bon Marche Mall
Baton Rouge, LA 70806
(504) 925-6922

Center for New Directions
51 Jefferson Ave.
Columbus, OH 43215-3859
(614) 461-6117

**Center for Women and Families
Creative Employment Project**
P. O. Box 2048
Louisville, KS 40201-2048
(502) 581-7237

**Central Arizona College
Displaced Homemaker Program**
8470 N Overfield Rd.
Coolidge, AZ 85004
(602) 426-4432

**Chicago City-Wide College
Displaced Homemaker Program**
226 W Jackson Blvd., 4th Fl.
Chicago, IL 60606-6997
(312) 368-8836

**Choices, Displaced Homemaker
Program of SE Minnesota**
851 30th Ave. SE
Rochester, MN 55904
(507) 280-5517

**College of Charleston Displaced
Workers Counseling and
Undergraduate Studies**
66 George St.
Charleston, SC 29424
(803) 792-5674

**Columbia Urban League Single
Parents/Displaced Homemaker
Programs**
P. O. Drawer J
Columbia, SC 29526
(803) 347-3186

**Community College of Allegheny
County, New Choice Program**
808 Ridge Ave.
Pittsburgh, PA 15208
(412) 237-2595

**Community College of Rhode
Island, Project Sphere**
Providence Campus
Providence, RI 02905
(401) 333-7206

**Community Colleges of Spokane
Displaced Homemaker Program**
W 3305 Ft. George Wright Dr.
Mail Stop 3090
Spokane, WA 98148
(206) 246-6142

Community Women's Education Project/New Horizons
Somerset at Franklin Ave.
Philadelphia, PA 19134
(215) 426-2200

Crossroads, Displaced Homemakers Program
403 N LaBree
Thief River Falls, MN 56701
(218) 681-8158

**D. C. Public Schools Office of Sex Equity
A Step Towards Employment Program**
415 12th St. NW, Room 1010
Washington, DC 20004
(202) 727-1037

Des Moines Area Community College Displaced Homemaker Program
1100 7th St.
Des Moines, IA 50314
(515) 244-4226

Displaced Homemakers Center of Tompkins County
301 S Geneva St.
Ithaca, NY 14850
(607) 272-1520

Displaced Homemakers Program
1 Armory Sq.
Springfield, MA 01105
(413) 737-6841

Displaced Homemakers Program
Cuyahoga Community College
Cleveland, OH 44116
(216) 987-4188

Displaced Homemakers Resource Center
865 Forest Ave.
Portland, ME 04103
(207) 773-3537

Displaced Homemakers Services
UMA Stoddard House
Augusta, ME 04330-9410
(207) 621-3433;
Fax: (207) 621-3429

Durham Technical Community College Single Parent/Displaced Homemaker Program
1637 Lawson St.
Durham, NC 27703
(919) 598-9206

Educational Services for Adults
1616 Walnut St., 1st Fl.
Philadelphia, PA 19103
(215) 787-1536

Employment Options, Incorporated/Forward View
2095 Winnebago St.
Madison, WI 53704
(608) 244-5181

**Essex Junction Area Vocational Center
Single Parent/Homemakers Program**
Essex Junction, VT 05452
(802) 879-5564

Everywoman Opportunity Centers of Western NY
237 Main St., #330
Buffalo, NY
(716) 847-1120

**Fairbanks Native Association
Careers in Non-traditional
Occupations for Single Parent
Homemakers**
201 1st Ave.
Fairbanks, AK 99701
(907) 452-1648

**Florissant Valley Community
College Careers for Homemakers**
3400 Pershall Rd.
St. Louis, MO 63135
(314) 595-4565

**Franklin Institute Displaced
Homemakers Program**
41 Berkeley St.
Boston, MA 02116
(617) 262-3240

Fresh Start Training Program
Project for Displaced Homemakers
1756 Ocean Ave.
Brooklyn, NY 11230

Futures Program
214 Main St.
Montpelier, VT 05602
(802) 223-7902

**Garland County Community
College
CHOICES: Career Development
Program**
Executive Bldg., Ste. 516
2020 W 3rd St.
Little Rock, AR 72205
(501) 372-7161

Gastinequ Human Services
Single Parent/Displaced
Homemaker Corrections Program
5597 Aisek St.
Juneau, AK 99801
(907) 780-4338

**Harrison Center for Career
Education**
624 9th St. NW, 6th Floor
Washington, DC 20005
(202) 628-5672

**Higher Education Information
Center
Bay State Center for Displaced
Homemakers**
666 Boylston St.
Boston, MA 02116
(617) 536-0200

**Hinds Community College Single
Parent/Displaced Homemaker
Program**
3925 Sunset Dr.
Jackson, MS 39213
(601) 366-1405

**Honolulu Community College
Single Parent/Homemaker
Program**
874 Dillingham Blvd.
Honolulu, HI 96817
(808) 845-9120

**Houston Area Women's Center/
WIRES: New Resources**
3101 Richmond Ave., Ste. 150
Houston, TX 77098
(713) 528-2121

**Institute for Human Research
and Development
Displaced Homemaker Center**
42 NW 27th Ave., Ste. 302
Miami, FL 33125
(305) 541-7887

**Institute for the Development of
Human Resources
Displaced Homemakers Program**
325 E Main St.
Newark, DE 19711
(302) 737-7488

**Interfaith Employment Services
Displaced Homemaker Network**
1200 E Capital Dr.
Milwaukee, WI 53211
(414) 963-1200

**Jeff Davis Community College
Displaced Homemakers and
Single Parent Program**
P. O. Box 1119
Atmore, AL 36504
(205) 368-8118

**J. Everett Light Career Center
Career Advancement Training
Center for Single Parents/
Homemakers**
1901 E 86th St.
Indianapolis, IN 46240
(317) 251-0041

**Jewish Social Service Agency
Displaced Homemakers Program**
6123 Montrose Rd.
Rockville, MD 20852
(301) 881-3700

**Job Training Service Displaced
Homemaker Program**
6201 N 35th Ave.
Phoenix, AZ 85017
(602) 841-9049

**J. Sargeant Reynolds Community
College
Single Parent/Homemaker
Center**
Downtown Campus
P. O. Box C-32040
Richmond, VA 23261-2040
(804) 786-1105

**Kansas City, Kansas Community
College Women's Resource Center**
7250 State Ave.
Kansas City, KS 66112
(913) 334-1100

**Kirkwood Community College
Displaced Homemaker Program**
6301 Kirkwood Blvd. SW
P. O. Box 2068
Cedar Rapids, IA 52406
(319) 398-5471

**Lane Community College
Transition to Success
Displaced Homemaker/Single
Parent Project**
4000 E 30th Ave.
Eugene, OR 97405
(503) 747-4501

**Laramie County Community
College Displaced Homemakers/
Single Parent Program**
1400 E College Dr.
Cheyenne, WY 82007
(307) 778-5222

Madison County Schools Single Parent Displaced Homemaker Program
Rte. 1, Box 47-A
Canton, MS 39046-4706
(601) 355-9893

Mainstam Inc.
P. O. Box 816
308 N 3rd St.
Marshall, MN 56358
(507) 537-1546

Manchester Community College Look Forward/Beginning Again
60 Bidwell Ave.
Manchester, CT 06040
(203) 647-6175

Maple Woods Community College Displaced Homemaker Program
2601 NE Barry Rd.
Kansas City, MO 64156
(816) 436-6500

Maryland New Directions, Incorporated
2220 N Charles St.
Baltimore, MD 21218
(410) 235-0350

Memphis City Schools Single Parent/Displaced Homemakers Program
320 Carpenter St.
Lester Annex
Memphis, TN 38112
(901) 425-5295

Metro Nashville Public Schools Career Directions Program
2601 Bradsford Ave.
Nashville, TN 37204
(615) 259-8545

Metro Tech Displaced Homemaker Program
1900 Springlake Dr.
Oklahoma City, OK 73111
(405) 424-8324

Missouri Shores Women Resource Center Single Parent/Homemaker Project
104 E Capital
Pierre, SD 57501
(605) 224-0256

Mountain View College Displaced Homemaker Program
4849 W Illinois Ave.
Dallas, TX 75211-6599
(214) 333-8672

New Choices
Community College of Philadelphia
1700 Spring Garden St.
Philadelphia, PA 19130
(215) 751-8922

New Choices Program
Erie County Technical School
8500 Oliver Rd.
Erie, PA 16509
(814) 868-0837;
Fax: (814) 864-9400

New Mexico Commission on the Status of Women Displaced Homemakers Project
P. O. Box 4368
Albuquerque, NM 87196
(505) 247-2329

New Orleans Regional Vocational Technical Institute Center for Displaced Homemakers
980 Navarre Ave.
New Orleans, LA 70124
(504) 483-4664

Nichols Career Center Displaced Homemaker Program
609 Union
Jefferson City, MO 65101
(314) 659-3049

Nine Star Enterprises, Incorporated Single Parent Career Enhancement
650 W International Airport Rd.
Anchorage, AK 99518
(907) 563-3174

Ogden-Weber Area Vocational-Technical School/Turning Point Program
559 A.V.C. La.
Ogden, UT 84404
(801) 621-2373

Palo Alto College Single Parent/ Homemaker Program
1400 W Villaret
P. O. Box 3800
San Antonio, TX 78224
(210) 921-5381

Pasadena Unified School District
SOLO Single Parent/ Displaced Homemaker Project
351 S Hudson
Los Angeles, CA 91109
(818) 793-2092

Pathfinders Displaced Homemakers Program
17 East Division, Box 127
Elbow Lake, MN 56531
(218) 987-4486

Pikes Peak Community College Displaced Homemaker Program
5675 S Academy Rd.
Colorado Springs, CO 80906
(719) 540-7112

Portland Community College Project Independence
Cascade Campus
P. O. Box 19000
Portland, OR 97280-0990
(503) 244-6111

Program Transitions
100 Cannon St.
Poughkeepsie, NY 12601
(914) 471-6665

Project Second Start
17 Knight St.
Concord, NH 03301
(603) 228-1341

Project SOAR of Northeast Minnesota
205 W 2nd St., Ste. 101
Duluth, MN 55802
(218) 722-3126

**Rhode Island Displaced
Homemaker Program**
275 Westminster Mall
Providence, RI 02905
(401) 277-2862

**Salt Lake City Community
College/Turning Point Program**
4600 S Redwood Rd.
P. O. Box 30808
Salt Lake City, UT 84130

**Santa Barbara City College
Single Parent/Displaced
Homemaker Project**
721 Cliff Dr.
Santa Barbara, CA 93109-2394
(805) 965-0581

**Santa Fe Community College
Focus on the Future:
Displaced Homemaker Program**
3000 NW 83rd St.
Gainesville, FL 32606

**Santa Fe Community College/
Women in Transition**
P. O. Box 4187
Santa Fe, NM 87502
(505) 471-8200

**Savannah Area Vocational-
Technical School New
Connections Program**
5717 White Bluff Rd.
Savannah, GA 31499
(912) 351-6362

**Schenectady/Fulmont Displaced
Homemakers Program**
237 State St.
Schenectady, NY 12305
(518) 374-9181

**Shelton State Community College
New Options Program**
202 Skyland Blvd.
Tuscaloosa, AL 35401
(205) 759-1541

**Single Parent/Homemakers
Program**
South Central High School
222 W Bowen
Bismarck, ND 58504
(701) 221-3790

**Single Parents & Homemakers
Program**
Kaplolani Community College
4304 Diamond Head Rd., #203
Honolulu, HI 96816
(808) 734-9500;
Fax: (808) 734-9456

Soundings
P. O. Box 7372
Ann Arbor, MI 48104
(313) 663-6689

**South Central Indiana PIC
Single Parent/Displaced
Homemaker Program**
405 W 7th St.
Bloomington, IN 47402
(812) 332-3777

**Southeast Community College
Single Parent/Displaced
Homemaker Program**
8800 O St.
Lincoln, NE 68520
(402) 471-3333

Southeast Vocational Technical Project Displaced Homemaker Program
2301 Career Pl.
Sioux Falls, SD 57104
(605) 339-7175

Step Up, Incorporated
983 Ingleside Rd., Ste. 2
Norfolk, VA 23502
(804) 461-8525

Transitions to Success: A Program for Displaced Home- makers & Single Parents
Indian Hill Community College
525 Grandview
Ottumwa, IA 52501
(515) 683-5172

Truckee Meadows Community College Single Parent/Displaced Homemaker Program
901 Elm St.
Elko, NV 89801
(702) 738-8493

Tulsa County Area Vocational Technical School Displaced Homemaker Program
3420 S Memorial
Tulsa, OK 74145-1390
(918) 627-7200

University of Arizona Project for Homemakers Seeking Employment
1230 N Park Ave., Rm. 209
Tucson, AZ 85721
(602) 621-3902

Urban League Displaced Homemaker Program
104-14th St.
Seattle, WA 98112
(206) 461-3792

Valencia Community College Displaced Homemaker Program
P. O. Box 3028 5-1
Orlando, FL 32802
(904) 237-2111

Wallace State Junior College Displaced Homemakers Program
P. O. Drawer 1418
Andalusia, AL 36420
(205) 222-6591

Wider Opportunities for Women
1325 G St. NW, Lower Level
Washington, DC 20005
(202) 638-3143

Women Employed Institute
22 W Monroe, Ste. 1400
Chicago, IL 60603
(312) 782-3902

Women in Transition at the Centennial Center
14750 SE Clinton St.
Portland, OR 97236
(503) 760-4007

Women's Center
128 E Hargett St., #10
Raleigh, NC 27601
(919) 829-3711

Women's Development Center
216 S 7th St., Ste. 2
Las Vegas, NV 89101
(702) 382-7311

Women's Job Counseling Service
34 Follen St.
Cambridge, MA 02138
(617) 547-1123

Women's Vocational Services
211 Carroll's Plaza
Dover, DE 19901
(302) 739-4540

Working Opportunities for Women
New Careers
2700 University Ave., Ste. 120
St. Paul, MN 55114
(612) 647-9961

YWCA Career Services Center
7201 Paseo del Norte NE
Albuquerque, NM 87113
(505) 266-9922

YWCA Discovery Program/ Displaced Homemaker Program
220 Union Ave. SE
Olympia, WA 98501
(206) 352-0593

YWCA Displaced Homemakers Center
222 S 29th St.
Omaha, NE 68131
(402) 345-6555

YWCA Displaced Homemakers Program
1600 M St.
Fresno, CA 93721
(209) 237-4701

YWCA Displaced Homemakers Program
P. O. Box 14163
Lansing, MI 48901
(517) 485-7201

YWCA Metropolitan Denver Displaced Homemakers Program
535 16th St., Ste. 700
Denver, CO 80202
(303) 825-7141

YWCA of Greater Bridgeport Job Re-entry Program Displaced Homemakers Program
753 Fairfield Ave.
Bridgeport, CT 06604
(203) 334-6154

YWCA of Greater New Haven Women in Transition Program
48 Howe St.
New Haven, CT 06511
(203) 865-5171

YWCA of New York City Re-entry Employment Program
610 Lexington Ave.
New York, NY 10022
(212) 735-9727

YWCA of Trenton Displaced Homemakers Program
140 E Hanover St.
Trenton, NJ 08608
(609) 989-2608

YWCA Turning Point Career Center
2600 Bancroft Way
Berkeley, CA 94704
(510) 848-6370

YWCA Woman's Center
Displaced Homemakers Program
167 Duke of Gloucester St.
Annapolis, MD 21401
(410) 269-0378

YWCA Women's Lifestrides
Opportunities Center
898 Walnut St.
Cincinnati, OH 45202
(513) 241-7090

YWCA Woman's Center
Displaced Homemakers Program
909 Wyoming Ave.
Billings, MT 59101
(406) 245-6879

YWCA Work Place
104 2nd St. S, Ste. 200
Great Falls, MT 59405
(406) 727-0966

Note: There may be a YWCA Displaced Homemakers/Career Assistance Program near you. Call your local YWCA for more information or contact the national headquarters at:

Young Women's Christian
Association of the USA
Career Assistance
726 Broadway
New York, NY 10003
(212) 614-2700

❑ Educational Services and Organizations

ADVOCACY AND RESEARCH

American Association of University Women
1111 Sixteenth St. NW
Washington, DC 20036
(202) 785-7712;
Fax: (202) 872-1425

A large, well-known organization that actively promotes educational equity for women and girls. Offers financial support to institutions and individuals. Conducts research to bolster opportunities and challenge discrimination.

American Educational Research Association
Research on Women and Educational Group
San Jose State Univ.
Dept. of Mathematics and Computer Science
San Jose, CA 95192-0103
(408) 924-5112

Promotes research concerning women in education and equity in education.

American Federation of Teachers Library
555 New Jersey Ave. NW
Washington, DC 20001
(202) 879-4481;
Fax: (202) 879-4545

Holds books, journals, and newspapers on labor, child care, education, and women's rights.

Black Women Organized for Educational Development
518 17th St., Ste. 202
Oakland, CA 94612
(510) 763-9501;
Fax: (510) 763-4327

Offers services and support to economically and socially disadvantaged women. Sponsors mentor programs, support groups, work-

44

shops, and seminars. See also Organizations Representing Women of Color.

Black Women's Educational Alliance
6625 Greene St.
Philadelphia, PA 19119

An organization for active and retired women in the field of education. Conducts public awareness programs to improve education standards, offers student scholarships, and maintains a speakers bureau. See also Organizations Representing Women of Color.

Clearinghouse on Women's Issues
P.O. Box 70603
Friendship Heights, MD 20813
(202) 363-9795

Provides educational information on gender and marital discrimination as it affects financial and educational matters as well as other areas of life. Members can request materials. Holds monthly meetings.

Council for the Advancement and Support of Education
11 Dupont Circle NW, Ste. 400
Washington, DC 20036-1207
(202) 328-5931

Works to achieve women's full access to educational opportunities and the benefits a solid education provides: career advancement, higher salaries, and recognition. Especially concerned with minor-

ities. Offers scholarships and holds career advancement forums. See also Work, Union, and Career Services.

Educational Equity Concepts
114 E 32 St., Rm. 701
New York, NY 10016
(212) 725-1803;
Fax: (212) 725-0947

A national organization that advocates educational equity through programs and materials that counteract bias due to sex, race, ethnicity, disability, and low income. Designs programs and materials, offers training and consulting services, and participates in public education activities.

Equals Project
Lawrence Hall of Science
UC Berkeley
Berkeley, CA 94720
(510) 642-1823;
Fax: (510) 643-5757

An educational equity program for elementary and secondary teachers, students, and parents. Provides information and materials to help especially women and minority students participate fully in mathematics and computer education. See also Science and Technology.

Foundation for Women's Resources
700 N Fairfax St., Ste. 302
Alexandria, VA 22314
(703) 549-1102;
Fax: (703) 836-9205

An education foundation that stresses women's achievements. Sponsors exhibits, publications, educational conferences, and the Leadership America program to advance women's status in our society.

National Association for Women in Education
1325 18th St. NW, Ste. 210
Washington, DC 20036
(202) 659-9330;
Fax: (202) 457-0946

A membership organization that promotes educational opportunities for all women. Sponsors programs that aid educational careers and continuing academic research. Also tries to influence legislation that responds to these goals. Holds an annual conference.

National Coalition for Women and Girls in Education
National Women's Law Center
1616 T Street NW
Washington, DC 20036
(202) 328-5160

Coalition of organizations dedicated to equity in education. Focuses on educational opportunities, gender equity in standardized testing, and public awareness of education issues concerning women. See also Women's Rights.

National Council of Administrative Women in Education
5190 Roxbury Rd.
Pittsburgh, PA 15235
(619) 223-3121

An organization of women educators in administrative or supervisory positions. Offers information and support, conducts research, and maintains a speakers bureau.

National Education Association Women's Caucus
1201 16th St. NW
Washington, DC 20036
(202) 373-1800

A group within the NEA that works to eliminate sexual and racial discrimination in education. Designs educational materials and programs, works to influence policymakers, sponsors programs for minorities. See also Women's Rights.

NOW Legal Defense and Education Fund
Project on Equal Education Rights
99 Hudson St., 12th Fl.
New York, NY 10013
(212) 925-6635

Works to ensure educational equity for all women and girls at both the national and local levels. Analyzes public policies, disseminates information to the public, and organizes local committees for equity. See also Women's Rights.

National Women Student's Coalition
815 15th St. NW, Ste. 838
Washington, DC 20005
(202) 347-8772

Lobbies for women students' issues at the national level.

Organization for Equal Education of the Sexes
P.O. Box 438
Blue Hill, ME 04614
(207) 374-2489;
Fax: (207) 374-2489

Offers information and publications to educate professionals, parents, and students on equal education opportunities and rights.

Sponsors a poster series on women's history.

United States Department of Education Equity and Educational Excellence Division, Women's Educational Equity
400 Maryland Ave. SW
Washington, DC 20202
(202) 401-1342

Promotes educational equity for women and provides financial assistance to educational agencies.

ALTERNATIVE AND CONTINUING EDUCATION

American Association for Adult and Continuing Education Women's Issues, Status and Education Unit
1112 16th St. NW, Ste. 420
Washington, DC 20036
(202) 463-6333;
Fax: (202) 797-7225

Provides support for women pursuing continued education. Sponsors an annual conference.

Feminist Women's Writing Workshop
P.O. Box 6583
Ithaca, NY 14851
(607) 272-6914

An eight-day conference for novice, emerging, and published women writers. Offers workshops, readings, critique sessions, and individual writing. See also Presses and Publishers.

The Flight of the Mind
622 SE 29th Ave.
Portland, OR 97214
(503) 236-9862

Sponsors week-long summer writing workshops for women on the McKenzie River in the Oregon Cascade Mountains. Past teaching staff has included Ursula K. LeGuin, Grace Paley, Naomi Shihab Nye, and Barbara Wilson.

National University Continuing Education Association
Division of Programs for Women
1 Dupont Cir. NW, Ste. 615
Washington, DC 20036
(202) 659-3130

Offers support and information to women seeking continued education.

Women's Education and Leadership Forum
918 16th St. NW, Ste. 701
Washington, DC 20006
(202) 223-2908;
Fax: (202) 835-0968

An educational network that offers day-long education conferences around the country. Focuses on helping women acquire independence, self-confidence, decision-making abilities, and other success-oriented skills.

Women's Learning Center
P.O. Box 2282
Sebastopol, CA 95473
(707) 823-1715

Provides educational programs and events for women. Topics include self-awareness, women's power, self-defense, and self-esteem.

COLLEGES AND UNIVERSITIES FOR WOMEN

Agnes Scott College
Decatur, GA 30030
(404) 371-6280

Alverno College
3401 S 39th St.
Milwaukee, WI 53215-4020
(414) 382-6000

Aquinas Junior College, Milton
303 Adams St.
Milton, MA 02186
(617) 969-4400

Aquinas Junior College, Newton
15 Walnut Park
Newton, MA 02158
(617) 969-4400

Bay Path College
588 Longmeadow St.
Longmeadow, MA 01106
(413) 567-0621

Bennett College
900 E Washington St.
Greensboro, NC 27401-3239
(919) 370-8607

Blue Mountain College
Box 338
Blue Mountain, MS 38610
(610) 685-4771

Brenau College
204 Boulevard
Gainesville, GA 30501
(404) 534-6299

Bryn Mawr College
Bryn Mawr, PA 19010
(215) 526-5000

Carlow College
3333 Fifth Ave.
Pittsburgh, PA 15213-3109
(412) 578-6000

Cedar Crest College
100 College Dr.
Allentown, PA 18104-6196
(215) 437-4471

Chatham College
Woodland Rd.
Pittsburgh, PA 15232
(412) 365-1100

Chestnut Hill College
9601 Germantown Ave.
Philadelphia, PA 19118
(215) 248-7000

College of New Rochelle
New Rochelle, NY 10801
(914) 632-5300

**College of Notre Dame of
Maryland**
4701 N Charles St.
Baltimore, MD 21210
(301) 435-0100

College of Saint Benedict
St. Joseph, MN 56374
(612) 363-5505

College of Saint Catherine
2004 Randolph Ave.
St. Paul, MN 55015
(612) 690-6000

College of Saint Elizabeth
Convent Station, NJ 07961
(201) 539-1600

College of Saint Mary
1901 S 72nd St.
Omaha, NE 68124
(402) 399-2438

Columbia College
Columbia College Dr.
Columbia, SC 29203
(803) 786-3012

Converse College
580 E Main St.
Spartansburg, SC 29301
(803) 596-9000

Cottey College
1000 W Austin
Nevada, MO 64772-1000
(417) 667-8181

Douglass College
Rutgers Univ.
New Brunswick, NJ 08903
(908) 932-9721

Elms College
291 Springfield St.
Chicopee, MA 01013-2839
(413) 594-2761

Emmanuel College
400 The Fenway
Boston, MA 02115
(617) 735-9825

Endicott College
376 Hale St.
Beverly, MA 01915
(508) 927-0585

Fisher Junior College
118 Beacon St.
Boston, MA 02116
(617) 262-3240

Georgian Court College
900 Lakewood Ave.
Lakewood, NJ 08701-2697
(908) 364-2200

Harcum Junior College
Morris & Montgomery Aves.
Bryn Mawr, PA 19010-3476
(215) 526-6050

Hartford College for Women
1265 Asylum Ave.
Hartford, CT 06105
(203) 236-1215

Hollins College
Hollins College, VA 24020
(703) 362-6321

Hood College
Rosemont Ave.
Frederick, MD 21701
(301) 663-3131

Immaculata College
Immaculata, PA 19345-0901
(215) 647-4400

Judson College
P.O. Box 120
Marion, AL 36756
(205) 683-6161

Lasell College
Newton, MA 02166
(617) 349-8500

Lesley College
29 Everett St.
Cambridge, MA 02138-2790
(617) 349-8500

Marian Court Junior College
35 Littles Point Rd.
Swampscott, MA 01907-2896
(617) 595-6768

Mary Baldwin College
Staunton, VA 24401
(703) 887-7000

Marymount College
Tarrytown, NY 10591
(914) 631-3200

Marymount Manhattan College
221 E 71st St.
New York, NY 10021
(212) 517-0400

Meredith College
Raleigh, NC 27607-5298
(919) 829-8600

Midway College
Midway, KY 40347-9731
(606) 846-5310

Mills College
5000 MacArthur Blvd.
Oakland, CA 94613
(415) 430-2255

Mississippi University for Women
P.O. Box W-1602
Columbus, MS 39701
(601) 329-7100

Moore College for Art and Design
20th and The Parkway
Philadelphia, PA 19103
(215) 568-4515

Mount Holyoke College
South Hadley, MA 01075-1496
(413) 538-2000

Mount Mary College
2900 N Menomonee River Pkwy.
Milwaukee, WI 53222
(414) 258-4810

Mount St. Mary's College
12001 Chalon Rd.
Los Angeles, CA 90049
(213) 476-2237

Mount Vernon College
2100 Foxhall Rd. NW
Washington, DC 20007
(202) 625-4600

Newcomb College
Tulane Univ.
New Orleans, LA 70118
(504) 865-5421

Notre Dame College of Ohio
4545 College Rd.
Cleveland, OH 44121
(216) 381-1680

Peace College
15 E Peace St.
Raleigh, NC 27604
(919) 832-2881

Pine Manor College
400 Heath St.
Chestnut Hill, MA 02167
(617) 731-7000

Radcliffe College
10 Garden St.
Cambridge, MA 02138
(617) 495-8601

Randolph-Macon Woman's College
2500 Rivermont Ave.
Lynchburg, VA 24503
(804) 846-7392

Regis College
235 Wellesley St.
Weston, MA 02193
(617) 893-1820

Rosemont College
Rosemont, PA 19010
(215) 527-0200

Russell Sage College
45 Ferry St.
Troy, NY 12180
(518) 270-2000

Saint Joseph College
1678 Asylum Ave.
West Hartford, CT 06117
(203) 232-4571

Saint Mary-of-the-Woods College
St. Mary-of-the-Woods, IN 47876
(812) 535-5151

Saint Mary's College
Notre Dame, IN 46556
(219) 284-4000

Saint Mary's College
900 Hillsborough
Raleigh, NC 27603-1689
(919) 828-2521

Salem College
Winston-Salem, NC 27108
(919) 721-2600

Scripps College
1030 Columbia Ave.
Claremont, CA 91711-3948
(714) 621-8000

Seton Hill College
Greensburg, PA 15601
(412) 834-2200

Simmons College
300 The Fenway
Boston, MA 02115
(617) 738-2000

Smith College
College Hall
Northampton, MA 01063
(413) 584-2700

**Southern Seminary
Junior College**
Buena Vista, VA 24416
(703) 261-6181

Spelman College
350 Spelman Ln. SW
Atlanta, GA 30314
(404) 681-3643

Stephens College
1200 E Broadway
Columbia, MO 65215-0001
(314) 442-2211

Sweet Briar College
Sweet Briar, VA 24595
(804) 381-6100

Texas Woman's University
Box 23925 TWU Station
Denton, TX 76204
(817) 898-3201

Trinity College
125 Michigan Ave. NE
Washington, DC 20017-1094
(202) 939-5000

Trinity College of Vermont
208 Colchester Ave.
Burlington, VT 05401
(802) 658-0337

Ursuline College
2550 Lander Rd.
Pepper Pike, OH 44124
(216) 449-4200

Wellesley College
Wellesley, MA 02181-8201
(617) 235-0320

Wells College
Aurora, NY 13026-0500
(315) 364-3370

Wesleyan College
4760 Forsyth Rd.
Macon, GA 31297-4299
(912) 477-1110

Westhampton College
Univ. of Richmond
Richmond, VA 23173-1903
(804) 289-8468

William Smith College
Smith Hall
Geneva, NY 14456
(315) 789-5500

William Woods College
200 W 12th St.
Fulton, MO 65251
(314) 642-2251

Wilson College
1015 Philadelphia Ave.
Chambersburg, PA 17201-1285
(717) 264-4141

Wood School
8 E 40th St.
New York, NY 10016
(212) 686-9040

EDUCATIONAL GRANTS, SCHOLARSHIPS, AND FELLOWSHIPS

See also Foundations and Funding Sources.

AAUW American Fellowships
American Assoc. of University Women, Educational Foundation
1111 16th St. NW
Washington, DC 20036
(202) 728-7603;
Fax: (202) 872-1425

Nine postdoctoral fellowships ranging from $20,000 to $25,000. Dissertation fellowships of $12,500 each.

AAUW Career Development Grants
American Assoc. of University Women, Wilmington, Delaware Branch
1800 Fairfax Blvd.
Wilmington, DE 19803
(302) 478-7058

Grants of $1000 to $5000 for women who, through higher education, are reentering the work force, making career changes, or advancing their careers.

AAUW Career Development Grants
American Assoc. of University Women, Educational Foundation
1111 16th St. NW
Washington, DC 20036
(202) 728-7603;
Fax: (202) 872-1425

Seed-money grants ranging from $1000 to $5000 to aid women who wish to reenter the job field after a prolonged leave, change career paths, or advance in their current fields. Applicants must enroll in courses that are prerequisites for professional employment plans.

AAUW Community Action Grants
American Assoc. of University Women, Educational Foundation
1111 16th St. NW
Washington, DC 20036
(202) 728-7603;
Fax: (202) 872-1425

Grants of $14,500 for projects that address women's issues and problems through community programs or public education.

AAUW Dissertation Fellowships in Engineering
American Assoc. of University Women, Educational Foundation
1111 16th St. NW
Washington, DC 20036
(202) 728-7603;
Fax: (202) 872-1425

Fellowship stipends of $12,500 for full-time work on dissertations in engineering.

AAUW Focus Professions Fellowship
American Assoc. of University Women, Educational Foundation
1111 16th St. NW
Washington, DC 20036
(202) 728-7603;
Fax: (202) 872-1425

Fellowship stipends from $5000 to $9500 for full-time study in the fields of business administration, law, and medicine.

AAUW Science/Technology Fellowships
American Assoc. of University Women, Educational Foundation
1111 16th St. NW
Washington, DC 20036
(202) 728-7603;
Fax: (202) 872-1425

Fellowship stipends of $5000 to $9500 for women in their final year of a master's degree program in architecture, computer information science, engineering, or mathematics.

Alexandria Apostolides Sonenfeld Award
Daughters of Penelope
AHEPA Senior Women's Auxiliary
1909 Q St. NW, Ste. 500
Washington, DC 20009

Scholarships of $1000 for women about to enter undergraduate studies. Must be of Greek descent, related to a Daughter of Penelope, or a member of the Maids of Athena.

Alice E. Smith Fellowship
State Historical Society of Wisconsin
816 State St.
Madison, WI 53706
(608) 264-6400

Grants available to women working on graduate-level research projects on women in American history.

Alpha Epsilon Iota Scholarship Fund
Trustcorp Society Bank
100 S Main St.
Ann Arbor, MI 48104
(313) 994-5555

Scholarships up to $3000 awarded to women medical students.

Amaranth Fund Awards
California Masonic Foundation
1111 California St.
San Francisco, CA 94108

Funds available up to $1000 to California women attending California colleges.

Amelia Earhart Fellowship Awards
Zonta International Foundation
557 W Randolph St.
Chicago, IL 60606-2284
(312) 930-5848;
Fax: (312) 930-0951

Forty fellowships of $6000 each awarded annually for women doing graduate work in aerospace-related fields.

Amelia Greenbaum Scholarship Fund
National Council of Jewish Women
Greater Boston Section
75 Harvard Ave.
Allston, MA 02134

Scholarships awarded to female Jewish students attending or planning to attend colleges or universities.

American Society for Microbiology Fellowships
American Society of Microbiology
1325 Massachusetts Ave. NW
Washington, DC 20005
(202) 737-3600

Offers grants and fellowships to women in science. Focuses on women in the fields of microbiology, immunology, and biochemistry.

America's National Teenager Scholarship
National Teenager Foundation
1001 W Euless Blvd., Ste. 208
Euless, TX 76040
(817) 540-0313

Offers cash, tuition scholarships, and other awards to females between thirteen and eighteen years old.

Anne O'Hare McCormick Scholarship
Newswomen's Club of New York
15 Gramercy Park S
New York, NY 10003
(212) 777-1610

Offers scholarships of between $2500 and $3100 to women students who have been accepted at Columbia University's Graduate School of Journalism.

AT&T Bell Laboratories Dual Degree Scholarships
AT&T Bell Laboratories, Special Programs
Crawfords Corner Rd., Room 1E-209
Holmdale, NJ 07733-1988
(908) 949-4301;
Fax: (908) 949-6800

Offers scholarships for women minorities, such as blacks, Hispanics, Native American Indians, etc. Women must be pursuing careers in engineering or computer science and be enrolled in an undergraduate engineering program.

AWIS Predoctoral Awards
Association for Women in Science, Educational Foundation
1522 K St. NW, Ste. 280
Washington, DC 20005
(202) 408-0742

Four $500 awards given to women in any life, physical, or social science or engineering program leading to a doctoral degree. Recipients are generally at the dissertation level of graduate work.

BPW Career Advancement Scholarships

Business and Professional Women's Foundation, Educational Programs
2012 Massachusetts Ave. NW
Washington, DC 20036
(202) 293-1200

Scholarships are awarded to women seeking reentry to the workplace and are seeking a master's degree in Business Administration. Scholarships range from $500 to $1000.

Bunting Fellowship

Mary Ingram Bunting Institute of Radcliffe College
34 Concord Ave.
Cambridge, MA 02138
(617) 495-8212;
Fax: (617) 495-8136

Stipends of $21,500 awarded to women scholars, creative writers, and visual artists for postdoctoral work.

Bunting Institute Peace Fellowships

Mary Ingram Bunting Institute of Radcliffe College
34 Concord Ave.
Cambridge, MA 02138
(617) 495-8212;
Fax: (617) 495-8136

Stipends of $21,500 awarded to women working on peaceful conflict-resolution projects on either an activist or academic basis. Applicants' work must be on the postdoctoral level.

Bunting Institute Science Scholars Fellowships

Mary Ingram Bunting Institute of Radcliffe College
34 Concord Ave.
Cambridge, MA 02138
(617) 495-8212;
Fax: (617) 495-8136

Stipends of $27,600 awarded to women scientists doing postdoctoral work.

Congressional Fellowships on Women and Public Policy

Women's Research and Education Institute
1700 18th St. NW, Ste. 400
Washington, DC 20009
(202) 328-7070

Fellowships of $11,000 for women interested in participation in and study of the formation of public policy.

Daughters of Penelope Past Grand Presidents Award

Daughters of Penelope
AHEPA Senior Women's Auxiliary
1909 Q St., Ste. 500
Washington, DC 20009

Scholarships of $500 awarded to females for undergraduate work. Must be of Greek descent, related to an *AHEPAN or a Daughter of Penelope, or a member of the Maids of Athena.*

David Sarnoff Research Center Scholarship

Society of Women Engineers
United Engineering Center,
Rm. 305
120 Wall St.
New York, NY 10005
(212) 509-9577, (800) 666-1SWE;
Fax: (212) 509-0224

A $1500 award to women entering their junior year of undergraduate work in engineering.

Digital Equipment Corporation Scholarship

Society of Women Engineers
United Engineering Center,
Rm. 305
345 E 47th St.
New York, NY 10017
(212) 705-7855

Scholarship of $1000 awarded at the end of the first year of college to a woman majoring in electrical, mechanical, or computer engineering and who is attending a university in New York or one of the New England states.

Doris Mullen Memorial Flight Scholarship

International Women Helicopter
Pilots
1619 Duke St.
Alexandria, VA 22314
(703) 683-4646

Scholarship of $5000 awarded to aid women in furthering education and experience in the helicopter industry.

Edith Nourse Rogers Scholarship Fund

Women's Army Corps Veterans
Association
P.O. Box 5577
McClellan, AL 36205
(205) 820-4019

A $1500 scholarship awarded to a woman attending a Massachusetts university. Must be a dependent of a United States veteran and major in government or political science.

Eleanor Roosevelt Teacher Fellowship

American Association of
University Women
1111 16th Ave. NW
Washington, DC 20006
(202) 728-7603;
Fax: (202) 872-1425

Fellowships range from $1000 to $10,000 for elementary and secondary school teachers working toward education and gender equity. Awards intended to aid recipients in programs to teach math and science to girls or to help girls and minorities at risk of dropping out.

Eleanor Scholar Grant

Eleanor Association
1550 N. Dearborn Pkwy.
Chicago, IL 60610
(312) 664-8245

Grants of $5000 to assist women in completing their undergraduate work. Must be attending participating Illinois universities.

Eloise Gerry Fellowships
Sigma Delta Epsilon Women in Science, Inc.
P.O. Box 4748
Ithaca, NY 14852
Fellowships from $1500 to $4000 awarded to women doing postdoctoral work in the fields of chemical and biological sciences.

ETS Postdoctoral Fellowship
Educational Testing Service
Mail Stop 30-B
Princeton, NJ 08541-0001
(609) 734-1124
Stipends of $27,000 granted to recent doctorates to aid in conducting research. Awarded to women in academic and occupational fields of psychology.

Foreign Policy Studies Advanced Research Fellowships
Social Science Research Council
605 Third Ave.
New York, NY 10158
(212) 661-0280
Fellowships awarded to women researching international relations.

General Electric Foundation Scholarships
Society of Women Engineers
United Engineering Center, Rm. 305
345 E 47th St.
New York, NY 10017
(212) 705-7855

Awards of $1000 given to women for undergraduate work in engineering and technology.

Georgia Harkness Scholarship
United Methodist Church
Office of Loans and Scholarships
General Board of Higher Education and Ministry
P.O. Box 871
Nashville, TN 37202
(615) 340-7344

Awards of up to $1000 granted to women over thirty-five preparing for the ordained ministry in the United Methodist Church.

Gladys Anderson Emerson Scholarship
Iota Sigma Pi
Dept. of Chemistry B-003,
Univ. of California
La Jolla, CA 92093
(619) 534-6479;
Fax: (619) 534-7687

Scholarships of $1000 awarded to women for undergraduate work in chemistry or biochemistry.

Gladys C. Anderson Scholarship
American Foundation for the Blind, Inc.
15 W 16th St.
New York, NY 10011
(212) 620-2000

Two $1000 scholarships awarded annually to women who are legally blind. Women must be studying religious or classical music at the undergraduate college level.

Harriett Barnhardt Wimmer Scholarship
Landscape Architecture Foundation
4401 Connecticut Ave. NW, Ste. 500
Washington, DC 20008
(202) 686-2752

Awards of $500 given to women in undergraduate landscape studies. Applicants must have design ability and have knowledge of and sensitivity to environmental issues.

Helen Miller Malloch Scholarship
National Federation of Press Women, Inc.
P.O. Box 99
Blue Springs, MD 64013
(816) 229-1666

Award of $1000 for female college students majoring in communication and seeking a degree in journalism. Must be junior, senior, or graduate-level students.

Helene Overly Scholarship
Women's Transportation Seminar
808 17th St. NW, Ste. 200
Washington, DC 20006-3953
(202) 223-9669

Scholarships of $3000 to female students in studies related to transportation.

Holly A. Cornell Scholarship
American Water Works Association
6666 W Quincy Ave.
Denver, CO 80235
(303) 794-7711;
Fax: (303) 794-7310

A $5000 award for women pursuing master's degrees in engineering.

IBM Fellowships for Women
International Business Machines
T.J. Watson Research Center
P.O. Box 218
Yorktown Heights, NY 10598

Fellowships awarded to women graduate students studying fields related to the electronics industry.

Iota Sigma Pi Undergraduate Award for Excellence in Chemistry
Dept. of Chemistry B-003,
Univ. of California
La Jolla, CA 92093
(619) 534-6479;
Fax: (619) 534-7687

Awards of $300 for women chemistry students in the senior year of undergraduate work.

Irene Stambler Vocational Opportunities Grant
Jewish Social Service Agency
6123 Montrose Rd.
Rockville, MD 20852
(301) 816-2676

Grant of $2500 to help Jewish women who are working toward financial self-sufficiency after a divorce, separation, or widowhood. Must demonstrate financial need and have a vocational plan that can be implemented within two years.

Ivy Parker Memorial Scholarship
Society of Women Engineers
United Engineering Center,
Rm. 345
345 E 47th St.
New York, NY 10017

Award of $1000 to women engineering students entering junior or senior year of undergraduate work.

Jeanne Humphrey Block Dissertation Award
Henry A. Murray Research Center,
Radcliffe College
10 Garden St.
Cambridge, MA 02138
(617) 495-8140

Grants of $2500 awarded to women doing postgraduate-level studies in fields related to women and psychology.

Jeannette Rankin Foundation
Women's Educational Foundation
P.O. Box 6653
Athens, GA 30604

Awards thirteen $1000 awards to women throughout the U.S. who are thirty-five years or older and are pursuing undergraduate education or a certified training course. Critical financial need and achievable goals are the criteria.

Judith Resnik Memorial Scholarship
Society of Women Engineers
United Engineering Center, Rm. 305
120 Wall St.
New York, NY 10005
(212) 509-9577, (800) 666-1SWE;
Fax: (212) 509-0224

A $1000 award given to undergraduate women pursuing degrees in an engineering field with a space-related major who want careers in the space industry.

Julia Kiene Fellowship
Electrical Women's Round Table
315 22nd Ave. S
Seattle, WA 98144

Awards for up to $2000 given to women doing graduate work in electrical fields.

Junior Native Daughter Scholarship
Native Daughters of the
Golden West
543 Baker St.
San Francisco, CA 94117-1405
(415) 563-9091

Awards of $100 for active members of the Junior Daughters for undergraduate work.

Kansas City Speech Pathology Award
Kappa Kappa Gamma Fraternity
P.O. Box 2079
Columbus, OH 43216-2079

Scholarships of $2000 awarded to women enrolled in a program of *clinical graduate training in speech pathology at the New York University Medical Center.*

Kathryn G. Siphers Scholarship
Women Band Directors National Association
344 Overlook Dr.
West Lafayette, IN 47906
(317) 463-1738

Scholarship given to young college women studying to be band directors. Must be instrumental music majors and working toward a degree in music education.

Lillian Moller Gilbreth Scholarship
Society for Women Engineers
United Engineering Center,
Rm. 305
120 Wall St.
New York, NY 10005
(212) 509-9577, (800) 666-1SWE;
Fax: (212) 509-0224

Award of $4000 for junior or senior women engineering students for undergraduate work.

Lucy Corbett Scholarship
Women in Communications, Inc.,
Detroit Chapter
35918 Rewa
Mt. Clemens, MI 48043
(313) 226-9282

Scholarships of $1000 for women pursuing undergraduate or graduate-level degrees in journalism or communications at a Michigan college or university.

Luise Meyer-Schutzmeister Award
Award for Women in Science-Educational Foundation
1522 K St. NW, Ste. 820
Washington, DC 20005
(202) 408-0742

Award of $500 to female graduate students in physics.

Lyle Mamer Fellowship
Electrical Women's Round Table
P.O. Box 292793
Nashville, TN 37229-2793

Offers awards up to $1000 to women doing graduate work. Awards given to women in fields related to electronics or mass communications.

Mary Isabel Sibley Fellowship
Phi Beta Society
1811 Q St. NW
Washington, DC 20009
(202) 265-3808

Fellowship of $7000 to women doing doctoral or postdoctoral work and research on Greek language, culture, or art, or French language or art.

McKnight Junior Faculty Development Fellowships
Florida Endowment Fund for Higher Education
201 E Kennedy Blvd., Ste. 1525
Tampa, FL 33602
(813) 221-2772;
Fax: (813) 224-0192

Fellowships of $15,000 for graduate work or professional development. Promotes teaching and research for minority junior faculty members with emphasis on African Americans and women.

NABWA Scholarship Award

National Association of Black Women Attorneys
3711 Macomb St. NW, 2nd Fl.
Washington, DC 20016
(202) 966-9693;
Fax: (202) 244-6648

Scholarships offered to provide financial assistance to African American female law students.

National Association for Women in Education Women's Research Awards

1325 18th St. NW, Ste. 210
Washington, DC 20036
(202) 659-9330

Awards of $500 for women graduate students who are involved in research for, by, and about women.

National League of American Pen Women Scholarships for Mature Women

1300 17th St. NW
Washington, DC 20036
(202) 785-1997

Scholarships of $1000 awarded to women in the fields of the arts, letters, or music. Scholarship is intended to encourage the creative and academic goals of older women.

National Miss Indian U.S. Scholarship

American Indian Heritage Foundation
6501 Arlington Blvd.
Falls Church, VA 22044
(703) 237-7500

A program established in 1985 and funded by the American Indian Heritage Foundation. Applicants must be high school graduates eighteen to twenty-six years of age. A woman is chosen each year to serve as a national spokesperson on American Indian issues.

NCAA Ethnic Minority and Women's Enhancement Programs

National Collegiate Athletic Association
6201 College Blvd.
Overland, KS 66211-2422
(913) 339-1906

Awards of $6,000 for minorities and women involved in intercollegiate sports. Candidates must be entering first year of postgraduate work.

New Mexico Graduate Fellowships

New Mexico Educational Assistance Foundation
3900 Osuna, NE
P.O. Box 27020
Albuquerque, NM 87125-7020
(505) 345-3371

Offers fellowships up to $7200 for women and minorities in academic *fields of regional and national priority in the New Mexico public universities.*

New York Life Foundation Scholarships for Women in the Health Professions
Business and Professional Women's Foundation,
Educational Programs
2012 Massachusetts Ave. NW
Washington, DC 20036

Scholarships from $500 to $1000 for women thirty years of age or older beginning a career in the health profession or for women seeking advancement in the health care profession.

NFPW Junior/Senior Scholarships
National Federation of Press Women, Inc.
P.O. Box 99
Blue Springs, MD 64013
(816) 229-1666

Scholarships of $1000 for female college students majoring in communication or journalism. Candidates must be juniors or seniors at the undergraduate level.

NIAAA Individual National Research Service Awards
National Institute on Alcohol Abuse and Alcoholism
5600 Fishers Ln.
Rockville, MD 20857
(301) 443-4223

Awards and stipends for women doing doctorate and postdoctorate research on alcohol projects. Candidates should intend to pursue careers in health-related research.

NRC/ACRS Science and Engineering Fellowships
U.S. Nuclear Regulatory Commission Advisory Committee on Reactor Safeguards
Washington, D.C. 20555

Fellowships from $32,000 to $65,000 awarded to women doing doctorate or postdoctorate work in nuclear power safety or nuclear power production.

NSF Graduate Research Fellowships for Women in Engineering
National Science Foundation
2101 Constitution Ave.
Washington, DC 20418
(202) 357-9598

Fellowships awarded to women doing graduate study and research in engineering fields.

NSF Minority Graduate Fellowships for Women
National Science Foundation
2101 Constitution Ave.
Washington, DC 20418
(202) 357-9498

Fellowships awarded to women who are members of an ethnic minority and are pursuing graduate or postgraduate study in an engineering field.

**Olive Lynn Salembier
Scholarship**
Society of Women Engineers
United Engineering Center,
Rm. 305
345 E 47th St.
New York, NY 10017
(212) 705-7855

*Award of $1500 for women doing
graduate or undergraduate studies
in engineering.*

**Patricia Robert Harris Public
Service Fellowship**
U.S. Dept. of Education
Office of Student Financial
Assistance
Washington, DC 20202
(202) 732-3154

*Awards of $10,000 for women or
minorities doing doctorate or postdoctorate work in academic areas.*

**Rocky Mountain Women's
Institute**
Foote Hall, Rm. 317
7150 Montview Blvd.
Denver, CO 80220
(303) 871-6923

*Offers seven to ten one-year associ-
ateships to women artists, writers,
and scholars annually. Sponsors
public lectures, readings, and art
exhibits.*

Root Foreign Languages
Kappa Kappa Gamma Fraternity
P.O. Box 2079
Columbus, OH 43216-2079

*Scholarships of $1000 to women
wishing to study a foreign language
in a country in which that language
is spoken. Applicants must be a
member of the Kappa Kappa
Gamma fraternity.*

**Sarah Bradley Tyson Memorial
Fellowship**
Woman's National Farm and
Garden Association
13 Davis Dr.
Saginaw, MI 48602
(517) 793-1714

*Awards of $500 for women study-
ing fields related to agriculture and
horticulture who demonstrate leadership and innovation in their academic and applied work.*

**Sigma Alpha Iota Inter-
American Music Awards**
165 W 82nd St.
New York, NY 10024
(212) 724-2809

*Award of $500 to women compos-
ers. Applicants must submit a com-
position for instrumental solo or
instrumental solo with piano to be
judged.*

Sportgirl of the Year Scholarship
Teen Magazine
8490 Sunset Blvd.
Los Angeles, CA 90069
(213) 854-2950

*Scholarship of $10,000 awarded to
teenage girls who have excelled in
athletics and who wish to seek a
career in postsecondary education.*

Applicants must also exhibit leadership skills and have a good academic record.

Syvenna Foundation
Rt. 1, Box 193
Linden, TX 75563
(903) 835-8252;
Fax: (903) 835-8252

Sponsors a writer-in-residence program for beginning and intermediate women writers. Offers four terms per year in which two women per term are offered a rent-and-utilities-free private cottage and a $300 per month stipend.

Women's Forum of Colorado Foundation
12501 WCR 74
Eaton, CO 80615
(303) 654-0094;
Fax: (303) 727-4504

Offers three $3000 grants annually to Colorado women pursuing graduate degrees in nontraditional fields.

Woodrow Wilson Women's Studies Research Grant
Woodrow Wilson National Fellowship Foundation
P.O. Box 642
Princeton, NJ 08542
(609) 924-4713; Fax: (609) 497-9064

Grants of $1000 for women doing doctoral work and research in the fields of science, history, psychology, or arts, as related to women.

STUDIES PROGRAMS

In many ways, women's studies programs can be considered the academic arm of the women's movement. They explore historical, social, and political contributions women have made throughout the decades. The following is a listing of some of these programs available in colleges and universities throughout the United States.

Africana Women's Studies Program
Clark Atlanta Univ.
223 James P. Brawley Dr.
Atlanta, GA 30314
(404) 880-8153;
Fax: (404) 880-8731

Albion College Women's Studies Program
Albion, MI 49224
(517) 629-1000;
Fax: (517) 629-0509

American University Women's Studies Program
4400 Massachusetts Ave. NW
Washington, DC 20016
(202) 885-2485;
Fax: (202) 885-2013

Amherst College
Dept. of Women and Gender Studies
14 Grosvenor House
Amherst, MA 01002
(413) 542-5781

Antioch University Women's Studies in Europe
Antioch Education Abroad
Yellow Springs, OH 45387
(513) 767-6366;
Fax: (513) 767-6469

Arizona State University Women's Studies Program
Tempe, AZ 85287-1801
(602) 965-2358;
Fax: (602) 965-1093

Auburn University Women's Studies Program
8030 Haley Center
Auburn, AL 36849
(205) 844-6373

Barnard College Women's Studies Program
203 Barnard Hall
New York, NY 10027
(212) 854-2108

Bates College Women's Studies Program
Lewiston, ME 04240
(207) 786-6335

Bellevue College Women's Studies Program
Dept. of English
Kearney, NE 68849
(308) 234-8294

Bennett College Women's Studies Program
900 E Washington St.
Greensboro, NC 27401
(919) 370-8690

Boston College Women's Studies Program
Dept. of Sociology
McGuinn Hall
Chestnut Hill, MA 02167
(617) 552-4139

Boston University Women's Studies Program
718 Commonwealth Ave., Rm. 405
Boston, MA 02215
(617) 353-2948

Bowling Green State University Women's Studies Program
Union Bldg.
Bowling Green, OH 43402
(419) 372-7133

Brandeis University
415 South St.
Waltham, MA 00254

Brigham Young University Women's Studies Program
970 SWKT
Provo, UT 84602
(801) 378-4636

Brown University Women's Studies Program
Pembroke Center for Teaching and Research on Women, Box 1958
Providence, RI 02912
(401) 863-2643

Bryn Mawr College Feminist and Gender Studies
Dept. of History
Thomas Hall
Bryn Mawr, PA 19010
(215) 526-5066;
Fax: (215) 525-4739

Burlington College Feminist Studies Program
95 N Ave.
Burlington, VT 05401
(802) 862-9616

Carroll College Women's Studies Program
Waukesha, WI 53186
(414) 547-1211

Casper College Women's Studies Program
125 College Dr.
Casper, WY 82601
(307) 268-2491

Central Washington University Women's Studies Program
Ellensburg, WA 98926
(509) 963-1858

Chaminade University
Women's Studies
3140 Walalae Ave.
Honolulu, HI 96816
(808) 735-4711

Colby College Women's Studies Program
Mayflower Hill Dr.
Waterville, ME 04901
(207) 872-3566

Colgate University Women's Studies Program
Hamilton, NY 13346-1398
(315) 824-1000;
Fax: (315) 824-1000

College of Charleston Women's Studies Program
Philosophy Dept.
Charleston, SC 29424
(803) 792-5687

Columbia University Women's Studies Program
763 Schermerhorn Extension
116th St. & Broadway
New York, NY 10027
(212) 854-1754

Cornell University Women's Studies Program
391 Uris Hall
Ithaca, NY 14853
(607) 255-6480

Dartmouth College Women's Studies Program
2 Carpenter Hall
Hanover, NH 03755
(603) 646-2722

Delaware State College Women's Studies Program
Dover, DE 19901
(302) 739-4000

**DePaul University Women's
Studies Program**
802 W Beldon Ave.
McGaw Bldg., Rm. 245
Chicago, IL 60601
(312) 781-9430

**DePauw University Women's
Studies Program**
109 Asbury Hall
Greencastle, IN 46135
(317) 658-4505

**Drake University Women's
Studies Program**
2700 University Ave.
Des Moines, IA 50311
(515) 271-3563

**Drew University Women's
Studies Program**
36 Madison Ave.
Bowne Bldg.
Madison, NJ 07940
(201) 408-3632;
Fax: (201) 408-3939

Duke University
Women's Studies Program
207 E Duke Bldg.
Durham, NC 27706
(919) 684-5683

Eastern Michigan University
Women's Studies Program
720 Pray-Harrold
Ypsilanti, MI 48197
(313) 487-1177

**Emerson College Women's
Studies Program**
100 Beacon St.
Boston, MA 02116
(617) 578-8600;
Fax: (617) 578-8509

**Emory University Women's
Studies Program**
210 Physics Bldg.
Atlanta, GA 30314
(404) 727-0096;
Fax: (404) 727-0251

**Evergreen State College
Women's Studies Program**
Library 2211
Olympia, WA 98505
(206) 866-6000

**Florida State University
Women's Studies Program**
R-2029
Tallahassee, FL 32306-2029
(904) 644-9514

**Fordham University Women's
Studies Program**
250 Bedford Park Blvd. W
Bronx, NY 10468
(718) 960-8847;
Fax: (718) 960-8935

**George Mason University
Women's Studies Program**
4400 University Dr.
Fairfax, VA 22030
(703) 993-1000

Georgetown University Women's Studies Program
Dept. of English
Washington, DC 20057
(202) 687-7558

George Washington University Women's Studies Program
2201 G St. NW
217 Funger Hall
Washington, DC 20052
(202) 994-6942

Gonzaga University Women's Studies Program
Spokane, WA 99258
(509) 484-6484

Great Lakes College Association Women's Studies Program
2929 Plymouth Rd.,
No. 207
Ann Arbor, MI 48105-3206
(313) 761-4833;
Fax: (313) 761-3939

Grinnel College Committee on Gender and Women's Studies
Women's Studies Program
Harry Hopkins House
Grinnell, IA 50112
(515) 269-4000

Harvard University Women's Studies Program
34 Kirkland St.
Cambridge, MA 02138
(617) 495-9199;
Fax: (617) 495-9855

Harvey Mudd College Women's Studies Program
Kingston Hall
301 E 21st
Claremont, CA 91711
(714) 621-8000;
Fax: (714) 621-8360

Haverford College Feminism and Gender Studies
Haverford, PA 19041
(215) 896-1156;
Fax: (215) 896-1224

Hofstra University
Women's Studies
1000 Fulton Ave.
Hempstead, NY 11550
(516) 463-5828

Hunter College of the City University of New York
Women's Studies Program
695 Park Ave.
New York, NY 10021
(212) 772-5680;
Fax: (212) 772-4941

Illinois State University
Women's Studies Program
604 S Main
Normal, IL 61761
(309) 438-2947

Indiana University Bloomington
Women's Studies Program
Memorial Hall E 131
Bloomington, IN 47405
(812) 855-0101

Iowa State University
Women's Studies Program
203 Ross Hall
Ames, IA 50011
(515) 294-3286

Johns Hopkins University
Women's Studies Program
300 Jenkins Hall
Baltimore, MD 21218
(301) 516-6166

Kalamazoo College Women's
Studies Program
1200 Academy St.
Kalamazoo, MI 49007
(616) 383-8494

Kansas State University
Women's Studies Program
22 Eisenhower Hall
Manhattan, KS 66506-1001
(913) 532-5738;
Fax: (913) 532-7004

Lewis and Clark College
Gender Studies
Palantine Hill Rd.
Portland, OR 97219
(503) 768-7000

Louisiana State University
Women's Studies
Box 65
6363 St. Charles Ave.
New Orleans, LA 70118
(504) 865-2567

Mankato State University
Women's Studies Program
P.O. Box 8400
Mankato, MN 56002
(507) 389-2077

Mary Washington College
Race and Gender Project
Fredricksburg, VA 22401
(703) 899-4117;
Fax: (703) 899-4373

Medgar Evers College of CUNY
International Cross-Cultural Black
Women's Studies Summer Institute
1150 Carroll St.
Brooklyn, NY 11225
Fax: (718) 270-5126

Michigan State University
Women's Studies Program
301 Linton Hall
East Lansing, MI 48824
(517) 355-4495;
Fax: (517) 353-5368

Mississippi University for
Women
Women's Studies Program
Box W-1603
Columbus, MS 39701
(601) 329-7142

Montana State University
Women's Studies Program
College of Letters and Science
Bozeman, MT 59717
(406) 994-4248

Mount Holyoke Women's
Studies Program
104 Dickinson House
South Hadley, MA 02193
(617) 893-1820

Northwestern University
Women's Studies Program
2000 Sheridan Rd.
Evanston, IL 60208
(708) 491-5871

Oberlin College Women's Studies Program
Rice Hall 16
Oberlin, OH 44074
(216) 775-8409;
Fax: (216) 775-8124

Oklahoma State University Women's Studies Program
College of Arts and Sciences
Stillwater, OK 74078
(405) 624-5663

Old Dominion University
Women's Studies Program
Norfolk, VA 23529
(804) 683-3823

Oregon State University Women's Studies Program
Social Science 200
Crovallis, OR 97331-6208
(503) 747-4501

Pitzer College Women's Studies Program
1050 N Mills Ave.
Claremont, CA 91711
(714) 621-8000

Princeton University Women's Studies Program
113 Dickinson
Princeton, NJ 08544
(609) 258-5430

Purdue University
Women's Studies Program
1361 Liberal Arts
Liberal Arts & Education Building,
Rm. 2238
West Lafayette, IN 47907-1361
(316) 494-4600

Radcliffe College, Women's Studies Program
Cambridge, MA 02138
(617) 253-8844

Sarah Lawrence College Women's Studies Program
Bronxville, NY 10708
(914) 395-2405

Scripps College Women's Studies Program
1030 Columbia Ave.
Claremont, CA 91711-3948
(714) 621-8000

Skidmore College Women's Studies Program
North Broadway
Saratoga Springs, NY 12866
(518) 584-5000

Smith College Women's Studies Program
Hatfield Hall
Northampton, MA 01063
(413) 585-3336;
Fax: (413) 585-2075

South Dakota State University Women's Studies Program
Political Science Dept.
Brookings, SD 57007
(605) 688-4914

Southern Methodist University
Women's Studies Program
217 CD Blocker Bldg.
College Station, TX 77843-4227
(409) 845-9670

Stanford University Program in Feminist Studies
Stanford, CA 94305-8640
(415) 723-2412

Syracuse University Women's Studies Program
Hall of Languages, Rm. 307
Syracuse, NY 13244-1170
(315) 443-3707

Towson State University
Women's Studies Dept.
Baltimore, MD 21204
(410) 830-2660

Tufts University Women's Studies Program
55 Talbot Ave.
Medford, MA 02155
(617) 381-3184

Tulane University Women's Studies Program
1229 Broadway
New Orleans, LA 70118
(504) 865-5238

University of Alabama Women's Studies Program
Humanities Bldg., Rm. 204
Birmingham, AL 35294
(205) 934-8599;
Fax: (205) 934-9896

University of Arizona Women's Studies Program
Douglass 102
Tucson, AZ 85721
(602) 621-7338;
Fax: (602) 621-9424

University of Arkansas Women's Studies Program
2801 S University
Little Rock, AR 72204
(501) 569-3234;
Fax: (501) 569-8775

University of Baltimore Women's Studies Program
Frostburg, MD 21532
(301) 689-4445;
Fax: (301) 689-4737

University of California, Berkeley
Women's Studies Dept.
301 Campbell Hall
Berkeley, CA 94720
(510) 642-2767;
Fax: (510) 642-4607

University of California, Davis
Women's Studies Program
307 Young Hall
Davis, CA 95616
(916) 752-4686

University of California, Irvine
Women's Studies Program
403 Social Science Tower
Irvine, CA 92717
(714) 856-4234;
Fax: 856-8441

**University of California,
Los Angeles**
Women's Studies Program
240 Kinsey Hall
405 Hilgard Ave.
Los Angeles, CA 90024-1453
(213) 206-8101

**University of California,
San Diego**
Women's Studies Program
c/o John Muir College-0006
La Jolla, CA 92093
(619) 534-7127

**University of California,
Santa Barbara**
Women's Studies Program
11 O'Connor Hall,
Rm. 329
Santa Clara, CA 95053
(408) 554-4461

**University of California,
Santa Cruz**
Women's Studies Program
186 Kresge College
Santa Cruz, CA 95064
(408) 459-4324

University of Cincinnati
Center for Women's Studies
Program
ML-164
Cincinnati, OH 45221
(513) 556-6776; Fax: (513) 556-0128

**University of Colorado,
Boulder**
Women's Studies Program
Campus Box 246
Boulder, CO 80309
(303) 492-8923

**University of Colorado,
Colorado Springs**
Women's Studies Program
Austin Bluffs Pkwy.
P.O. Box 7150
Colorado Springs, CO 90833
(719) 593-3538

University of Connecticut
Women's Studies Program
2131 Hillside Rd.
U-181
Storrs, CT 06269-3181
(203) 486-3970;
Fax: (203) 486-4789

**University of Delaware Women's
Studies Program**
333 Smith Hall
Newark, DE 19716
(302) 831-8474

University of Denver
Women's Studies Program
3401 S University Blvd.
2130 S Race, Rm. 119
Denver, CO 80208
(303) 871-2406

**University of Detroit Women's
Studies Program**
4001 W McNichols
Detroit, MI 48221
(313) 993-1000

**University of Florida Women's
Studies Program**
8 Anderson Hall
Gainesville, FL 32611
(904) 392-3365

University of Georgia, Athens
Women's Studies Program
230-F Main Library
Athens, GA 30602
(404) 542-2846

University of Hawaii at Hilo
Women's Studies Program
Chancellor's Office
Hilo, HI 96720-4091
(808) 933-3422

University of Hawaii at Honolulu
Women's Studies
3140 Walalae Ave.
Honolulu, HI 96816
(808) 735-4711

University of Hawaii at Manoa
Women's Studies Program
2424 Maile Way, Porteus 722
Honolulu, HI 96822
(808) 956-7464;
Fax: (808) 942-5710

University of Kansas Women's Studies Program
2120 Wescoe Hall
Lawrence, KS 66045-2117
(913) 864-4011

University of Kentucky Women's Studies Program
241 Patterson Office Tower
Lexington, KY 40506-0027
(606) 257-1388

University of Louisville Women's Studies Program
College of History
Louisville, KY 40292
(502) 588-6831

University of Maine Women in the Curriculum, Women's Studies Program
5278 Fernald Hall
Orono, ME 04469
(207) 581-1228

University of Maryland Women's Studies Program
1121 Mill Bldg.
College Park, MD 20742
(301) 405-6877

University of Michigan Women's Studies Program
550 University, Rm. 234
West Engineering
Ann Arbor, MI 48109-1092
(313) 763-2047

University of Minnesota, Duluth
Women's Studies Program
469 AB Anderson Hall
10 University Dr.
Duluth, MN 55812-2496
(218) 726-7953;
Fax: (218) 726-6386

University of Mississippi Women's Studies Program
Sarah Isom Center
Oxford, MS 38677
(601) 232-5916

University of Missouri, Columbia
Women's Studies Program
309 Switzler Hall
Columbia, MO 65211
(314) 882-2703

**University of Missouri,
Kansas City**
Women's Studies Program
5700 Rock Hill Rd.
Kansas City, MO 64110
(816) 235-1000

**University of Montana Women's
Studies Program**
Philosophy Dept.
Missoula, MT 59812
(406) 243-2845

University of Nebraska, Lincoln
Women's Studies Program
202 Andrews Hall
Lincoln, NE 68588-0333
(402) 472-6357

University of Nevada, Las Vegas
Women's Studies Program
4505 Maryland Pkwy.
Las Vegas, NV 89154
(702) 739-3322

University of Nevada, Reno
Women's Studies Program
090 UNR
Reno, NV 89557
(702) 784-1560

**University of New Hampshire
Women's Studies Program**
304A Dimond Library
Durham, NH 03824
(603) 862-2194

**University of New Mexico
Women's Studies Program**
2142 Mesa Vista Hall 2130
Albuquerque, NM 87131
(505) 277-3854

**University of North Carolina at
Chapel Hill**
Women's Studies Program
207 Caldwell Hall/CB 3135
Chapel Hill, NC 27599-3135
(919) 962-3908

**University of North Carolina at
Charlotte**
Women's Studies Program
301 Kennedy
Charlotte, NC 28223
(704) 547-4312

**University of North Carolina at
Greensboro**
Women's Studies Program
200 Foust Blvd.
Greensboro, NC 27410-5001
(919) 292-5511

University of North Dakota
Women's Studies Program
Box 42, University Sta.
Grand Forks, ND 58202
(701) 777-4115

**University of North Florida
Women's Studies Program**
College of Arts and Sciences
4567 St. John's Bluff Rd.
Jacksonville, FL 32216
(904) 646-2666

**University of Oklahoma
Women's Studies Program**
530 Physical Science Center
Norman, OK 73019
(405) 325-3481

University of Oregon Women's Studies Program
636 Prince L. Campbell Hall
Eugene, OR 97403
(503) 346-5529;
Fax: (503) 346-3127

University of Pennsylvania Women's Studies Program
3440 Market, Rm. 590
Philadelphia, PA 19104-3325
(215) 898-8740

University of Pittsburgh Women's Studies Program
4200 Fifth Ave.
Pittsburgh, PA 15260
(412) 624-6485

University of Rhode Island Women's Studies Program
315 Roosevelt Hall
Kingston, RI 02881-0806
(401) 792-5150;
Fax: (401) 792-2892

University of South Carolina Women's Studies Program
1710 College St.
Columbia, SC 29208
(803) 777-4007

University of South Dakota Women's Studies Program
414 E Clark St.
Vermillion, SD 57069
(605) 677-5229;
Fax: (605) 677-5073

University of Tennessee, Knoxville
Women's Studies Program
2012 Lake Ave.
Knoxville, TN 37996-4102
(615) 974-2409

University of Tennessee, Memphis
Women's Studies Program
Memphis, TN 38163
(901) 528-5560

University of Texas at Arlington Center for Women's Studies Program
Dept. of Psychology
Box 19529
Arlington, TX 76019-0529
(817) 273-2861;
Fax: (817) 273-3392

University of Texas at Austin Women's Studies Program
WMB 206B
Austin, TX 78712
(512) 471-1122

University of Texas at El Paso Women's Studies Program
401 Liberal Arts
University Ave.
El Paso, TX 79968
(915) 747-5200

University of Utah Women's Studies Program
217 Bldg. 44
Salt Lake City, UT 84112
(801) 581-8094;
Fax: (801) 581-5580

**University of Vermont Women's
Studies Program**
Colchester Ave.
Burlington, VT 05401
(802) 658-0337

**University of Virginia Women's
Studies Program**
11 Miner Hall
Charlottesville, VA 22901
(804) 982-2961

**University of Washington
Women's Studies Program**
GN-45
Seattle, WA 98195
(206) 543-6900

**University of Wisconsin,
Green Bay
Women's Studies Program**
2420 Nicolet Dr.
Green Bay, WI 54311-7001
(414) 465-2355

**University of Wisconsin, Madison
Women's Studies Program**
209 N Brooks St.
Madison, WI 53715
(608) 263-4703;
Fax: (608) 263-6448

**University of Wyoming Women's
Studies Program**
P.O. Box 4297
Laramie, WY 82071
(307) 766-6870

**Utah State University Women's
Studies Committee**
Logan, UT 84322-3510
(801) 750-1256;
Fax: (801) 750-1240

**Vanderbilt University Women's
Studies Program**
Box 86, Sta. B
Nashville, TN 37203
(615) 898-2645

**Vassar College Women's
Studies Program**
Raymond Ave.
Box 205
Poughkeepsie, NY 12601
(914) 437-7144

**Villanova University Women's
Studies Program**
Villanova, PA 19085
(215) 645-4483

**Washington State University
Women's Studies Program**
Pullman, WA 99164-4171
(509) 335-1794;
Fax: (509) 335-4032

Weaton College
Women's Studies Program
Norton, MI 02766
(508) 285-7722

**Wellesley College Women's
Studies Program**
106 Central St.
Wellesley, MA 02181-8201
(617) 235-0320

**Wesleyan University Women's
Studies Program**
287 High St.
Middletown, CT 06459
(203) 347-9411

**West Virginia University
Women's Studies Program**
218 Eiesland Hall
Morgantown, WV 26506
(304) 293-2339

**Whitman College Women's
Studies Program**
P.O. Box 1647
Yakima, WA 98907
(509) 575-2915

**Wilkes University Women's
Studies Program**
Liberal Arts and Human Sciences
South River St.
P.O. Box 111
Wilkes-Barre, PA 18766
(717) 824-4651

**Williams College Women's
Studies Program**
Dept. of English
Stetson Hall
Williamstown, MA 02167
(413) 597-2567

**Yale University Women's Studies
Program**
Yale Sta.
80 Wall St.
P.O. Box 5046
New Haven, CT 06520
(203) 432-0845

❏ Family, Children, and Youth Services

Aid to Incarcerated Mothers.
See Special Interests: Prisoners' Services.

Advocacy Press
P.O. Box 236
Santa Barbara, CA 93102
(805) 962-2728 .

A publisher of numerous titles of nonsexist children's literature. Write for catalog.

American Mothers, Inc.
The Waldorf Astoria
301 Park Ave.
New York, NY 10022
(212) 755-2539;
Fax: (212) 755-2539

An organization dedicated to honoring motherhood and strengthening home life and family values. Sponsors a mother's network and several educational programs. Each year it publicizes and promotes Mother's Day and selects a mother of the year.

Chain of Life
Box 8081
Berkeley, CA 94707

Works on the issue of adoption from a feminist perspective. Publishes a newsletter that addresses such topics as birth parents' rights, birth mothers' rights, open adoptions, etc.

Children's Defense Fund
122 C St. NW
Washington, DC 20001
(202) 628-8787

A national public charity that serves as a voice for children. Offers monthly newsletter, calendars, and posters. Addresses child health, education, child care, youth employment, and adolescent pregnancy prevention.

Children's Foundation
725 15th St. NW, Ste. 505
Washington, DC 20005
(202) 347-3300;
Fax: (202) 347-3382

Advocacy group for children and their families. Committed to helping legislators reform child welfare laws, custody and child support rulings, day care, federal food as-

sistance programs and health care, among other issues.

Child Support & Custody Project
Women's Legal Defense Fund
2000 P St. NW, #710
Washington, DC 20036

Provides legal assistance to policy-makers regarding the issues of child support and custody. See also Legal Services.

Committee for Mother and Child Rights
Rt. 1, Box 256A
Clear Brook, VA 22624
(703) 722-3652

An organization for mothers with custody-related problems. Helps mothers and children going through contested custody. Educates the public about injustices they believe occur to mothers and children. See also Violence Against Women.

Compleat Mother.
See Newspapers, Newsletters, and Magazines.

Custody Action for Lesbian Mothers.
See Lesbian and Gay Organizations.

Delaware Association of Mothers
8428 Society Dr.
Claymont, DE 19703
(302) 798-8801

An organization of mothers united

to strengthen moral and spiritual values related to families. See also Religious and Spiritual Groups.

Depression After Delivery.
See Health Organizations: Mental Health Services.

Families First
250 Baltic St.
Brooklyn, NY 11201
(718) 237-1862;
Fax: (718) 237-1862

Offers support groups, children's activities, parenting workshops, and regular daily drop-in hours where parents can meet and children can play. Primarily for preschool-age children, but also occasionally offers after-school classes for older children. See also Special Interests.

Family Next Door.
See Lesbian and Gay Organizations.

Family of the Americas Foundation
P.O. Box 219
Mandeville, LA 70470-0219
(504) 626-7724;
Fax: (504) 626-4981

Teaches a birth regulation method. Assists parents in providing effective sex education for their children. Teaches adolescents about fertility and the importance of accepting responsibility for their sex-

ual behavior. See also Health Organizations.

FEMALE (Formerly Employed Mothers at Loose Ends)
P.O. Box 31
Elmhurst, IL 60126
(708) 941-3553

A national organization of women who have left the paid work force to raise their children at home. Members reject the superwoman myth (doing it all at one time) in favor of sequencing (doing it all, one at a time). Local chapters offer support and companionship through meetings, events, "Mom's Night Out Dinners," children's play groups, and other activities.

Gay & Lesbian Parents Coalition International.

See Lesbian and Gay Organizations.

Girl Scouts of the USA
830 Third Ave.
New York, NY 10028
(212) 940-7500

Helps girls ages six to seventeen develop potential, make friends, gain confidence and self-esteem, and participate in the community. Local chapters of volunteers are located nationwide.

Girls Incorporated
30 E 33rd St.
New York, NY 10016
(212) 683-1253

Helps young women to gain confidence, self-sufficiency, and overcome gender discrimination. Sponsors programs on self-esteem, careers, drug abuse, pregnancy prevention, and sports, and issues a quarterly publication. Formerly called the Girls Club of America.

La Leche League International, Incorporated
P.O. Box 1209
Franklin Park, IL 60131
(708) 455-7730, (800) LALECHE
(Breastfeeding Helpline);
Fax: (708) 455-0125

A nonprofit organization that helps mothers breastfeed their babies through a support network, interaction with health care providers, a breastfeeding helpline, educational literature, and breastfeeding support products. Chapters exist in many states and cities.

Momazons: Lesbians Choosing Children.

See Lesbian and Gay Organizations.

Mothers' Home Business Network.

See Professional and Business Associations and Networks.

Mothers Without Custody
P.O. Box 27418
Houston, TX 77227-7418
(800) 457-6962

Works to strengthen the role of the

noncustodial parent in regard to custody, child support, visitation, and parenting. Provides a network, education, and information.

Mountain Meadow
63 W Washington Ln.
Philadelphia, PA 19144
(215) 843-0332

A feminist summer camp for girls and boys aged nine to fourteen. Welcomes lesbian and gay, biracial, and single-parent families. Offers one and two week wilderness programs featuring vegetarian food, craft projects, theater, music, sports, and other activities. See also Recreation, Fitness, and Sports Groups.

National Organization of Single Mothers
P.O. Box 68
Midland, NC 28107
(704) 888-2337;
Fax: (704) 888-1752

Works to help single mothers meet the challenges of daily life. Offers support groups and self-help programs. Publishes a bimonthly newsletter. See also Newspapers, Newsletters, and Magazines.

New Moon Publishing
New Moon Magazine for Girls and New Moon Parenting of Girls
P.O. Box 3587
Duluth, MN 55803
(218) 728-5507

Publishes two periodicals, one for young girls through puberty, written exclusively by the girls themselves and gives voice to their interests and concerns. New Moon Parenting of Girls is a sensitive and informative publication for parents.

Single Mothers by Choice
P.O. Box 1642
New York, NY 10028
(212) 988-0993

Provides support and information for single women in their thirties who are considering motherhood or who have chosen to be single mothers. Publishes a quarterly newsletter.

Sisterhood of Black Single Mothers
1504 Bedford Ave.
Brooklyn, NY 11216
(718) 638-0413

Organized to give voice to the special concerns—social, economic, and emotional—of black single mothers. Publishes a newsletter.

Sister's Choice
1450 Sixth St.
Berkeley, CA 94710
(510) 524-5804;
Fax: (510) 524-9342

An organization started as a team of traveling storytellers that publishes fiction and audio recordings. Focuses on the art of storytelling and on making available nonsexist multicultural stories and songs for children and adults. See also Art and Media.

❏ Foundations and Funding Sources

*U*nlike educational grants, scholarships, and fellowships that support individuals pursuing personal educational or research goals, foundations and funds generally bestow awards to groups, projects, or individuals working for a particular cause. The following is a list of sources dedicated to funding women's concerns.

Amazon Autumn
P.O. Box 2104
Union, NJ 07083

Makes grants from $100 to $1000 to lesbians and lesbian organizations for projects that build, strengthen, and enrich the lesbian community. Preference is given to those projects based in New Jersey, New York, Pennsylvania, and Delaware. Contact them by mail for more information. See also Lesbian and Gay Organizations.

Astrea Foundation
Astrea National Lesbian Action Foundation
666 Broadway, Ste. 520
New York, NY 10012
(212) 529-8021

Funds projects that seek to end all forms of discrimination against lesbians.

Atlanta Women's Fund
The Hart Building, #449
Atlanta, GA 30303
(404) 688-5525

Offers grants to women's organizations that assist women and girls. Has already funded groups that deal with social issues, education, teenage pregnancy, and breast cancer.

Barbara Deming Memorial Fund
Money for Women
Box 40-1043
Brooklyn, NY 11240-1043

Offers small grants for feminists in the arts whose work addresses women's concerns. Grants awarded twice per year. Write to this group for more information.

Boston Women's Fund
31 St. and James Ave.
Boston, MA 02116
(617) 542-5955

Offers grants up to $2500 to women's organizations that are working to create a more just and humane society free from all inequalities.

Bucks County Women's Fund
812 N Easton Rd.
Doylestown, PA 18901
(215) 345-5440

Provides grants to organizations devoted to women and children in the local county.

Chicago Women's Foundation
230 W Superior, #400
Chicago, IL 60610
(312) 266-1176

Raises money and distributes funds to women's and girls' organizations.

Dallas Women's Foundation
9400 N Central Expressway
Dallas, TX 75231
(214) 750-6363

Offers grants to nonprofit organizations that fund women's programs.

Feminist Health Fund
P.O. Box 323
Yellow Springs, OH 45387
(513) 767-8771

Offers funds from $35 to $3500 to help Ohio women with medical and related expenses during critical ill-

ness. Aids women with cancer, heart disease, severe allergies, and depression. See Also Health Organizations.

Florida Women's Foundation
P.O. Box 1281
San Antonio, FL 33576

A foundation that distributes monies to women's groups within the state.

Foundation for a Compassionate Society
227 Congress Ave., Ste. 100
Austin, TX 78701
(512) 473-8339;
Fax: (512) 472-1043

Dedicated to creating social change by funding projects that express feminist ethical values. Sponsors a variety of projects and a grant program.

Global Fund for Women
2480 Sand Hill Rd., #100
Menlo Park, CA 94025
(415) 854-0420;
Fax: (415) 854-8050

An international fund-raising and grant-making organization that provides funds to women's groups working on women's issues. Seeks to connect groups around the globe and fund those projects that seem particularly difficult or controversial. See also Global Feminism and World Peace.

Greater Houston Women's Foundation
3 Riverway, Ste. 725
Houston, TX 77054
(713) 623-4493;
Fax: (713) 623-0733

Works to help women become productive, self-sufficient, and economically independent. Gives grants to local and nonprofit organizations that serve women, provides free courses in money management for women, and funds research on issues that affect women.

Harmony Women's Fund
P.O. Box 30015
Minneapolis, MN 55403
(612) 377-8431

A private foundation that funds local nonprofit organizations or projects that are committed to creating feminist change and are run by women. Committed to diversity and underrepresented populations such as women with disabilities, older women, rural women, lesbians, and women of color.

Illinois Women's Funding Federation
22 W Monroe, #1400
Chicago, IL 60603
(312) 762-3902

An umbrella organization of seventeen groups that provide funds to women's organizations in Illinois. They raise funds in the workplace.

Kentucky Foundation for Women, Incorporated
332 W Broadway, #1215
Louisville, KY 40202
(502) 562-0045;
Fax: (502) 561-0420

Administers a grant program for feminists in Kentucky who are using the arts for social change. Publishes a literary magazine and operates a country house used for meetings of women's groups. See also Art and Media.

Long Island Fund for Women and Girls
1740 Old Jericho Turnpike
Jericho, NY 11753
(516) 681-5156

Dedicated to encouraging philanthropy and leadership among women and girls on Long Island and to building a permanent fund to support projects that will support women and girls.

Maine Women's Fund
P.O. Box 5135
Portland, ME 04101
(207) 774-5513

Provides funding for grass-roots organizations serving the interests of women and girls.

Michigan Women's Foundation
119 Pere Marquette Dr., #2A
Lansing, MI 48912
(517) 374-7270;
Fax: (517) 374-6217

A statewide fund directed to wom-

en's nonprofit organizations in Michigan. Grant priorities include women's economic self-sufficiency, leadership development for women, and management and assistance for women's organizations. Also conducts research on issues that impact women and works to increase philanthropic support for women's needs.

Minnesota Women's Fund
821 Marquette, #A200
Minneapolis, MN 55402
(612) 337-5010

Mission is to remove barriers to women and girls in every area of life. Working to effect changes in various systems. Also grants money to benefit women, conducts workshops, and holds meetings.

Ms. Foundation for Women
141 5th Ave., Ste. 6S
New York, NY 10010-7105
(212) 353-8580;
Fax: (212) 475-4217

Funds and assists women's self-help organizing efforts and promotes full equality for women and girls in all walks of life. Seeks to influence public awareness on a broad range of issues including gender discrimination, self-sufficiency, furthering career aspirations, leadership, and raising self-esteem. Also addresses the special concerns of low-income women, women of color, and lesbians.

National Network of Women's Funds
1821 University Ave., Ste. 409N
St. Paul, MN 55104
(612) 641-0742

The national network of local and regional women's funds. Advocates and educates on behalf of philanthropy that supports projects for women and girls, and monitors the level of financial support given for this purpose by corporate and national philanthropic organizations. Holds conferences, publishes a newsletter, aids in program development, and provides research to its member funds.

Nebraska Women's Foundation
P.O. Box 94744
Lincoln, NE 68509
(402) 471-2039

Sister organization of the Nebraska Commission on Women. Raises money for projects of the commission.

New Mexico Women's Foundation
5200 Cooper NE
Albuquerque, NM
(505) 268-3996

Raises funds and provides grants to nonprofit women's and girls' organizations throughout New Mexico.

New York Women's Foundation
120 Wooster St.
New York, NY 10012
(212) 226-2220

Offers grants to community organizations primarily serving young girls and women. Helps these organizations to become self-sufficient.

Nurses Educational Funds
555 W 57th St.
New York, NY 10019
(212) 582-8820

A nonprofit corporation awarding scholarships to nurses for graduate education. Funds available for people seeking a master's or doctoral degree.

Open Meadows Foundation
P.O. Box 197
Bronx, NY 10464
(718) 885-1119

A national funding organization for women's projects. Offers small grants up to $1500 to projects that have limited funds, are designed and implemented by women, and reflect the cultural and ethnic diversity of society.

Sister Fund
1255 Fifth Ave., #C-2
New York, NY 10029
(212) 722-7606

Provides monies to women's projects that otherwise might not receive funding or receive limited funds. Small grants are provided, usually up to $1500.

**Thanks Be to Grandmother
Winifred Foundation**
P.O. Box 1449
Wainscott, NY 11975
(516) 725-0323

Through individual grants, encourages the creativity of women over fifty-four years of age. Grant receivers use money to create a project or improve a literary, artistic, scientific, or teaching skill or talent that will contribute to the benefit of their communities. See also Special Interests: Older Women's Services.

Valentine Foundation
900 Old Gulph Rd.
Bryn Mawr, PA 19010
(215) 525-6272

Makes one to two grants a year to women's organizations working to improve the status of women. Grants are allocated as funding for innovative programs that offer a new approach to working to change attitudes, policies, or social patterns that oppress women.

Vermont Women's Fund
c/o Peat, Marwick
P.O. Box 1307
Burlington, VT 05402
(802) 864-7491

Funds nonprofit organizations that improve the lives of women and children.

Women and Foundations
Corporate Philanthropy
322 Eighth Ave., Rm. 702
New York, NY 10001
(212) 463-9934;
Fax: (212) 463-9417

A membership association of individuals who work in philanthropy.

Dedicated to increase funding to women's groups and to advance the involvement of other people in this cause. Also sponsors an internship program for undergraduate women of color to work in foundations.

Women's Community Foundation
12200 Fairhill Rd.
Cleveland, OH 44120
(216) 229-5001;
Fax: (216) 229-5029

Works to empower women and girls in the Cleveland area. Promotes diversity and increasing resources and opportunities for women through the provision of grants, technical assistance, education, and advocacy.

Women's Foundation
3543 18th St.
San Francisco, CA 94110
(415) 431-1290;
Fax: (415) 431-9634

Works for women's social justice and economic equality. Develops and funds programs that empower low-income women, women of color, lesbians, older women, physically challenged women, and other women and girls whose needs have not been met by traditional funding sources.

Women's Foundation of Colorado
1580 Logan, #500
Denver, CO 80203
(303) 832-8800

Mission is to ensure the economic self-sufficiency of women and girls. Raises money and provides grants to direct service agencies that are working toward this goal.

Women's Foundation of Oregon
921 SW Morrison, Ste. 422
Portland, OR 97205-2723

Raises money to fund programs for advancement of women and girls. Allocates grants designed to effect social change.

Women's Fund of Greater Omaha
222 S 15th St., #2
Omaha, NE 68102
(402) 342-3458

A foundation that is working to develop a permanent endowment for the advancement of women and girls in the Omaha area.

Women's Fund of Southern Arizona
6601 E Grant Rd., #111
Tucson, AZ 85715
(602) 722-1707

Grants money to groups of five people or more that serve women and girls in southern Arizona.

Women's Funding Alliance
219 1st Ave. S, Ste. 120
Seattle, WA 98104
(206) 467-6733;
Fax: (206) 467-7537

A federation of ten nonprofit organizations that provides services to women and children in Seattle and the surrounding area. The organizations address difficult social conditions that include domestic violence, sexual assault, and discrimination. Maintains a Washington-state community funding program.

Women's Way
1233 Locust St., Ste. 300
Philadelphia, PA 19107
(215) 592-7212;
Fax: (215) 592-1169

A fund-raising coalition that allocates monies to member organizations and offers grants to nonmember groups in and around Philadelphia. All recipients serve the well-being of women and children. Currently is working on Women's Way, USA, which will fund groups helping women around the country.

❑ Global Feminism and World Peace

*O*wing in part to the United Nations sponsored "International Decade of Women" from 1980–1990, women of different nationalities have come together to share ideas and learn from each other. This strong sense of worldwide sisterhood and the ability to network internationally continues to grow and the movement that supports it has become known as Global Feminism.

African American Women's Association
P.O. Box 55122
Brightwood Sta.
Washington, DC 20011
(202) 882-8263

Seeks to build an alliance of friendship, understanding, and appreciation between the women of Africa and the Americas. Sponsors charitable activities, scholarships, and other services.

Alliance of American and Russian Women
P.O. Box 328
Washington Depot, CT 06794
(203) 868-9089;
Fax: (203) 868-9768

Develops entrepreneurism, small business ownership, and financial empowerment of women. Promotes and supports joint ventures between American women and women of the former U.S.S.R.

Amnesty International/Women and Human Rights Project.

See Women's Rights.

Arab-Jewish Women's Dialogue for Peace
2116 Henderson Ave.
Wheaton, MD 20902
(301) 946-9311

An organization of Jewish and Arab women working to foster communication between their communities and promote their cultures. Conducts discussion groups, teen programs, and cultural events to educate and help end prejudice and stereotypes.

Coalition for Women in International Development
1717 Massachusetts Ave. NW, 8th Fl.
Washington, DC 20036
(202) 466-3430;
Fax: (202) 775-0596

A coalition of organizations and individuals working to increase and enhance the involvement of American women in U.S. foreign policy. Promotes and supports women and their involvement in social and political issues worldwide. Conducts research programs and lobbying efforts.

Committee on South Asian Women
Texas A & M Univ.
Dept. of Psychology
College Station, TX 77843
(409) 845-3211;
Fax: (409) 845-4727

Organizes and participates in conferences, seminars, and workshops on issues pertaining to women in developing countries and immigrant women. Coordinates lectures and films concerning South Asian women. Supports the efforts of women's groups in South Asia and establishes links between these groups and Western counterparts.

Connexions.

See Newspapers, Newsletters, and Magazines.

Delegation for Friendship Among Women
2219 Caroline Ln.
South St. Paul, MN 55075
(612) 455-5620;
Fax: (612) 445-5620

An education and networking organization of leading women in the fields of architecture, academics, business, law, journalism, and science. Sponsors activities to promote communication and networking of women worldwide. Programs focus on issues such as health, education, and general welfare of women.

Feminist Issues International Journal.

See Newspapers, Newsletters, and Magazines.

Global Fund for Women
2480 Sand Hill Rd., #100
Menlo Park, CA 94025-6941
(415) 854-0420;
Fax: (415) 854-8050

Offers grants, educational activities, fund-raising events, international conferences, and organizational counseling seminars for women's organizations worldwide.

Global Women of African Heritage
P.O. Box 1033
Cooper Station, NY 10003
(718) 655-1657;
Fax: (718) 547-5696

A networking organization for women of African Heritage.

Grandmothers for Peace International
9444 Medstead Way
Elk Grove, CA 95758
(916) 684-0394

Participates in demonstrations, awards scholarships, and circulates petitions to help work for peace worldwide.

Hadassah, The Women's Zionist Organization of America
50 W 58th St.
New York, NY 10019
(212) 355-7900

A large, well-known international Zionist women's organization that supports health and educational programs in Israel. Sponsors youth resettlement programs of Soviet and Ethiopian Jews and initiates action for medical work in Israel.

Institute for Policy Studies Third-World Women's Project
1601 Connecticut Ave. NW
Washington, DC 20009
(202) 234-9382

Seeks to advance the causes of human rights, world peace, and so-cial welfare throughout the world, particularly in third-world countries. Brings third-world women speakers to universities in the U.S.

International Alliance of Business and Professional Women.

See Professional and Business Associations and Networks.

International Center for Research on Women
1717 Massachusetts Ave. NW, Ste. 302
Washington, DC 20036
(202) 797-0007;
Fax: (202) 797-0020

A private research organization that seeks to promote understanding and advance earning ability, health, and social status of poor women living in developing countries. Advises policymakers on such topics as economic self-sufficiency, health care, nutrition, affordable housing, agriculture, and training. Sponsors a fellows program and offers publications and a library.

International Women's Forum
1146 19th St. NW, Ste. 700
Washington, DC 20036
(202) 775-8917

A coalition of international women's organizations and networks. Works for the empowerment and leadership of women worldwide.

International Women's Health Coalition.

See Health Organizations.

International Women's Rights Action Watch
301 19th Ave. S.
Minneapolis, MN 55455
(612) 625-5093;
Fax: (612) 625-6351

A global network of activists and scholars that monitors changes in law and policy in accordance with the principles of the Convention of Elimination of All Forms of Discrimination Against Women.

International Women's Tribune Center
777 United Nations Pl., 3rd Fl.
New York, NY 10017
(212) 687-8633;
Fax: (212) 661-2704

Offers technical assistance, networking, and training in communications skills and media production to individuals and groups working to benefit women in the South Pacific, the Caribbean, Latin America, Africa, and Asia. Provides assistance with technology, and developing low-cost media.

Israel Women's Network
c/o New Israel Fund
111 W 40th St., #2300
New York, NY 10018
(212) 302-0066;
Fax: (212) 302-7629

A coalition of Israeli women united to improve the status of women in Israel. Acts through advocacy, legal activity, and education.

Madre, Incorporated
121 W 27th St., #301
New York, NY 10001
(212) 627-0444; Fax: (212) 675-3704

Works to link the problems women and children face in the U.S. with the challenges women and children in other parts of the world face as a result of U.S. policies. Works for human rights, peace, and justice.

Najda, Women Concerned About The Middle East
Box 7152
Berkeley, CA 94707
(510) 549-3512

Provides aid to people in need in the Arab world. Publishes a quarterly newsletter and provides cultural and educational materials pertaining to the Arab world.

OEF International
1815 H St. NW, 11th Fl.
Washington, DC 20006
(202) 466-3430; Fax: (202) 775-0596

Sponsors training and technical assistance programs to address the economic and social needs of third-world women. Offers handbooks, reports, brochures, and studies.

PanAmerican Liaison Committee of Women's Organizations
3202 Beech St. NW
Washington, DC 20015
(202) 362-3274

An organization of women's networks in Western Hemisphere countries. Conducts cultural, educational, and research projects to promote women's rights and women's agendas. Offers leadership training, training for literacy teachers, and scholarships.

PanPacific and Southeast Asia Women's Association of the U.S.A.

1 Lexington Ave.
New York, NY 10159
(212) 228-5307

Works to strengthen ties between Asian and Pacific women and women of the U.S. Conducts studies, offers educational programs, and sponsors lectures.

Peace Links

747 Eighth St. SE
Washington, DC 20003
(202) 544-0805;
Fax: (202) 544-0809

Networks women who are active in working for peaceful resolution of conflicts. Holds a letter-writing exchange between Americans and Russians.

Rutgers University Center for Women's Global Leadership

Douglass College
27 Clifton Ave.
New Brunswick, NJ 08903
(908) 932-8782

Seeks to deepen an understanding of the way gender affects the exer-cise of power and the conduct of public policy internationally. Campaigns for other women's organizations to incorporate women's rights into the international human rights agenda, and promotes women's leadership worldwide. Sponsors an annual two-week residential women's leadership seminar and a visiting associates program.

U.S. Committee for the U.N. Fund for Women (UNIFEM)

252 N Washington St.
Falls Church, VA 22046
(703) 241-8405;
Fax: (703) 241-8405

Supports the work of UNIFEM through education, fund-raising, and advocacy. Helps women living in poverty in developing countries.

WINGS: Women's International News Gathering Service

P.O. Box 33220
Austin, TX 78764
(512) 416-9000

Produces audiocassettes on news and current affairs topics related to women for noncommercial radio worldwide. Special focus on women covering their native regions. Offers catalogs to individuals and free samples to radio stations.

Women Against Military Madness

3255 Hennepin Ave.
Minneapolis, MN 55408
(612) 827-5364;
Fax: (612) 827-6433

A nonviolent, nonhierarchical feminist organization. Purpose is to dismantle militarism and its system of oppression and to create a system of social equality and justice through education and empowerment of women.

Women and Global Corporations
c/o AFSC Women's Project
1501 Cherry St.
Philadelphia, PA 19102
(215) 241-7181

Analysis and experience of the impact of globalized economics on women with emphasis on women of color both in the U.S. and internationally.

Women's Action for New Directions
P.O. Box B
Arlington, MA 02174
(617) 643-6740;
Fax: (617) 643-6744

A national membership organization working to empower women to act politically to reduce violence and militarism and redirect military resources toward human and environmental needs. Supports research and education.

Women's Environment and Development Organization.

See Environmental Groups; Special Interests.

Women's Feature Service and Bulletin
245 E 13th St.
New York, NY 10003
(212) 477-1216;
Fax: (212) 477-2674

A news-feature service of views and analyses of women and their perceptions of local, national, and international development. Articles are distributed internationally.

Women's International League for Peace and Freedom
United States Section
1213 Race St.
Philadelphia, PA 19107
(215) 563-7110;
Fax: (215) 564-2880

Works on international issues of women's equal rights, racial prejudice, and disarmament. Seeks a reorientation of government ideals that would end spending on violence in favor of projects supporting human rights. Has offices worldwide and sponsors the Jane Addams Peace Association education fund.

Women's International Network
187 Grant St.
Lexington, MA 02173
(617) 862-9431

Facilitates communication among international women's organizations about women and women's issues. Publishes a quarterly news magazine.

Women's International Resource Exchange
122 W 27th St., 10th Fl.
New York, NY 10001
(212) 741-2955

Reprints or distributes booklets and articles concerning women in the third world. Most publications are in English, with some in Spanish as well.

Women Strike for Peace
110 Maryland Ave. NE, Ste. 302
Washington, DC 20002
(202) 543-2660

A feminist organization working to end the arms race and all nuclear testing and reduce the military budget. Supports nonintervention by the U.S. in the affairs of other countries.

Women to Women International
1298 Orchid Dr.
Santa Barbara, CA 93111
(805) 964-6688;
Fax: (805) 964-3336

Offers seminars led by professional American women for professional women in Russia and other Eastern European countries.

World Feminist Commission
13 Oaks Ct.
Bloomfield Hills, MI 48304
(313) 540-8885

An international feminist network of contacts that can organize feminists to be advocates for women worldwide.

World Peace Begins at Home
3002 Wilson Ave.
Bronx, NY 10469
(718) 655-5273

An organization working to stop violence in the family. Teaches that positive conflict resolution in the family has global ramifications. See also Violence Against Women.

World Women in the Environment.

See Special Interests: Environmental Groups.

❑ Health Organizations

ADVOCACY, EDUCATION, AND RESEARCH ORGANIZATIONS

Boston Women's Health Book Collective
240A Elm St.
Somerville, MA 02144
(617) 625-0277;
Fax: (617) 625-0294

A well-known health organization that conducts education, advocacy, and consulting in women's health. Contributes to Ms. *magazine, and sponsors numerous projects on health education, disability, and reproductive rights. Authored* Our Bodies, Our Selves. *See also* Women's Rights; Special Interests.

Federation of Feminist Women's Health Centers
633 E 11th St.
Eugene, OR 97401
(503) 342-5940

Brings together women's health activists and women's clinics to advocate women's participation in and control of their health care, reproduction, and sexuality. Challenges medical, legal, and social institutions to expand options, alternatives, and access in women's health care.

Health House
420 Lake Ave.
St. James, NY 11780
(516) 862-6743

A women's health resource center serving women on Long Island, NY. Has over 250 files on an assortment of women's health care topics, from physical health to spiritual health. Also offers support groups, workshops, and individual and short-term counseling.

Institute for Research on Women's Health
1616 18 St. NW, #109
Washington, DC 20009
(202) 483-8643;
Fax: (301) 216-2157

Dedicated to research, education, and policy work related to the health and mental health of women. Gender-sensitive pharmacology and workplace abuse are among the specialties.

Institute of Women's Health
Indiana Univ., School of Medicine
Dept. of Obstetrics and Gynecology
926 W Michigan St.
Indianapolis, IN 46202
(317) 274-2014;
Fax: (317) 274-2014

Advocates self-care and studies women's health practices. Conducts community education research projects and sponsors educational demonstration projects. See also Research Centers and Organizations.

International Dalkon Shield Victims Education Association
225 Pioneer Bldg.
Seattle, WA 98104
(206) 329-1371;
Fax: (206) 623-4251

A support and educational network of Dalkon Shield victims worldwide. Offers information on legal claims, seminars, a speakers' bureau, and information on Dalkon Shield injuries, claims, and resolutions.

International Women's Health Coalition
24 E 21st St.
New York, NY 10010
(212) 979-8500

A private, nonprofit organization supporting quality reproductive health care for women in third-world countries. Works with health care workers, policy makers, and women's groups. Offers professional and technical assistance to third-world health organizations. Provides financial support and offers educational materials. See also Global Feminism and World Peace.

Jacobs Institute of Women's Health
409 12th St. SW
Washington, DC 20024-2188
(202) 863-4990;
Fax: (202) 484-5107

Concerned with all issues of women's health, particularly with the interaction between physicians and their patients. Offers workshops to medical professionals and others involved with women's health on surgery, obstetrical medicine, breast health, reproductive medicine, and so on. Publishes a peer-review journal.

Melpomene Institute for Women's Health Research
1010 University Ave.
St. Paul, MN 55104
(612) 642-1951;
Fax: (612) 642-1871

A nonprofit, membership-based organization that studies and helps women understand the link between physical activity and health. Sponsors a large and very active re-

search center that focuses on women's eating and sleeping habits, menstrual patterns, medical history, psychological well-being, attitudes toward body image, activity, and exercise programs. Packets of information available free to members. Research center is open to nonmembers for a small fee. See also Research Centers and Organizations.

National Black Women's Health Project
1237 Gordon St. SW
Atlanta, GA 30310
(404) 753-0916;
Fax: (404) 752-6756

A public education health organization for black women. Advocates personal involvement and encourages black women to take charge of their physical, mental, and emotional health. Also addresses issues such as rural health, health care for homeless women, and health care for women in developing countries.

National Council on Women's Health
1300 York Ave.
Box 52
New York, NY 10021
(212) 535-0031

Seeks to improve all areas of women's health through public and professional education. Sponsors conferences and publishes educational material. Council is comprised of general consumers and individuals involved in health care.

National Women's Health Network
1325 G Street NW, Lower Level
Washington, DC 20005
(202) 347-1140;
Fax: (202) 347-1168

Devoted exclusively to women's health issues. Advocates women's involvement in the system and their right to receive informed, unbiased health care. Also seeks to educate policymakers and the public about special issues involving older women and women of color.

National Women's Health Resource Center
Columbia Hospital for Women Foundation
2440 M Street NW, Ste. 325
Washington, DC 20037
(202) 293-6045;
Fax: (202) 293-7256

Serves the health needs of all women, particularly groups that are underserved by the current system. Conducts research, designs programs and services for use by other health organizations, and supports the exchange of ideas among health care professionals and the public. Also works to educate and empower women. See also Research Centers and Organizations.

Native American Women's Health Education Resource Center
P.O. Box 572
Lake Andes, SD 57356
(605) 487-7072;
Fax: (605) 487-7964

A grass-roots, community-based organization that provides education and empowerment skills to women and children and self-help skills to the Native American community. Projects include AIDS education, diabetes education, domestic violence programs and a shelter, an adult learning center, child development, a reproductive rights coalition, and education programs in several other health areas. See also Women's Centers.

New Jersey Women and AIDS Network
5 Elm Row, #112
New Brunswick, NJ 08901
(908) 846-4462;
Fax: (908) 846-2674

A statewide network of organizations devoted to education and advocacy concerning issues affecting women in the AIDS epidemic. Provides publications, training, resources, and referral information.

Organizacion Nacional de la Salud National Latina Health Organization
P.O. Box 7567
Oakland, CA 94601
(510) 534-1362

Concerned with the health issues of Latinas. Provides information and referrals.

Society for Menstrual Cycle Research
10559 N 104th Pl.
Scottsdale, AZ 85258
(602) 457-9731

Researches the menstrual cycle and its impact on women's health needs and life-styles. Serves as a communication link among researchers to exchange information. Offers seminars and publishes papers on menstruation. See also Research Centers and Organizations.

Women's Health Education Project
2271 Second Ave.
New York, NY 10035
(212) 987-0066

Provides weekly health education workshops for women living in shelters. Encourages and facilitates empowerment by teaching holistic and alternative medical approaches.

Women's Health Policy Project
1325 S Wabash, #205
Chicago, IL 60605
(312) 939-3636;
Fax: (312) 939-4187

An advocate for women's health programs in the public sector including breast and cervical center, HIV-related services, and violence against women. Reviews and evalu-

ates services within the Chicago Department of Health that address the health needs of women and their children and in turn makes recommendations to the Chicago Board of Health. Publishes Well Woman Journal.

Women's Health Resources
1003 W Wellington
Chicago, IL 60657
(312) 525-1177

Offers articles, resource guides, brochures, magazines, and other materials on issues of women's health and mental health. Topics include battered women, breast cancer, disabled women, stress, and occupational health.

Women's International Public Health Network
7100 Oak Forest Ln.
Bethesda, MD 20817
(301) 469-9210

An international network of women's groups that supports the exchange of ideas on all women's health issues. Offers a newsletter. See also Global Feminism and World Peace.

ALTERNATIVE HEALTH SERVICES

Blazing Star Herbal School
Women's Herbal Conference
P.O. Box 6
Shelburne Falls, MA 01370
(413) 625-6875

Offers workshops and retreats that teach women how to use herbs for medicinal use. Holds an annual herbal conference.

Center for Traditional Medicine
P.O. Box 1526
Cambridge, MA 02238
(617) 489-3806

Offers international workshops to study indigenous healing practices.

Center of the Web
Jade Hill Farmstead
Box 175
Manchaug, MA 01526-0175
(508) 476-7081

A teaching center for herbal medicine, women's spirituality, and earth awareness. Brings together ancient teachings and modern knowledge to create a matrix for women's empowerment and healing.

**Informed Homebirth/
Informed Birth and Parenting**
P.O. Box 3675
Ann Arbor, MI 48106
(313) 662-6857;
Fax: (313) 662-9381

An educational organization that supports women's reproductive rights. Advocates, educates, and informs regarding childbirth and birthing at home. Newsletter published regularly.

Massachusetts Friends of Midwives
P.O. Box 3188
Boston, MA 02130
(508) 369-1468

Assists midwives in establishing midwifery as a recognized, self-regulating profession. Also works to remove barriers that prevent women from making fully informed choices regarding reproductive care.

Menstrual Health Foundation/ New Cycle Products
104 Petaluma Ave.
Sebastopol, CA 95472
(707) 829-2744

Advocates for women using noncommercial natural menstrual care products. Write for their informative catalog.

Sage: The Spirit and Essence of Herbs
P.O. Box 420
East Barre, VT 05649
(802) 479-9825

Offers workshops in herbalism and earth awareness. Classes feature medicinal herbalism, wild plant identification, and earth ceremonies. Located on five hundred wilderness acres in Vermont.

Wholistic Health for Women
8235 Santa Monica Blvd., #308
West Hollywood, CA 90046
(213) 650-1508

A women's clinic offering a full range of wholistic alternative women's health care.

Wise Woman Center
Healing Intensives
P.O. Box 64
Woodstock, NY 12498
(914) 246-8081;
Fax: (914) 246-8081

Offers workshops, correspondence courses, and retreat lodges to teach ancient methods of women's healing and spirituality. Workshops cover healing through sound, herbal oils, and herbal remedies, and address women's sexuality, power, and identity. See also Religious and Spiritual Groups.

CANCER RESOURCES

African-American Breast Cancer Alliance
1 W Lake St., #423
Minneapolis, MN 55408

An alliance of mutual support among African-American women who suffer from breast cancer.

Bosom Buddies
RD 4, Box 58
Bedford, PA 15522
(814) 847-2446

A local support group for women who have had breast cancer and mastectomies.

Massachusetts Breast Cancer Coalition
P.O. Box 383
Newton Highland, MA 02161
(617) 423-6222;
Fax: (617) 423-2115

An alliance of individuals and organizations committed to changing the course of the breast cancer epidemic. Holds forums, participates in panels, networks groups, and offers information.

Mautner Project for Lesbians with Cancer
P.O. Box 90437
Washington, DC 20090
(202) 332-5536;
Fax: (202) 544-7876

A volunteer organization dedicated to assisting lesbians with cancer and their families. Provides sup-port, services, education, and information at no cost. See also Lesbian and Gay Organizations.

National Alliance of Breast Cancer Organizations
1180 Ave. of the Americas, 2nd Fl.
New York, NY 10036
(212) 719-0154;
Fax: (212) 719-0263

A coalition of breast centers, hospitals, health offices, and research organizations dealing with breast cancer and breast diseases. Offers educational materials, relevant public policy information, and support group contacts.

National Breast Cancer Coalition
P.O. Box 66373
Washington, DC 20035
(202) 296-7477;
Fax: (202) 592-4329

A national grass-roots organization that works to educate the public and to lobby federal lawmakers for increased support of breast cancer research, diagnosis, and treatment. Also dedicated to eliminating breast cancer by focusing national attention on this common form of cancer.

Northern California Breast Cancer Organization
19305 Crist Ave.
Saratoga, CA 95070

Educates and supports breast cancer victims.

Reach to Recovery
c/o American Cancer Society
1599 Cliffton Rd. NE
Altanta, GA 30329
(404) 320-3333

Provides support, information, and short-term programs for women suffering from breast cancer. Offers services for those who have undergone treatments such as chemotherapy, radiation treatment, and breast reconstruction.

Self-Help for Women with Breast or Ovarian Cancer
19 W 44 St., #311
New York, NY 10036
(212) 719-0364

A self-help organization for women with breast or ovarian cancer that provides support groups; hotlines in Spanish, English, and Chinese; educational forums; and wellness programs. All programs are free of charge.

Susan G. Komen Breast Cancer Foundation
5005 LBJ, Ste. 730
Dallas, TX 75244
(214) 450-1777,
(800) IM-AWARE;
Fax: (214) 450-7710

Conducts research on breast diseases. Provides funding for research and treatment programs and offers public education activities.

See also Research Centers and Organizations.

Womancare: Women's Cancer Advocacy, Resources, and Education
P.O. Box 944
Santa Cruz, CA 95061
(408) 457-2273

A community-based, nonprofit resource center for women with cancer. Designed and directed by women with cancer or with cancer histories.

Women's Cancer Resource Center
3023 Shattuck Ave.
Berkeley, CA 94705
(510) 548-9272;
Fax: (510) 548-2155

A grass-roots, nonprofit organization dedicated to empowering women with cancer to be active and informed consumers and survivors. Provides practical and emotional support and free services to women with cancer and their families.

Women's Community Cancer Project
46 Pleasant St.
Cambridge, MA 02139
(617) 354-8807

Provides education and support services for Boston-area women with cancer.

Y-Me National Organization for Breast Cancer Information and Support
18220 Harwood Ave.
Homewood, IL 60430
(708) 799-8338; Fax: (708) 799-5937

Provides information, hotline counseling, educational programs, and self-help meetings for breast cancer patients, their families and friends, and the general public.

EATING DISORDER SERVICES

American Anorexia/Bulimia Association
418 E 76th St.
New York, NY 10021
(212) 734-1114

Offers information, referrals, and publications on eating disorders. Serves and supports individuals with eating disorders, health care professionals, and families of anorexics and bulimics.

ANAD, National Association of Anorexia Nervosa and Associated Disorders
Box 7
Highland Park, IL 60035
(708) 831-3438

Works to prevent and offers education on anorexia. Serves as a resource center and advocacy agency on eating disorders. Conducts a referral service, surveys, education, and early detection programs.

Anorexia Nervosa and Related Eating Disorders
P.O. Box 5102
Eugene, OR 97405
(503) 344-1144

Offers information on anorexia nervosa, bulimia, and other eating disorders. Provides support groups, medical referrals, counseling, seminars, and training programs. Conducts educational programs for schools, clubs, civic organizations, churches, and women's health or counseling agencies.

Gurze Catalogue
Box 2238
Carlsbad, CA 92008
(619) 434-7533

A catalog of over 125 books, cassettes, and videos about eating disorders and other self-esteem issues.

International Association of Eating Disorders Professionals
123 NW 13th St., #206
Boca Raton, FL 33432
(407) 338-6494

An organization of eating disorder counselors and therapists. Develops curricula, provides certification, offers public education and information, and sponsors workshops.

National Anorexic Aid Society
1925 E Dublin-Granville Rd.
Columbus, OH 43229
(614) 436-1112

Offers information and referrals to *anorexics and their families. Sponsors educational programs and organizes self-help groups. Publishes a quarterly newsletter. See also* Newspapers, Newsletters, and Magazines.

FAMILY PLANNING AND REPRODUCTIVE RIGHTS

Atlanta Pro-Choice Action Committee (APAC)
P.O. Box 57104
Atlanta, GA 30343
(404) 239-8016

Part of the clinic defense movement. Organizes to keep abortion clinics open and aids women seeking abortions by escorting them through anti-abortion demonstrations.

Bay Area Coalition for Our Reproductive Rights
750 La Playa, #730
San Francisco, CA 94121
(415) 252-0750

Active in abortion clinic defense work and escorting women through picket lines to preserve their rights to have a legal abortion. Meets weekly.

Brooklyn Pro-Choice Network
P.O. Box 150736
Brooklyn, NY 11215
(212) 629-1950

Protects women seeking abortions and defends clinics that are under attack.

Buffalo United for Choice
P.O. Box 871
Amherst, NY 14226
(716) 855-4033

Works to assure that women seeking a legal abortion may be able to terminate their pregnancies without harassment or intimidation. Provides escort services and organizes a strong pro-choice presence at clinics to counteract assaults by anti-abortion demonstrators.

Catholics For a Free Choice
1436 U St. NW, Ste. 301
Washington, DC 20009
(202) 986-6093;
Fax: (202) 332-7995

An educational organization whose Catholic members support women's right to reproductive health care, especially as it concerns birth control and abortion. Also seeks to reduce the number of abortions. Provides educational materials to the public and supports pro-choice policymakers. Publishes Conscience, *a news journal.*

Center for Choice
16 N Huron
Toledo, OH 43604
(419) 255-7769

An activist organization working to keep abortion clinics open and to protect and escort women who use them. Committed to ensuring women reproductive freedom.

Cesareans/Support, Education, and Concern
22 Forest Rd.
Framingham, MA 01701
(508) 877-8266

Provides information and support on cesarean childbirth, cesarean prevention, and vaginal birth after cesarean to parents and professionals.

Chicago Abortion Fund
P.O. Box 578307
Chicago, IL 60657
(312) 248-4807

A nonprofit organization aimed at guaranteeing the reproductive freedom of low-income women. Provides financial assistance to low-income women seeking safe abortion services and educates the public about economic barriers to reproductive choice.

Choice
4228 N Central Expwy., Ste. 206
Dallas, TX 75206
(214) 821-4495;
Fax: (214) 826-2508

An independent, nonprofit organization working politically and educationally to safeguard the rights of women to make reproductive choices. Provides training for volunteers who wish to participate in clinic support activities and coordinate communication among area abortion providers.

Clinic Defense Committee
2930 McClure St.
Oakland, CA 94609

Engages in a wide variety of clinic support activities when a clinic has been targeted for attack.

Committee to Defend Reproductive Rights
25 Taylor St.
San Francisco, CA 94402
(415) 441-4434

Works to ensure that women may continue to exercise their right to reproductive choice. Active through legislation and clinic support work.

Council on Abortion Rights Education and Minnesota Abortion Rights Council
430 Oak Grove St., #108
Minneapolis, MN 55403

Works to keep abortions safe and legal and to protect women's reproductive rights.

80% Majority Campaign
P.O. Box 1315
Hightstown, NJ 08520

Seeks to elect or raise money for pro-choice candidates.

Hudson County Reproductive Rights Network

P.O. Box 3292
Hoboken, NJ 07030
(201) 217-2610

A group of activists available to support and defend clinics that are under attack.

Hysterectomy Educational Resources

422 Bryn Mawr Ave.
Bala Cynwd, PA 19004
(215) 667-7757

Provides information and counseling nationally about the alternatives to and consequences of getting a hysterectomy. Publishes a quarterly newsletter, holds semiannual conferences, and has a lending library that holds books, audiotapes, and videotapes. Gives physician and lawyer referrals.

Illinois Pro-Choice Alliance Education Fund

203 N La Salle St., #1405
Chicago, IL 60601
(312) 357-0084;
Fax: (312) 201-9760

A statewide coalition of organizations committed to ensuring and providing reproductive rights and services for all women.

Informed Homebirth/Informed Birth and Parenting.

See Health Organizations: Alternative Health Services.

International Cesarean Awareness Network

P.O. Box 152
Syracuse, NY 13210
(315) 424-1942

Provides women with education and support about cesarean prevention, cesarean recovery, and vaginal birth after cesarean. Eighty chapters established nationwide.

Mid-Hudson Coalition for Free Choice

Box 5142
Poughkeepsie, NY 12602-5142
(914) 431-6727

A grass-roots organization fighting for reproductive freedom for women. Works to influence elections at the state and local levels, runs a political action committee, and sponsors a voter identification project. See also Political Groups.

Montgomery County Alliance for Women

2011 Birchwood Dr.
Morristown, PA 19401
(215) 277-1076

Works to insure a woman's right to make her own reproductive choices.

National Abortion Federation

1436 U St. NW, Ste. 103
Washington, DC 20009
(202) 667-5881, (800) 772-9100;
Fax: (202) 667-5890

A professional association of abortion providers that works to ensure access to safe, quality abortion

care throughout the United States
and Canada. Offers educational
materials, violence and disruption
statistics, and continuing education
meetings.

**National Abortion Rights Action
League (NARAL)**
1101 14th St. NW, 5th Fl.
Washington, DC 20009
(202) 973-3000;
Fax: (202) 973-3096

The major national organization
whose mission is to keep abortions
safe and available to all women.
Activities include lobbying, supporting pro-choice policymakers,
and insuring that legal rights are
maintained in the judicial system
and in clinics around the country.
With chapters in most states,
NARAL is considered the political
arm of the pro-choice movement.

**National Center for the
Pro-Choice Majority**
P.O. Box 1315
Hightstown, NJ 08520
(609) 443-8780;
Fax: (609) 448-9550

A clearinghouse for pro-choice information, resources, and opposi-
tion research, particularly research
into the activities and participants
of the direct-action militants. Maintains a database of those who are
arrested at abortion clinics and all
others who are identified as having
been involved with blockades, ha-

rassment, and intimidation. Publishes Pro-choice Report.

National Clinic Defense Project
Feminist Majority Foundation
8105 W 3rd St., #1
Los Angeles, CA 90048
(213) 651-0495

Sets up projects on a national level
to counter the activities of Operation Rescue and other anti-abortion
clinic groups.

**National Coalition Against
Surrogacy**
1130 17th St. NW, Ste. 630
Washington, DC 20036
(202) 466-2823

A coalition of individuals and organizations that seeks to outlaw
surrogate births. Advocates on behalf of birth mothers.

**National Women's Rights
Organizing Coalition.**
See Women's Rights.

**Northeast Philadelphia
Pro-Choice Coalition**
2751 Comley Rd.
Philadelphia, PA 19154
(215) 676-9002

A coalition of individuals and reproductive rights organizations that
actively supports clinics to help
them stay open and assist women
seeking their services.

Planned Parenthood Federation of America
810 7th Ave.
New York, NY 10019
(212) 261-4660

A large, long-established organization offering reproductive health care and information to individuals across the country. Operates more than eight hundred centers that provide medically supervised family planning services. Also sponsors programs for health care professionals. Chapters exist in most major cities; write for the chapter nearest you.

Pro-Choice Network of Western New York
P.O. Box 461
Buffalo, NY 14209
(716) 882-2029

A grass-roots women's reproductive rights organization formed to combat attempts to block entrance to abortion clinics. Maintains an escort service and a speaker's bureau. Conducts fund raising, endorses pro-choice political candidates, monitors abortion rights issues, and publishes a monthly newsletter, Speak Out.

Pro-Choice Resources
3255 Henepin Ave. S, #255
Minneapolis, MN 55408
(612) 825-9122;
Fax: (612) 827-6433

Offers pro-choice education, conducts lobbying efforts, sponsors workshops and outreach programs, gives referrals, and grants loans to women in need of abortions.

Religious Coalition for Abortion Rights
100 Maryland Ave. NE, #307
Washington, DC 20002-5625
(202) 543-7032;
Fax: (202) 543-7820

A nonprofit coalition of groups from various religions working to preserve freedom of choice. Offers public education materials and seeks to mobilize support at the state and national levels.

Religious Coalition for Abortion Rights Women of Color Partnership Program
100 Maryland Ave. NE, #307
Washington, DC 20002
(202) 543-7032;
Fax: (202) 543-7820

A program dedicated to increasing the participation of women of color in the fight for reproductive freedom. Its goal is to help the pro-choice movement become racially inclusive and to reflect the needs of all women. Offers videotapes, brochures, filmstrips, and other publications.

Reproductive Health Technologies Project
1601 Connecticut Ave. NW, #801
Washington, DC 20009

Monitors, studies, and analyzes the impact of new reproductive health technologies like genetic engineering and sex selection procedures.

Reproductive Rights Project
New York Civil Liberties Union
132 W 43rd St.
New York, NY 10036
(212) 382-0557;
Fax: (212) 354-2583

Works to protect women's reproductive rights through litigation, public education, and advocacy. Seeks to increase young and poor women's access to comprehensive reproductive health care. See also Women's Rights; Legal Services.

Richmond Coalition for Choice
P.O. Box 950
Richmond, VA 23207
(804) 355-0936

Original goal was to defend the local clinic. Continues to fight for reproductive freedom and works for pro-choice candidates.

Right to Choose
P.O. Box 343
East Brunswick, NJ 08816
(908) 254-8665

A statewide group of individuals and organizations dedicated to preserving women's rights to choose a safe, legal, accessible abortion. Publishes a newsletter, provides speakers, and offers fact sheets to high schools, colleges, and civic and religious groups.

Rockland Coalition for Choice
P.O. Box 504
Nanuet, NY 10954

Works to maintain reproductive freedom for all women.

Sacramento Area Coalition for Our Reproductive Rights
P.O. Box 19261
Sacramento, CA 95819
(916) 763-7705

Involved in numerous local activities that protect women's right to choose under the law.

South Mountain Women's Health Alliance
P.O. Box 1523
Morgantown, NC 28680
(704) 438-4594

Provides education, counseling, and financial aid to women for management and prevention of unintended pregnancies. Gives grants to women needing abortion services who have no other resources. Also offers a relationship-building course and individual counseling.

South Texas for Choice
P.O. Box 81304
Corpus Christi, TX 78468

Actively works to protect reproduction rights and to elect pro-choice candidates.

This Ain't Kansas Escorts
1929 E Main St.
Madison, WI 53704
(608) 246-2737

Activists providing escort services for women exercising their right to choose an abortion.

Voters for Choice
2604 Connecticut Ave. NW, #200
Washington, DC 20008

A political action committee that raises money and works to support the election of pro-choice candidates.

Washington State National Abortion Rights Action League
811 1st Ave., #456
Seattle, WA 98104-1434
(206) 624-1990;
Fax: (206) 624-4505

A pro-choice grass-roots political organization working to keep abortion safe, legal, and accessible for all women.

Westchester Coalition for Legal Abortion
237 Mamaroneck Ave.
White Plains, NY 10605
(914) 946-5363

An action group that identifies pro-choice individuals in Westchester County to vote for candidates who support legal abortion.

Women's Health Action and Mobilization
P.O. Box 733
New York, NY 10009
(212) 713-5966

An action group committed to demanding, securing, and defending reproductive freedom and quality health care for all women. Holds weekly meetings.

HEALTH CENTERS

Many of the following health centers are members of the Federation of Feminist Women's Health Centers. Most of the centers included in this list provide gynecological and other health services; some offer abortions. Contact the specific center for details and changing services.

Aradia Women's Health Center
112 Boylston Ave. E
Seattle, WA 98102
(206) 323-9388

Offers gynecological services, abortion services, and counseling.

Berkeley Women's Health Center
2908 Ellsworth
Berkeley, CA 94705
(510) 843-6194;
Fax: (510) 843-6297

Offers primary care services, gen-

eral medicine, gynecologic services, family planning, and preventative services for females age twelve and up.

Boulder Valley Women's Health Center
2855 Valmont
Boulder, CO 80301
(303) 442-5160

Offers all gynecological services except mammograms. Counseling and abortions for women who are up to fourteen weeks pregnant.

Buena Vista Women's Services
2000 Van Ness
San Francisco, CA 94109
(415) 771-5000

Offers general gynecological services for women and performs abortions.

Cedar Rapids Clinic for Women
86½ 16th Ave. SW
Cedar Rapids, IA 52404
(319) 365-9527

Provides a full range of gynecological and health educational services for women, including abortions.

Chicago Women's Health Center
3435 N Sheffield
Chicago, IL 60657
(312) 935-6126

A woman-operated feminist collective that provides health care to women. Services include Ob/Gyn services, self-help, education, and counseling.

Choices Women's Medical Center
97–77 Queens Blvd.
Forest Hills, NY 11374
(718) 275-6020;
Fax: (718) 997-1206

Offers full reproductive health care services, including abortion to twenty-four weeks. Provides speakers on feminist issues for both local and national schools and organizations. Also offers rape treatment counseling to victims and their families. Publishes On the Issues, *a magazine of feminist thought. See also* Violence Against Women; Newspapers, Newsletters, and Magazines.

Commonwoman's Health Project
2200 County Center Dr., #H
Santa Rosa, CA 95403
(707) 578-1700

Provides low-cost quality health care to women and children. Services include pregnancy testing, birth control, gynecological care, and first trimester abortions. Also serves as a center for education, information, meetings, and referrals.

Concord Feminist Health Center
38 S Main St.
Concord, NH 03301
(603) 225-2739

Offers gynecological services and has a first trimester abortion clinic. Also provides STD services for women and men, anonymous HIV testing, and educational services on women's issues, reproductive rights, and lesbian and gay rights. Publishes WomanWise Health Journal.

Elizabeth Blackwell Health Center for Women
1124 Walnut St.
Philadelphia, PA 19107
(215) 923-7577;
Fax: (215) 923-2237

Offers gynecological care, pregnancy testing services and options counseling, insemination services for fertile women, HIV testing and AIDS counseling, health education programs, and first trimester abortions.

Emma Goldman Clinic for Women
227 N Dubuque
Iowa City, IA 52245
(319) 337-2112;
Fax: (319) 337-2754

A feminist health center. Services include first trimester abortions and gynecological services.

Feminist Women's Health Center
330 Flume St.
Chico, CA 95928
(916) 891-1911

A women's clinic offering abortion, gynecological services, self-help, pregnancy testing, and birth control. Also does speaking engagements on all women's health issues.

Feminist Women's Health Center
241 E 6th Ave.
Tallahassee, FL 32303
(904) 224-9600;
Fax: (904) 574-0054

Provides birth control, pregnancy tests, general health screening, infectious diseases counseling, and abortions.

Feminist Women's Health Center
580 14th St. NW
Atlanta, GA 30318
(404) 875-7115;
Fax: (404) 875-7644

Offers reproductive health care, counseling, public education, outreach programs, and self-help education to women in Atlanta and the southeast states.

Feminist Women's Health Center
633 E 11th Ave.
Eugene, OR 97401
(503) 342-5940

Offers a variety of gynecological services for women.

Feminist Women's Health Center
4300 Talbot Rd. S, #403
Renton, WA 98055
(206) 255-0471;
Fax: (206) 277-3640

Provides health care services and education programs. Offers reproductive health services, including abortion.

Gainesville Women's Health Center
720 NW 23 Ave.
Gainesville, FL 32609
(904) 377-5055

A full-service gynecology center that also offers walk-in pregnancy exams, HIV screening, STD treatment, and school and work physicals for people age ten and older. Performs first and second trimester abortions.

Haight-Ashbury Women's Clinic
1825 Haight St.
San Francisco, CA 94117
(415) 221-7371

Offers gynecological services to low-income women, including pregnancy tests and referrals, birth control screening, pelvic and annual exams, and HIV and infectious disease testing.

Hamot Women's Health Connection
3330 Peach St., #LL2
Erie, PA 16508
(814) 877-6145

A resource and reference center for women. Services include a health information library, educational classes, health counseling, psychological services, therapeutic massage, and breast health services.

Health House Women's Resource Center
420 Lake Ave.
Saint James, NY 11780
(516) 862-6743

A health education and resource center for women. Services include short-term counseling, support groups, workshops, health information, and referrals.

Lifespan Center for Women's Health
1506 S Oneida St.
Appleton, WI 54915
(414) 738-2623;
Fax: (414) 738-0949

Offers Lamaze, parenting, exercise classes, physician referrals, and maintains an extensive library for public use.

Lower East Side Women's Center
53 Stanton St.
New York, NY 10002
(212) 353-1924

Provides gynecological and health services to women.

Lyon-Martin Women's Health Services
1748 Market St., #201
San Francisco, CA 94102
(415) 565-7667

A health clinic providing a range of services to lesbians.

Mabel Wadsworth Women's Health Center
334A Harlow
P.O. Box 20
Bangor, ME 04402
(207) 947-5337

Provides reproductive and sexual

health eduction and medical ser-vices to all women. Clinical ser-vices include basic gynecological services with referrals for preg-nancy options. Presents semiannual women's health conferences and sponsors a lesbian health project.

Memphis Center for Reproductive Health
1462 Poplar
Memphis, TN 38104
(901) 274-3550

Provides free pregnancy testing, of-fers birth control and family plan-ning information, performs ultra-sound, Pap and pelvic exams, and performs abortions.

New Hampshire Women's Health Center
559 Portsmouth Ave.,
P.O. Box 456
Greenland, NH 03840
(603) 436-7588

Provides all gynecological services, pregnancy testing, STD and HIV screening and counseling, and weekly abortion clinics.

North Country Clinic for Women and Children
785 18th St.
Arcata, CA 95521
(707) 822-2481

Offers a full range of gynecological and family health services such as prenatal and well child care. Also provides counseling services.

North Florida Women's Health and Counseling Services, Incorporated
126 B. Salem Ct.
Tallahassee, FL 32301
(904) 877-3183

Provides gynecological care, preg-nancy testing, and abortion ser-vices, as well as sexuality and contraceptive education.

Portland Women's Health Center
1020 NE 2nd Ave., #200
Portland, OR 97232
(503) 233-0808

Provides walk-in pregnancy testing, abortions, annual exams, and cer-vical cap and diaphragm fittings.

Redding Feminist Women's Health Center
1901 Victor Ave.
Redding, CA 96002
(916) 221-0193

Provides annual exams, birth con-trol, and other gynecological ser-vices. Performs abortions and STD testing.

Rhode Island Women's Health Collective
90 Printery St.
Providence, RI 02904
(401) 861-0030

Offers a hotline people can call about any health issue, provides physician referrals, sends health care literature upon request, and sponsors lectures and workshops for women.

Sacramento Feminist Women's Health Center
3401 Folsom Blvd., #A
Sacramento, CA 95816
(916) 451-0621

Provides reproductive services including pregnancy tests, phone counseling, birth control, abortion, gynecological care, and fertility health services. Also offers health education, self-help, and home remedies.

Santa Cruz Women's Health Center
250 Locust St.
Santa Cruz, CA 95060
(408) 427-3500

Feminist primary medical care and health education center. Provides general medical care, family planning, and gynecological services, as well as advocacy and education activities.

Southern Vermont Women's Health Center
187 North Main St.
Rutland, VT 05701
(802) 775-1946

Offers complete gynecological services to women, in addition to abortions.

Vermont Women's Health Center
336 North Ave.
Burlington, VT 05401
(802) 863-1386;
Fax: (802) 863-1774

Provides obstetrical and gyneco-

logical health care for women. Also offers consulting services for health care policy, educational services, legislative leadership and testimony, and training of health care professionals.

Washington Free Clinic, Women's Health Collective
1525 Newton St. NW,
P.O. Box 43202
Washington, DC 20010
(202) 667-1106

Provides general medicine, Ob/Gyn services, STD testing and treatment, and HIV screening.

Westside Women's Health Center
1711 Ocean Park Blvd.
Santa Monica, CA 90405
(310) 450-2191;
Fax: (310) 450-0873

Provides family planning, gynecological services, prenatal care, well baby care, STD testing, and anonymous HIV testing.

Womancare Clinic South
688 Hollister St., #B
San Diego, CA 92154
(619) 424-9944

Provides birth control information, gynecological services, abortions, and donor insemination procedures.

Womancare Feminist Women's Health Center
2850 6th Ave., #311
San Diego, CA 92103
(619) 298-9352

Provides abortions, birth control and family planning, gynecological exams, and donor insemination.

Woman's Choice Clinic
4415 Sonoma Hwy., #D
Santa Rosa, CA 95409
(707) 537-1173

Offers both abortion and well woman clinics. Services include basic gynecology exams and testing, and HIV and STD screening.

Women and Wellness
701 Foulk Rd.
Foulk Pl., #E–1
Wilmington, DE 19803
(302) 654-5604

A nonprofit organization offering wellness through educational programs and lecture series. Maintains a consumer-oriented health library.

Women's Choices Health Clinic
2930 McClure
Oakland, CA 94609
(510) 444-5676

Offers gynecological exams, first and second trimester abortions, STD screening, and family planning and contraceptive advice.

Women's Community Clinic
696 E Santa Clara St., #204
San Jose, CA 95112
(408) 287-4090

Offers Ob/Gyn exams and family planning. Performs gynecological surgeries such as tubal ligations and hysterectomies. Also provides

abortions. Has a Personal Family Development Center that offers psychological therapies.

Women's Community Health Center
131 Longwood Dr.
Huntsville, AL 35801
(800) 666-9228

Provides gynecological services, abortions, HIV screening, and STD testing. The center does not provide prenatal care.

Women's Health Center
205 W 2nd St., #500
Duluth, MN 55802
(218) 727-3352, (800) 735-7654;
Fax: (218) 720-6976

Offers STD testing, pregnancy tests, abortions, birth control, vasectomies, cholesterol screening, morning-after treatments, and HIV testing.

Women's Health Center
60 Central Ave.
Cortland, NY 13045
(607) 753-5027

Provides general gynecological care, including exams and Pap smears as well as STD testing. Also offers referrals for prenatal care.

Women's Health Center of West Virginia
3418 Staunton Ave. SE
Charleston, WV 25304
(304) 344-9834

Women's Health Organization
2123 W Newport Pike
Wilmington, DE 19804
(302) 652-3410

Staff sees gynecological patients and performs abortions.

Women's Health Services
500 W San Francisco
Santa Fe, NM 87501
(505) 988-8869

Has family physicians and nurse practitioners on the staff that provide family health and gynecological services. Also offers accupressure and massage therapies.

Women's Health Services, Incorporated
911 State St.
New Haven, CT 06511
(203) 789-1272

A private, nonprofit organization that provides low-cost health care to women and men. Services include gynecology, family planning, pregnancy testing, counseling, abortion, food and body image counseling, STD screening and treatment, and vasectomy.

Women's Needs Center
A Women's Resource Center
1825 Haight St.
San Francisco, CA 94117
(415) 487-5607

Provides gynecological and family planning services to low-income women.

MENTAL HEALTH SERVICES

American Psychological Association, Division of the Psychology of Women, Women's Program Office
750 First St. NE
Washington, DC 20002-4242
(202) 336-6044;
Fax: (202) 336-6040

Works for equitable treatment of women within the discipline of psychology. Concerns include policy initiatives, research on women, and publications. See also Research

Centers and Organizations; Women's Rights.

American Women in Psychology Roster.
See Professional and Business Associations and Networks.

Boston Psychological Center for Women
20 Park Pl., #451
Boston, MA 02216
(617) 422-0788

Provides counseling services that

are particularly designed for women and the issues they face.

Catalyst—A Program for Women
310 E 38th St.
Minneapolis, MN 55409
(612) 822-7393

Offers counseling services for women in transition.

Chrysalis Center for Women.

See Women's Centers.

Counseling Center of Milwaukee
2038 N Bartlett
Milwaukee, WI 53202
(414) 271-2565

Provides individual couple and family counseling as well as support groups. Fees are paid on a sliding scale and all counselors have master's degrees.

Depression After Delivery
P.O. Box 1282
Morrisville, PA 19067
(215) 295-3994

A national self-help organization that provides support, education, information, and referral for women and families coping with anxiety, depression, and psychosis associated with the arrival of a baby. Promotes awareness of these issues to all sectors of the community and advocates for changes to ensure the well-being of women and their families.

Elizabeth Stone House
Box 59
Jamaica Plain, MA 02130
(617) 522-3417;
Fax: (617) 522-4321

Offers three residential programs: a five-month mental health alternative, an eight-week battered women's program, and an eighteen-month transitional housing program. Also holds workshops and training on women's mental health issues. See also Displaced Homemakers' Services; Violence Against Women.

Family Institute,
Crowley Library
680 N Lake Shore Dr., Ste. 1306
Chicago, IL 60611
(312) 908-7854

Holds books, videos, and audiocassettes on mental health issues. Topics include family, marriage, divorce, adolescent pregnancy, adoption, contraception, and reproductive health. See also Family, Children, and Youth Services.

Feminist Expressive Therapies Program
Northwest Institute for the Creative Arts Therapies, Inc.
33 E 20th Ave.
Eugene, OR 97405
(503) 683-4483

Provides counseling services, training programs, and consultations in art therapy, dance/movement therapy, psychodrama, and feminist

*theory and therapy. Training
ranges from short workshops to degree programs.*

**Grove Institute for
Psychotherapy and Training**
10 2nd St. NE, E #100
Minneapolis, MN 55414
(612) 379-2640

*A center for feminist therapy serv-
ing adults and family groups. Provides training for clinicians and
workshops for clients addressing
issues such as family, sexuality,
abuse, incest, relationships, and
parenting.*

**Irene Josselyn Clinic,
Mental Health Library**
405 Central
Northfield, IL 60093
(708) 441-5600;
Fax: (708) 441-7968

*Offers information and materials
on child development, parenting,
divorce, and other mental health issues, theories, and research information. Also holds films and
videotapes on suicide.*

**Journeywomen, A Feminist
Psychotherapy Collective**
240A Elm St., Davis Sq.
Somerville, MA 02144
(617) 776-9232

*A feminist therapy collective dedi-
cated to serving the psychotherapy
needs of women. Expertise includes
addictions, abuse, relationships,
grief, loss, and family issues.*

**Lesbian Resource and
Counseling Center.**
See Lesbian and Gay Organizations.

Love-N-Addiction
P.O. Box 759
Willimantic, CT 06226
(203) 423-2344

*Offers self-help support groups on
relationships, codependence, and
emotionally addictive behavior for
women.*

**National Coalition for Women's
Mental Health**
Arizona State Univ.
Women's Studies Program
Tempe, AZ 85287-1801
(602) 965-2358

*A network that promotes a women's
mental health agenda. Analyzes
current issues from a psychological
perspective and provides information to the public.*

**Postpartum Support,
International**
927 N Kellogg Ave.
Santa Barbara, CA 93111
(805) 967-7636

*Promotes public awareness about
the mental health issues of child-
bearing. Provides educational programs and encourages research
and support groups.*

**Pregnancy and Infant Loss
Center**
1421 Wayzata Blvd., #30
Wayzata, MN 55391
(612) 473-9372

Provides counseling and support for those suffering from miscarriage, stillbirth, and Sudden Infant Death Syndrome (SIDS).

Psychology of Women Quarterly.

See Newspapers, Newsletters, and Magazines.

Stone Center

Wellesley College
106 Central St.
Wellesley, MA 02181
(617) 283-2838;
Fax: (617) 283-3646

Works to prevent and address psychological problems of women and to enhance psychological well-being of women, children, and families. Develops theory, conducts research, and offers public education, consultation, action programs, and counseling. See also Research Centers and Organizations.

Womankind Counseling Center

15 Warren St.
Concord, NH 03301
(603) 225-2985

Provides individual, family, and group psychotherapy to women, men, and children. Offers special topic groups, weekend retreats, consultations, and training.

Woman Reach, Inc.

The Gallery Outlet Square Shopping Center, Ste. 605
Charlotte, NC 28204
(704) 334-3614;
Fax: (704) 334-4689

A women's resource center that provides peer counseling, support groups, workshops, and seminars on issues of interest to women.

Women's Counseling and Therapy Center

112–11 68 Dr.
Forest Hills, NY 11375
(718) 268-3077;
Fax: (718) 261-5961

Offers counseling and referral services, as well as special programs for sex abuse recovery.

Women's Growth and Therapy Center

2607 Connecticut Ave. NW, 3rd Fl.
Washington, DC 20015
(202) 483-9376

A mental health counseling center for women and their partners.

Women's Institute of Boulder

207 Canyon Blvd., #201
Boulder, CO 80302
(303) 449-2856

A feminist collective offering psychotherapy, counseling, education, and body-oriented therapies.

Women's Mental Health Collective

61 Roseland
Somerville, MA 02143
(617) 354-6270

Offers counseling services and psychotherapy from a feminist perspective.

Women's Psychotherapy Institute
1301 20th St. NW
Washington, DC 20036
(202) 833-9026

*Offers mental health counseling
and psychotherapy for women.*

Women's Therapy Center
1930 Chestnut St., Ste. 1703
Philadelphia, PA 19103
(215) 567-1111

*A mental health center for adult
women. Offers counseling and psychotherapy, referral and information,
education, outreach programs, advocacy, and professional training.*

SELF-HELP HEALTH

There are a growing number of self-help organizations by and for
women who share similar health crises. Please note that many of these
that pertain to cancer have been listed in the section on Cancer Resources.

Advocacy Institute
Women vs. Smoking Network
1730 Rhode Island Ave NW,
Ste. 600
Washington, DC 20036
(202) 659-8475

*Offers information to women on the
adverse effects of tobacco use. Mo-
bilizes women to fight for tobacco
control.*

Endometriosis Association
8585 N 76 Pl.
Milwaukee, WI 53223
(414) 355-2200, (800) 992-3636;
Fax: (414) 355-6065

*A self-help organization of women
with endometriosis. Offers mutual
support, education for the public
and the medical community, research, and publications.*

**LifeCycles for Women PMS
Self-Help Center**
101 First St., #441
Los Altos, CA 94022
(800) 862-9876;
Fax: (415) 965-4311

*Provides education, programs, and
products for women's health. Priority is given to common female
health concerns including PMS,
menopause, fibroids, chronic fa-
tigue, endometriosis, cramps, ane-
mia, and estrogen therapy.
Publishes a quarterly newsletter.*

Menstrual Health Foundation
104 Petaluma Ave.
Sebastopol, CA 95472
(707) 829-2744;
Fax: (707) 829-1753

Offers programs for menstrual and menopausal empowerment. Also publishes a menstrual catalog featuring organic cotton menstrual pads and accessories.

Pregnancy and Infant Loss Center
1421 Wayzata Blvd., #30
Wayzata, MN 55391
(612) 473-9372;
Fax: (612) 473-8978

A nonprofit center that offers support, resources, and education on issues of miscarriage, stillbirth, and newborn death.

Silicone Problem Awareness
P.O. Box 965
Eldridge, CA 95431

A northern California support group for women who have or have had silicone or saline breast implants. Meets once per month and provides emotional support and education. Write to them for specific information.

SUBSTANCE ABUSE SERVICES

Alcoholism Center for Women
1147 S Alvarado St.
Los Angeles, CA 90006
(213) 381-8500;
Fax: (213) 381-8525

Supports the recovery from and prevention of alcoholism and other drug-related problems among women at high risk, including lesbians, adult daughters of alcoholics, incest and battering survivors, homeless women, and women of color. Offers residential and outparticipant services, as well as workshops.

Friendly Peersuasion
33 E 33rd St.
New York, NY 10016
(212) 689-3700;
Fax: (212) 683-1253

Works to prevent drug and alcohol abuse among young women and teens. Offers peer leadership training programs dealing with how to manage stress, make decisions, and refuse alcohol and drugs.

Gay Alcoholism Center
11918 Garden Grove Blvd.
Garden Grove, Ca 92643
(714) 534-5820

Runs an alcoholism recovery program designed for gays and lesbians.

Healy & Associates
121 Springfield Ave.
Joliet, IL 60435-6561
(815) 741-0102
Offers consulting to help women and their families deal with alcoholism and drug abuse. Offers pro-

grams on stress, smoking cessation, and weight control. Sponsors educational forums and public information workshops.

Human Services Institute, Incorporated
4301 32nd St. W, No. C8
Bradenton, FL 34205-2743
(813) 746-7088

Publishes a national directory of alcohol and drug abuse treatment services and prevention programs for women.

Institute on Black Chemical Abuse
2614 Nicollet Ave. S
Minneapolis, MN 55408
(612) 871-7878

Provides assessment and referrals, and has an outpatient program for individual counseling.

Iris Center, Women's Counseling and Recovery Services
333 Valencia St., #222
San Francisco, CA 94103
(415) 864-2364

A center designed for the recovery needs of women. Provides multicultural, lesbian-sensitive services to women of all economic backgrounds.

Lapis Program
c/o Alcoholism Center for Women
1147 S Alvarado St.
Los Angeles, CA 90006
(213) 381-8500;
Fax: (213) 381-8525

An alcohol and drug prevention component of the Alcoholism Center for Women. Designed to do specific outreach to lesbians of African American or Latina descent.

Lavender Waves
Box 44
Seal Rock, OR 97376
(503) 563-3643

A lesbian recovery retreat center.

National Women's Christian Temperance Union
1730 Chicago Ave.
Evanston, IL 60201
(708) 864-1396

An old, well-established organization of women from many faiths. Their mission is to educate people about what alcohol, narcotics, and tobacco do to individuals as well as to society. Produces films on temperance, promotes essay and poster contests, maintains a research library, and holds youth abstinence camps.

Project Return Foundation, Incorporated
Women in Crisis, Incorporated
10 Astor Pl.
New York, NY 10003
Fax: (212) 979-0100

Concerned with educating African American and Latina women and others on the correlations between alcohol and drug use and HIV infection. Advocates a wholistic approach throughout its programs. Teaches women numerous life skills to reduce their health risks. See also Organizations Representing Women of Color.

Recovering Hearts, Books and Gifts.

See Booksellers: Bookstores.

Sobering Thoughts
P.O. Box 618
Quakertown, PA 18951
(215) 536-8026, (800) 333-1606

A monthly newsletter that offers articles for women on substance abuse and mental health issues dealing with substance abuse.

Solutions, A Recovery Bookstore.

See Booksellers: Bookstores.

Step by Step Books.

See Booksellers: Bookstores.

Task Force on Women and Addiction
P.O. Box 33
Leetsdale, PA 15056
(412) 766-8700, Ext. 127

A nonprofit group of professional women whose mission is to educate and support women affected by addiction and the professionals who serve them in the region. Provides community education, advocacy, professional development, support groups, and a networking service.

Womanfocus
656 Elmwood Ave., #300
Buffalo, NY 14222
(716) 884-3256;
Fax: (716) 844-3279

A substance abuse program for women and adolescent girls. Designed to address the problems inherent in the woman's role in society which may lead to masking feelings through use of alcohol and other drugs. Offers six-week workshops on topics such as self-esteem and assertiveness for women.

Womanspace
112 Ardmore Ave.
Ardmore, PA 19003
(215) 649-8136

Focuses primarily on helping women with drug and alcohol dependencies. Also sponsors support groups and education programs in parenting, nutrition, and health to help women during the recovery process.

Woman's Program
1751 Cattlemen Rd.
Sarasota, FL 34232
(813) 377-8583; Fax: (813) 377-4901

Offers outpatient and educational services for women dealing with substance abuse problems.

Woman-to-Woman
4214 Market
Youngstown, OH 44512
(216) 740-2850

A drug and alcohol outpatient treatment center. Offers both group and individual counseling sessions for women in treatment or their families or friends. Also has placement referrals for those needing live-in facilities.

Women and Recovery
c/o Woman-to-Woman
Communications
P.O. Box 161775
Cupertino, CA 95016

Publishes a recovery newsletter.

Women for Sobriety
P.O. Box 618
Quakertown, PA 18951
(215) 536-8026;
Fax: (215) 536-8026

A program for women with alcohol or drug problems. Teaches women self-esteem and empowerment. Offers self-help groups, a monthly newsletter, and literature. Chapters throughout the U.S.

Women, Incorporated
244 Townsend St.
Dorchester, MA 02121
(617) 442-6166;
Fax: (617) 427-1359

A nonprofit agency that helps women with drug or alcohol dependency problems. Offers residential substance abuse treatment, shelter for homeless women and their children, and a variety of outpatient services, such as AIDS education and referrals to other agencies.

Women's Alcoholism Center
2261 Bryant St.
San Francisco, CA 94110
(415) 285-4484

One of the earliest feminist-oriented alcohol treatment centers for women. Offers a full range of programs from residential treatment to outpatient services.

Women's Alcoholism Program
Cambridge and Summerville
6 Camelia Ave.
Cambridge, MA 02139
(617) 661-1316

Offers group and individual counseling throughout the day and evening.

Women's Drug Research Project
Univ. of Michigan,
School of Social Work
1065 Frieze Bldg.
Ann Arbor, MI 48109-1285
(313) 763-5958

Conducts research on women and drug abuse and drug treatment.

Women's Outreach for Women
1950 N 4th St.
Columbus, OH 43201
(614) 291-3639

Offers a variety of twelve-step groups, including AA, AlAnon, and Survivors of Incest Anonymous, as well as educational workshops for women in recovery.

Women's Recovery Network
P.O. Box 141554
Columbus, OH 43214
(614) 268-5847

A bimonthly newsletter for and about women in recovery. Articles deal with such issues as alcoholism, drug addiction, eating disorders, violence, and rape.

❏ **Land Trusts**

Women's land trusts are nonprofit entities that either own or are attempting to buy land that will be held for the benefit and use of women. All hold strong environmental ethics and make decisions based on consensus. If an entry does not include a description, simply write to the address listed for more information.

**Daughters of the Earth Farm
(DOE)**
Rte. 2, Box 42
Norwalk, WI 54648
(608) 269-5301

An eighty-acre land trust for women members. Offers camping, farmhouse lodging, and workshops.

**Howl: Vermont Women's
Land Trust**
P.O. Box 242
Winooski, VT 05404
(802) 658-0199

**New Mexico Women's
Land Trust**
P.O. Box 707
Tesuque, NM 87574
(505) 989-8627

Oregon Women's Land Trust
P.O. Box 133
Days Creek, OR 97429

One hundred and forty-seven acres

in rural southern Oregon open to women visitors. No male children over five years old allowed.

Sisters Homelands on Earth
She Land Trust
P.O. Box 5285
Tucson, AZ 85703
(602) 883-9085

Works to acquire and hold land for the use of present and future generations of women and children. Gives access to land especially to those denied access because of racism, ableism, classism, and other oppressions.

**Southern Oregon Lesbian
Country Archival Project**
200 King Mountain Trail
Sunny Valley, OR 97497
(503) 679-4655

WomLand
P.O. Box 55
Troy, ME 04987

❏ Legal Services

American Bar Association Commission on Women in the Profession
750 N Lakeshore Dr.
Chicago, IL 60611
(312) 988-5676;
Fax: (312) 988-6281

Promotes the advancement of women in the law. Develops educational materials, programs, and research to address discrimination against women lawyers.

Connecticut Women's Education and Legal Fund
135 Broad St.
Hartford, CT 06105
(203) 247-6090;
Fax: (203) 524-0804

Works through legal and public policy strategies and community education to end sex discrimination and empower all women. Offers an information and referral program, an education and training program, and publications.

Custody Action for Lesbian Mothers.
See Lesbian and Gay Organizations.

Equal Rights Advocates
1663 Mission St., Ste. 550
San Francisco, CA 94103
(415) 621-0672

A women's law center. Litigates lawsuits on women's rights, offers advice and counseling, and publishes information on legal rights.

Family Law Project
Univ. of Michigan Law School
Ann Arbor, MI 48109
(313) 763-6591

A nonprofit organization that provides legal services to indigent survivors of domestic violence. Helps women obtain restraining orders, divorces, and custody.

Family Violence Law Center
P.O. Box 2529
Berkeley, CA 94702
(510) 540-5354

Provides legal assistance in obtaining restraining orders.

Lambda Legal Defense and Education Fund
666 Broadway
New York, NY 10012
(212) 995-8585;
Fax: (212) 995-2306

A nonprofit organization working to protect and advance the legal and civil rights of lesbians, gay men, and people with HIV/AIDS. With offices in New York, Los Angeles, and Chicago, has regional and national expertise in all aspects of sexual orientation and HIV-related law and policy. See also Lesbian and Gay Organizations.

Legal Aid Society Domestic Violence Victim Assistance
225 S 200 E, Ste. 230
Salt Lake City, UT 84111
(801) 355-2804

Provides legal assistance and advice to women affected by domestic violence.

Legal Awareness for Women
Box 35H
Scarsdale, NY 10583
(914) 472-2371

Educates women on their rights within the legal system. Provides information and referrals.

NAACP Legal Defense and Educational Fund Law Library
99 Hudson St., 16th Fl.
New York, NY 10013
(212) 219-1900

A library holding publications and information on civil rights law. Deals with issues of discrimination against blacks, other racial minori-

ties, and women from a legal standpoint. See also Organizations Representing Women of Color; Women's Rights.

National Association of Black Women Attorneys
3711 Macomb St. NW
Washington, DC 20016
(202) 966-9693

Mission is to advance justice by increasing opportunities for all women. Also helps women students remain in law school by offering grants and scholarships. See also Business and Professional Associations and Networks.

National Center for Lesbian Rights.

See Lesbian and Gay Organizations.

National Center for Women and Family Law
799 Broadway, Rm. 402
New York, NY 10003
(212) 674-8200;
Fax: (212) 533-5104

A national legal organization addressing women's issues in the family law area. Provides legal assistance to advocates for poor women and addresses battery, child custody, incest, child support, wife support, and division of property. Also offers training and education on family law issues. See also Violence Against Women.

National Women's Law Center
1616 P Street NW, Ste. 100
Washington, DC 20036
(202) 328-5160;
Fax: (202) 328-5137

Advocates for the advancement and protection of women's legal rights. Focuses on major policy areas of importance to women and their families, including health and reproductive rights, education, employment, income security, and family support. Special attention given to the concerns of low-income women. See also Family, Children, and Youth Services.

Northwest Women's Law Center
119 S Main St., #330
Seattle, WA 98104-2515
(206) 682-9552;
Fax: (206) 682-9556

A nonprofit public interest law center focusing on women's legal issues. Works to advance women's rights through litigation, legislation, education, and information and referral by telephone. Publications available for purchase. See also Women's Rights.

NOW Legal Defense and Education Fund
99 Hudson St., 12th Fl.
New York, NY 10013
(212) 925-6635;
Fax: (212) 226-1066

Provides legal information and litigates cases regarding sex discrimination. Projects include violence against women, poverty issues, educational equity, gender equity in the courts, and incest. See also Women's Rights.

Women's Law Project
125 S Ninth Ave., Ste. 401
Philadelphia, PA 19107
(215) 928-9848

A public interest law center dedicated to improving the economic status of women through public policy development, litigation, education, and advocacy. Offers a speakers' bureau, telephone counseling, referrals, and publications on family law.

Women's Legal Defense Fund
2000 P Street NW, Ste. 400
Washington, DC 20036
(202) 986-2600;
Fax: (202) 861-0691

Advocates public policies that focus on work and family concerns, provides assistance to activists and policymakers, and participates in litigation to challenge gender bias. Offers public education about the social costs of gender discrimination. See also Women's Rights.

❑ Lesbian and Gay Organizations

ACHE.

See Newspapers, Newsletters, and Magazines.

ALA Gay and Lesbian Task Force Clearinghouse
c/o American Library Assoc.
50 E Huron
Chicago, IL 60611
(312) 944-6780

Holds books, periodicals, and other materials on homosexuality, lesbianism, feminism, and gay rights. Offers occasional educational programs.

Amazon Autumn.

See Foundations and Funding Sources.

American Civil Liberties Union, Gay Rights Chapter
1663 Mission St., #460
San Francisco, CA 94103
(415) 621-2493

Supports and promotes lesbian and gay rights in the San Francisco Bay area. Sponsors programs, activities, and meetings.

Associated Lesbian Professionals of Seattle
P.O. Box 20424
Seattle, WA 98102
(206) 233-8145

Serves as a social and educational network for lesbians in Seattle.

Association for Gay, Lesbian, and Bisexual Issues in Counseling
Box 216
Jenkintown, PA 19046

An organization of counselors, personnel, and guidance workers concerned with lesbian and gay issues. Works to eliminate discrimination against gays and lesbians. Provides referrals and networking opportunities. Write to them for further information.

Astrea Foundation.

See Foundations and Funding Sources.

Atlanta Lesbian Feminist Alliance Southeastern Lesbian Archives
Box 5502
Atlanta, GA 30307
(404) 378-9769

Sponsors numerous social and lesbian rights activities. The archives holds books and periodicals on lesbian feminism, women's theory, and women's issues. Publishes newsletter.

Black Lace.

See Newspapers, Newsletters, and Magazines.

Common Lives/Lesbian Lives.

See Newspapers, Newsletters, and Magazines.

Conference for Catholic Lesbians.

See Religious and Spiritual Groups.

Custody Action for Lesbian Mothers
P.O. Box 281
Narberth, PA 19072
(215) 667-7508

A litigation support service for lesbian mothers. Offers free representation in the Delaware Valley and offers consultation nationally. See also Legal Services.

Damron Co., Incorporated
P.O. Box 4224
San Francisco, CA 94142-2458
(415) 255-0404

Publishes a gay and lesbian travel guide. Lists bars, baths, hotels, and restaurants frequented by lesbians and gays.

Dignity, Incorporated
1500 Massachusetts Ave. NW,
Ste. 11
Washington, DC 20005
(202) 861-0017

An organization for lesbians and gays who are members of the Roman Catholic church. Offers programs, education, and social events.

Dykes, Disability & Stuff.

See Special Interests: Physically Challenged Services.

Entre Nous: Between Us.

See Newspapers, Newsletters, and Magazines.

Entre Nous, Windy City Times.

See Newspapers, Newsletters, and Magazines.

Family Next Door
P.O. Box 21580
Oakland, CA 94620
(510) 482-5778

A newsletter for lesbian and gay parents. Addresses topics such as medical and health issues, legal and social concerns, and schooling. See also Newspapers, Newsletters, and Magazines.

Gay Alcoholism Center.

See Health Organizations: Substance Abuse Services.

Gay and Lesbian Community Center of Orange County
12832 Garden Grove B1
Garden Grove, CA 92643
(714) 534-0862

Sponsors a wide range of social, political, and support activities for the lesbian and gay community.

Gay and Lesbian Parents Coalition International
P.O. Box 50360
Washington, DC 20091

Publishes Just For Us *newsletter for the children of gay and lesbian parents. Holds annual conferences. Chapters in most cities.*

Gay, Lesbian and Bisexual Speakers Bureau
Public Education Services, Inc.
11 P.O. Box 2232
Boston, MA 02117
(617) 354-0133

Offers educational speaking engagements on gay, lesbian, and bisexual issues as well as a speaker's manual entitled Speaking Out. *The above address is for ordering the speaker's manual. However, call for specific ordering instructions as well as information on scheduling speakers and membership.*

Hikane: The Capable Woman.

See Newspapers, Newsletters, and Magazines.

Homosexual Information Center Library
115 Monroe St.
Bossier City, LA 71111
(318) 742-4709

Offers a collection of books, periodicals, original manuscripts, legal briefs, and papers. Specializes in civil liberties, censorship, sexual freedom, and abortion. Also provides information and referrals.

June Mazer Lesbian Collection
Connexus Women's Center
626 N Robertson Blvd.
West Hollywood, CA 90069
(213) 659-2478

Offers books, dissertations, tapes, manuscripts, periodicals, and videos on lesbian history and culture.

Labrys Productions.

See Art and Media: Music.

Lambda Legal Defense and Education Fund.

See Legal Services.

Lavender Morning.

See Newspapers, Newsletters, and Magazines.

Lavender Waves.

See Health Organizations: Substance Abuse Services.

Lesbian Alliance
130 N Madison
Iowa City, IA 48244
(319) 335-1486

An organization of lesbians in Iowa. Offers support, resources, and social activities.

Lesbian Contradiction.

See Newspapers, Newsletters, and Magazines.

Lesbian Feminist Liberation
Gay Community Center
208 W 13th St.
New York, NY 10011
(212) 620-7310

Works to promote and enhance lesbian and women's rights. Networks with other organizations, conducts lobbying efforts, organizes demonstrations, and offers educational programs. Also hosts dances, concerts, sports events, and conferences.

Lesbian Herstory Archives
Lesbian Herstory Educational
Foundation
484 14th St.
Brooklyn, NY 11215
(718) 768-DYKE

An archive that collects and preserves original documents, manuscripts, books, and other material written by or about lesbians. Also sponsors public lectures. See also Women's History.

Lesbian Mothers' National Defense Fund
P.O. Box 21567
Seattle, WA 98111
(206) 325-2643

Provides attorney referrals, legal information, and personal support for lesbians involved in custody disputes. Offers information about current developments in custody and visitation, child rearing, donor insemination, and adoption, and educates mothers, attorneys, judges, and the public about lesbian family issues. See also Legal Services.

Lesbian Resource Center
1208 E Pine St.
Seattle, WA 98122
(206) 322-3953

Provides information and services to lesbian community groups. Maintains a lending library, offers referrals, and operates a speakers' bureau. Publishes LRC Community News.

Lesbian Resource and Counseling Center
Whitman/Walker Clinic
1407 S St. NW
Washington, DC 20009
(202) 332-5935

Offers phone and individual counseling, a lesbian drop-in rap group resource and listings of lesbian events and referrals.

Lesbian Resource Project and Women's Center, Incorporated
P.O. Box 26031
Tempe, AZ 85285-6031
(602) 966-6152

Offers a resource and lending li-

brary of lesbian and feminist materials, an art gallery, and a workshop series. Also offers information on health care issues.

Lesbian Visionaries
P.O. Box 191443
Dallas, TX 75219
(214) 528-2426

A nonprofit membership organization that promotes the welfare of Texas lesbians through communication and educational activities. Publishes the New Vision.

Lesbian Visual Artists.

See Art and Media: Visual Art, Galleries, and Museums.

Mautner Project for Lesbians with Cancer.

See Health Organizations: Cancer Resources.

Media Fund for Human Rights
P.O. Box 8185
Universal City, CA 91608
(818) 902-1476

An educational foundation of the Gay and Lesbian Press Foundation. Offers information and services to the public about lesbians and gay issues. Promotes gay and lesbian history.

Midwest Lesbian and Gay Resource Library
3238 N Sheffield Ave.
Chicago, IL 60657
(312) 883-3003

Offers resources and information on lesbianism and homosexuality. Subjects include AIDS, health, and legal rights of homosexuals.

Momazons: Lesbians Choosing Children
P.O. Box 02069
Columbus, OH 43202
(614) 267-0193

A national organization for lesbian mothers and for lesbians who want children in their lives. Offers referrals and produces a newsletter. See also Newspapers, Newsletters, and Magazines.

National Association of Women for Understanding
1017 N La Cienega Blvd., #106
Los Angeles, CA 90069
(310) 657-1115;
Fax: (310) 657-1116

Offers educational and social activities for lesbians. Advocates equal rights for lesbians and works to eradicate negative lesbian stereotypes through public education. See also Women's Rights.

National Center for Lesbian Rights
1663 Mission St., 5th Fl.
San Francisco, CA 94103
(415) 621-0674;
Fax: (415) 621-6744

A feminist, lesbian, and multicultural legal resource center. Works through the courts, the legal system, and in the community to erad-

icate discrimination against lesbians and their families. Provides legal representation and advocacy, advice and counseling, technical assistance, and community education about lesbian and gay rights. See also Legal Services.

National Gay and Lesbian Task Force

1517 U St. NW
Washington, DC 20009
(202) 332-6483

One of the leading lesbian/gay rights advocacy organizations in the U.S. Lobbies at the federal level for appropriate legislation. Researches and publishes resource materials concerning the lesbian/gay community and publishes a quarterly newsletter.

Parents and Friends of Lesbians and Gays (PFLAG)

P.O. Box 44–4
West Sommerville, MA 02144
(617) 547-2440

Provides a helpline of PFLAG members that people can call in confidence for information, support, and referrals. Also offers brochures and booklets on such topics as general parenting, religious issues, and coming out to your parents. PFLAG maintains a speakers bureau, holds meetings for its members, and has a number of chapters throughout the country.

Tacoma Lesbian Concern

Box 947
Tacoma, WA 98401
(206) 472-0422

An organization for lesbians in the Tacoma area. Offers social and educational programs and events, as well as support groups.

United Sisters

P.O. Box 41
Garwood, NJ 07027

Sponsors research and offers social services, educational opportunities, and civil rights activities for lesbians. Also offers peer counseling and legal, medical, religious, and psychiatric referrals.

❏ **Newspapers, Newsletters, and Magazines**

AAUW Outlook
American Association of University Women
1111 16th St. NW
Washington, DC 20036
(202) 785-7728

A quarterly magazine addressing women's concerns. Topics cover political issues, education, and legislative issues.

ACHE: A Journal for Black Lesbians
P.O. Box 6071
Albany, CA 94706
(510) 849-2819

Covers issues of concern to black lesbians. Published six times per year.

Affilia: Journal of Women and Social Work
Columbia Univ.
622 W 113th St.
New York, NY 10025
(212) 854-5183;
Fax: (212) 854-2975

A feminist journal that addresses the interests of women in social work. Includes research reports, book reports, fiction, and feminist articles.

Albuquerque Woman
P.O. Box 6133
Albuquerque, NM 87197
(505) 247-9195

A bimonthly magazine dealing with women's issues and business in Albuquerque. Also publishes Albuquerque Women in Business Directory annually.

Alleluia Press
P.O. Box 103
Allendale, NJ 07401

A feminist publisher. Write to them requesting further information and a description of services.

American Voice
Kentucky Foundation for Women, Inc.
332 West Broadway, Ste. 1215
Louisville, KY 40202

A quarterly journal that contains fiction, poetry, essays, and photographs for women.

American Women Motorsports Magazine
Ladylike Enterprise, Inc.
2830 Santa Monica Blvd.
Santa Monica, CA 90404
(310) 829-0012

A magazine for women who ride motorcycles. Articles also on other adventure sports. Published six times per year.

BBW: Big Beautiful Women
BBW Publishing Co.
9171 Wilshire Blvd., Ste. 300
Beverly Hills, CA 90210
(310) 271-8442

A monthly fashion magazine for large-size women.

Belles Lettres: A Review of Books by Women
11151 Captains Walk Ct.
North Potomac, MD 20878
(301) 294-0278;
Fax: (301) 294-0023

A quarterly magazine devoted to literature by or about women. Includes reviews, interviews, essays, theme sections, and columns on publishing news, reprints, and non-fiction titles.

Beltane Papers
1333 Lincoln St., #240
Bellingham, WA 98226

A biannual journal of women's mysteries. Includes poetry and articles about the mysteries of women, in addition to articles on food and music and book excerpts. See also Religious and Spiritual Groups.

Berkeley Women's Law Journal
c/o Boalt Hall School of Law
Univ. of California, Berkeley
Berkeley, CA 94720
(415) 642-6263

An annual law journal for women. Specifically addresses concerns of women of color, lesbians, disabled women, and economically disadvantaged women.

Birth Gazette
Farm Midwifery Center
42 The Farm
Summertown, TN 38483
(615) 964-2519

An independent magazine published by practicing midwives about issues, concerns, and information related to midwifery.

Birth Notes
Association for Childbirth at Home, International
P.O. Box 430
Glendale, CA 91205-1025

A quarterly magazine that presents information about childbirth at home, alternative technologies of childbirth, and perinatology.

Bitch: The Women's Rock Magazine
San Jose Face
478 W Hamilton Ave., Ste. 164
Campbell, CA 95008
(408) 374-8073

A monthly music magazine covering rock music for and by women.

Black Lace
P.O. Box 83912
Los Angeles, CA 90083
(310) 410-0808;
Fax: (310) 410-9250

An erotic quarterly for African American lesbians. Features a collection of poetry, short stories, fantasy letters, an advice column, artwork, and erotic photography. Also included are politically focused feature articles.

Bridges: A Journal for Jewish Feminists and Our Friends
P.O. Box 18437
Seattle, WA 98118
(206) 721-5008

A journal committed to integrating analyses of class, race, and sexual identity into Jewish feminist thought. Publishes the work of Jewish feminists as well as writing of particular relevance to Jewish feminism by non-Jewish women and men.

Broomstick
3543 18th St., #3
San Francisco, CA 94110
(415) 552-7460

Quarterly journal by, for, and about women over forty. Publishes personal experiences of midlife and long-living women and the feminist politics of their lives.

Buenhogar
America Publishing Group
Vanidades Continental Bldg.
6355 NW 36th St.
Virginia Gardens, FL 33166
(305) 871-6400

A bimonthly magazine for Hispanic and Latina women. Articles cover entertainment and general interest topics.

Bulletin: Committee on South Asian Women
Texas A & M Univ.,
Dept. of Psychology
College Station, TX 77843
(409) 845-2576

Features articles by and about South Asian women. Published two to three times per year.

Business Women's Directory
5225 Boyd Ave.
Oakland, CA 94618
(510) 654-7557

A women's resource guide of organizations offering support to women in business in the Bay area.

California Women
California Federation of Business and Professional Women's Clubs
1100 N St., No. 50
Sacramento, CA 95814-5627
(916) 442-2633

A quarterly journal for business and professional women.

Calyx, A Journal of Art and Literature by Women
P.O. Box B
Corvallis, OR 97339
(503) 753-9384;
Fax: (505) 247-9195

A journal that publishes the art and literature of women in a beautiful format. Includes the contributions of women of color, lesbians, and older women.

Camera Obscura: A Journal of Feminism and Film Theory
Johns Hopkins University Press
Journals Publishing Division
701 W 40th St., Ste. 275
Baltimore, MD 21211-2190

Contains articles on feminism and the film industry. Published three times per year.

Carolina Woman Today
Nason & Assoc.
P.O. Box 8204
Asheville, NC 28814
(704) 258-1322

A monthly magazine for women in North and South Carolina.

Challenging Media Images of Women Newsletter
P.O. Box 902
Framingham, MA 01701
(508) 879-8504

A newsletter that protests sexism in the media through articles by activ-ists and educators. Publishes names and addresses of companies that perpetuate narrow and biased depictions of women.

Chrome Rose's Review
7 Lent Ave.
Leroy, NY 14482
(716) 768-6054

A publication for women motorcy-clists. Prints articles relating to women motorcyclists, travel, and technical tips.

Colorado Women News
1900 Wazee St., #205
Denver, CO 80202
(303) 296-3447

A monthly news magazine for women in Colorado.

Columbia Journal of Gender and Law
Columbia Univ. School of Law
435 W 116th St.
New York, NY 10027-7297

Offers legal and interdisciplinary writings on feminism, gender is-sues, and feminist jurisprudence.

Common Lives/Lesbian Lives
P.O. Box 1553
Iowa City, IA 52244
(319) 335-1486

A quarterly magazine for lesbians. Articles present lesbian history, so-cial conditions, and analysis of les-bian culture.

Compleat Mother, USA
Box 209
Minot, ND 58702
(701) 852-2822

A resource magazine of pregnancy, birth, and breastfeeding for parents and health care providers.

Connexions
Interop Co.
480 San Antonio Rd., Ste. 100
Mountain View, CA 94040
(415) 941-3399

A quarterly magazine that features news and interviews about women, translated from international publications that are otherwise unattainable in the English-language press.

Country Woman
5400 S 60th St.
Greendale, WI 53129
(414) 423-0100

A magazine that features articles on rural living and concerns of country women. Published six times per year.

Creative Woman
Governors State Univ.
University Pkwy.
University Park, IL 60466
(708) 534-4485;
Fax: (708) 534-5459

A magazine that focuses on creative achievements by women. Articles feature fiction, poetry, and reviews.

Crone Chronicles
P.O. Box 81
Kelly, WY 83011
(307) 733-1726

A quarterly national networking journal activating the archetype of the Crone within Western culture. The Crone is identified as the third aspect of being female as described by the ancient Triple Goddess, Maiden/Mother/Crone.

Dallas Woman
Paradigm Publishing
14275 Midway Rd., Ste. 280
Dallas, TX 75244
(214) 458-7383

A monthly general interest magazine for women in the Dallas area.

Daughters of Sarah
3801 N Keeler
P.O. Box 416790
Chicago, IL 60641
(312) 736-3399

A magazine for Christian feminists. Published six times per year.

Deneuve Magazine
2336 Market St., #15
San Francisco, CA 94114
(415) 863-6538

Glossy lesbian life-style magazine.

Detroit Metropolitan Woman
North Park Pl.
17117 W 9 Mile Rd., Ste. 1115
Southfield, MI 48075-4517
(313) 443-6500;
Fax: (313) 443-6501

A monthly magazine for women in the Detroit area. Contains news, features, and information.

Differences: A Journal of Feminist Cultural Studies
Indiana Univ. Press
10th and Morton
Bloomington, IN 47405
(812) 855-9449; Fax: (812) 855-7931

A journal published three times per year that focuses on issues of cultural studies and feminism.

Dinah
P.O. Box 1485
Cincinnati, OH 45201

Bimonthly lesbian magazine based on reader-contributed articles.

Durham County Directory of Women-Owned Businesses
P.O. Box 15657
Durham, NC 27704
(914) 220-8177

Annual publication listing the women's businesses in the Durham area.

Dyke Review
584 Castro, #456
San Francisco, CA 94114
(415) 621-3769

A magazine for lesbians that publishes literary, controversial, informative, and humorous articles.

Dykes, Disability, & Stuff
P.O. Box 8773
Madison, WI 53703
(608) 256-8883

A quarterly newsletter devoted to the health and disability concerns of lesbians. Available in standard print, large print, audiocassette, braille, DOS diskette, and modem transfer.

Earth's Daughters
Box 41, Central Park Sta.
Buffalo, NY 14215

A feminist literary and art periodical. Focuses on the experience and creative expression of women.

Eidos: Erotica for Women by Women
P.O. Box 96
Boston, MA 02137
(617) 262-0096

A quarterly erotic journal for women of all sexual preferences and their partners. Published quarterly.

Entre Nous: Between Us
P.O. Box 412
Santa Clara, CA 95052
(408) 275-0834

Monthly lesbian newspaper with events calendar.

Entre Nous, Windy City Times
970 W Montana
Chicago, IL 60614
(312) 935-1974

Lesbian section of the Windy City Times.

Entrepreneurial Woman
Entrepreneur, Inc.
2392 Morse Ave.
Irvine, CA 92714
(714) 261-2325

A monthly magazine for women business owners.

Equal Means: Women Organizing Economic Solutions
2512 9th St., #3
Berkeley, CA 94710
(510) 549-9931;
Fax: (510) 549-9995

Provides a forum for women to develop an analysis of the economy, to share women's models of leadership, training, and organization, and to foster strategies of development that empower communities and respect the environment. Covers women's strategies for economic justice, economic development, and empowerment.

Esto No Tiene Nombre Magazine
4700 NW 7 St., #463
Miami, FL 33126
(305) 541-6097

A quarterly publication acting as a forum for Latina experience. Features reviews, poetry, interviews, essays, and news.

Ethnic Woman
United Nations Press Div., 3rd Fl.
New York, NY 10017

A biannual networking periodical and quarterly newsletter. Covers women and information about women that is not covered by mainstream media.

Executive Female
National Assoc. for Female Executives
127 W 24th St., 4th Fl.
New York, NY 10011
(212) 645-0770

A magazine that offers career and financial management information for women professionals and entrepreneurs. Published six times per year.

Fairfield County Woman
FCW, Inc.
15 Bank St.
Stamford, CT 06901
(203) 323-3105;
Fax: (203) 323-4112

A tabloid primarily geared for professional women covering topics that range from careers and finances to life-style and fitness.

The Family Next Door.

See Lesbian and Gay Organizations.

Feelin' Good
Ware Publishing, Inc.
400 Corporate Point, No. 580
Culver City, CA 90230
(213) 649-3320

A magazine that covers health and life-style for black women. Published six times per year.

Feminist Bookstore News
P.O. Box 882554
San Francisco, CA 94118
(415) 626-1556;
Fax: (415) 626-8970

This trade magazine, published every other month, reviews or announces new books from feminist, independent, university, and mainstream publishers dealing with women's topics. Includes news, debates, and issues of feminist bookselling and publishing. Can provide international lists of feminist bookstores for a nominal charge.

Feminist Broadcast Quarterly of Oregon
P.O. Box 19946
Portland, OR 97280
(503) 220-6413

A multicultural, multiracial magazine for, by, and about women. Covers issues such as sexism, racism, rape, violence, poverty, and misogyny.

Feminist Free Press
Box 81226
Lincoln, NE 68501
(402) 476-9855

A feminist publication that examines and promotes feminism, creativity, and culture. Articles cover racism, class division, oppression, and sexuality.

Feminist Issues International
2948 Hillegass
Berkeley, CA 94705
(415) 843-7659

A biannual journal of feminist social and political theory. Concentrates on international issues relating to feminism.

Feminist Periodicals: A Current Listing of Contents
Univ. of Wisconsin, Women's Studies Librarian
430 Memorial Library
729 State St.
Madison, WI 53706
(608) 263-5754

A quarterly reference journal containing tables of contents from feminist periodicals. Geared toward people in women's studies.

Feminist Studies
c/o Women's Studies
Univ. of Maryland
College Park, MD 20742
(301) 405-7415;
Fax: (301) 314-9190

A scholarly journal published three times per year. Offers analytic response to feminist issues and addresses new areas of research, criticism, and feminist analysis.

Feminist Teacher
Indiana Univ.
Ballantine 442
Bloomington, IN 47405
(812) 855-5597

Publishes multidisciplinary articles that challenge traditional teaching practices, disciplinary methods, research techniques, and approaches to classroom interactions. Includes reviews of books that address pedagogical issues from a feminist perspective.

Fighting Woman News Magazine
6741 Tung Ave. W
Theodore, AL 36582
(205) 653-0549

Provides a communications medium for women in martial arts and self-defense.

Financial Woman Today
Financial Women International, Inc.
7910 Woodmont Ave., Ste. 1430
Bethesda, MD 20814-3015
(301) 657-8288

A monthly magazine for women financial executives. Covers career, financial services industry, and work force issues.

Free Focus
Women's Literary Guild
224 82nd St.
Brooklyn, NY 11209
(718) 680-3899

A quarterly literary magazine that promotes and publishes women writers.

Friendly Woman
84889 Harry Taylor Rd.
Eugene, OR 97405
(503) 686-3530

A quarterly journal for Quaker women.

Frontiers: A Journal of Women's Studies
Univ. of New Mexico, Women's Studies Program
Mesa Vista Hall 2142
Albuquerque, NM 87131-1586
(505) 277-1198; Fax: (505) 277-0267

Publishes scholarly and feature articles, essays, poetry, fiction, book reviews, and art. Published three times per year.

Gender and Society
Sage Publications, Inc.
2455 Teller Rd.
Newbury Park, CA 91320
(805) 499-0721; Fax: (805) 499-0871

A quarterly journal that addresses the study of gender and its relationship to social order. Emphasizes feminist scholarship, theory, and research.

Genders
Univ. of Colorado, English Dept.
Campus Box 226
Boulder, CO 80309
(202) 492-2853

Publishes articles that examine the experiences of girls and women in education, highlights feminist research, and discusses international feminist issues.

Genesis
American Society for Psychoprophylaxis in Obstetrics, Inc.
1101 Connecticut Ave. NW,
Ste. 700
Washington, DC 20036-4303
(703) 524-7802

A journal that contains research data and teaching aids for health professionals and individuals who promote and support the ASPO/ Lamaze method of childbirth.

GFWC Clubwoman Magazine
General Federation of Women's Clubs
1734 N St. NW
Washington, DC 20036
(202) 347-3168;
Fax: (202) 835-0246

Offers community service project information and women's club news. Published six times per year.

Girl Scout Leader
Girl Scouts of the U.S.A.
830 3rd Ave.
New York, NY 10028
(212) 940-7500

A quarterly magazine offering information and news for Girl Scout adult volunteers and staff.

Glowing Lamp
Chi Eta Phi Sorority, Inc.
3029 13th St. NW
Washington, DC 20009
(202) 232-3858

An annual journal for women in the nursing profession.

Golden Isis Magazine
Bldg. 105, Box 137
23233 Saticoy St.
West Hills, CA 91304

A quarterly journal of mystical surrealism and the occult.

Golden Threads
P.O. Box 3177
Burlington, VT 05401-0031
(802) 658-5510

A quarterly international networking publication for middle-aged lesbians.

Harley Women Magazine
Asphalt Angels Publications, Inc.
P.O. Box 374
Streamwood, IL 60107
(708) 888-2645

A motorcycle magazine for women. Offers profiles, technical information, photographs, fiction, and information on national events. Published six times per year.

Harvard Women's Law Journal
Harvard Law School
Publications Center
Cambridge, MA 02138
(617) 495-3726;
Fax: (617) 495-1110

An annual journal that offers articles on feminist jurisprudence and women's legal issues.

Healing Woman Newsletter for Women Survivors of Child Sexual Abuse
P.O. Box 3038
Moss Beach, CA 94038
(415) 728-0339;
Fax: (415) 728-1324

A monthly newsletter that offers self-help for women survivors of childhood sexual abuse. Contents include feature articles on recovery from childhood sexual abuse, interviews with survivors, poetry, book reviews, recent research, journal exercises, and resources.

Health
Family Media, Inc.
3 Park Ave.
New York, NY 10016
(212) 779-6441

A health and nutrition magazine for women. Published ten times per year.

Health Care for Women International
Hemisphere Publishing Corp.
1101 Vermont Ave. NW, No. 200
Washington, DC 20005
(202) 289-2174

A quarterly journal on women's health care. Covers psychology, alternative life-styles, aging, abuse, parenting, and ethics.

Hembra: A Journal of Southwest Feminist Thought
P.O. Box 40572
Albuquerque, NM 87196
(505) 256-3740

The feminist newspaper containing articles, poetry, and prose serving the women of the southwest.

Hera: A Forum for the Binghamton Women's Community
c/o Women's Center
P.O. Box 354
Binghamton, NY 13902
(607) 724-3462

A feminist newspaper offering local news, articles, book reviews, a calendar of women's events, and fiction pieces.

Heresies: A Feminist Publication on Art and Politics
Heresies Collective, Inc.
280 Broadway, Ste. 412
New York, NY 10013
(212) 227-2108

Offers poetry, fiction, criticism, interviews, and art. Published twice per year.

Hikane: The Capable Womon
P.O Box 841
Great Barrington, MA 01230

A grass-roots magazine for the networking and empowerment of disabled lesbians. Contents include the politics, experience, ideas, creativity, and culture of disabled women. Write to them for more information.

Hotwire
5210 N Wayne
Chicago, IL 60640
(312) 769-9009;
Fax: (312) 728-7002

A journal promoting women in the arts, particularly music. Priority is given to lesbian and feminist ideals.

Housewife-Writer's Forum
P.O. Box 780
Lyman, WY 82937
(307) 786-4513

A literary magazine for house-wives. Published six times per year.

Hurricane Alice
207 Lind Hall
207 Church St. SE
Minneapolis, MN 55455
(612) 625-1834

A quarterly magazine that pub-lishes a range of feminist work. Ar-ticles challenge assumptions under-lying culture, gender, art, and language.

HW: Hartford Woman
Gamer Publishing Group
20 Isham Rd.
West Hartford, CT 06107-2291
(203) 278-3800

A monthly magazine for business and professional women in the Hartford area.

Hypatia
Univ. of South Florida
Soc-107
Tampa, FL 33620-8100
(813) 974-5531;
Fax: (813) 974-2668

A quarterly journal offering arti-cles and criticism on feminist phi-losophy.

Hysteria: A Magazine of Women, Humor and Social Change
P.O. Box 8581
Brewster Sta.
Bridgeport, CT 06605
(203) 333-9399

A feminist humor magazine pub-lished quarterly. Writings and car-toons that have fun with the whole spectrum of women's real-life issues.

Ikon
P.O. Box 1355
Stuyvesant Sta.
New York, NY 10009
(212) 673-4104

A biannual feminist magazine with articles on the experiences of women in third-world countries, lesbians, Jewish women, and work-ing women. Particularly focuses on politics and culture of these women.

Indianapolis Woman
Media Management Group
P.O. Box 68699
Indianapolis, IN 46268
(317) 297-7465

A monthly magazine for women in the Indianapolis area.

Initiatives: Journal of NAWE
National Assoc. of Women
in Education
1325 18th St. NW, Ste. 210
Washington, DC 20036-6511
(202) 659-9330

A quarterly journal on women's ed-ucation issues and the personal and professional development of women.

Inner Woman
Silver Owl Publications, Inc.
P.O. Box 51186
Seattle, WA 98115-1186
(206) 524-9071

A quarterly tabloid on women's spirituality, healing, and personal growth.

Intercambios Femeniles
National Network of Hispanic Women
12021 Wilshire Blvd., Ste. 353
Los Angeles, CA 90025
(213) 225-9895

A quarterly magazine that profiles the careers of successful Hispanic and Latina women. Offers career and resource information.

Interracial Books for Children
1841 Broadway
New York, NY 10023
(212) 757-5339

A journal offering book recommendations for people interested in the elimination of racism, sexism, and other bias in children's books. Published eight times per year.

Iowa Woman
P.O. Box 2938
Waterloo, IA 50704
(319) 987-2879

A quarterly literary magazine of fiction, essays, memoirs, poetry, book reviews, and visual art by women residents of Iowa.

IRIS: A Journal About Women
Univ. of Virginia, Women's Center
Box 323, HSC
Charlottesville, VA 22908
(804) 924-4500

A biannual journal that offers articles on women's political, social, and empowerment issues and concerns.

Issues in Reproductive and Genetic Engineering
Pergamon Press
82 Richdale Ave.
Cambridge, MA 02140
(617) 491-4038

Publishes articles and essays on international feminist analysis. Published three times per year.

Journal of Feminist Family Therapy
The Haworth Press
10 Alice St.
Binghamton, NY 13904
(607) 722-2493

A quarterly journal that provides analysis on feminist theory and family therapy practice and theory.

Journal of Feminist Studies in Religion
Harvard Divinity School
45 Francis Ave.
Cambridge, MA 02138
(617) 495-5751

A biannual journal of feminist scholarship.

Journal of Reprints of Documents Affecting Women
Today Publications & News Service, Inc.
621 National Press Bldg.
Washington, DC 20045
(202) 628-6663

A quarterly journal offering articles and analysis of women's rights and feminism.

Journal of the American Medical Women's Association
American Medical Women's Assn.
801 N Fairfax St.
Alexandria, VA 22314
(703) 838-0500; Fax: (703) 549-3864

A medical journal for women. Published six times per year.

Journal of the History of Sexuality
Univ. of Chicago Press
5720 S Woodlawn
Chicago, IL 60637
(312) 702-7600;
Fax: (312) 702-0172

Offers articles and information on the historical context of sexual politics, prostitution, homophobia, and gender roles.

Journal of the National Association of University Women
1553 Pine Forest Dr.
Tallahassee, FL 32301
(904) 878-4660

The annual publication of the National Association of University Women that reports on the activities of the NAUW members.

Journal of Women and Aging
The Haworth Press
10 Alice St.
Binghamton, NY 13904
(607) 722-2493

A quarterly journal that covers the health and life-styles of women as they age.

Journal of Women and Religion
2400 Ridge Rd.
Berkeley, CA 94709
(510) 649-2490;
Fax: (510) 649-1417

Offers articles that promote equity and justice for women in religious institutions. Includes articles on women's spirituality, culture, and experience.

Journal of Women's History
Indiana Univ., History Dept.
742 Ballantine Hall
Bloomington, IN 47405
(812) 855-1320;
Fax: (812) 855-5678

A journal for students and others interested in women's history. It's published three times a year and contains articles, trends, abstracts, and dialogues.

Kalliope: A Journal of Women's Art
Florida Community College
3939 Roosevelt Blvd.
Jacksonville, FL 32205
(904) 381-3511

Publishes the poetry, fiction, interviews, and visual art of women three times per year.

Labyrinth
4722 Baltimore Ave.
Philadelphia, PA 19143
(215) 724-6181

A feminist monthly newspaper that promotes understanding among women of different races, classes, and sexual orientations.

La Gazette
P. O. Box 671
Santa Cruz, CA 95061
(408) 426-7828

A feminist newspaper combining art, adventure, sports, politics, and personal accounts.

Lambda Book Report
1625 Connecticut Ave. NW
Washington, DC 20009
(202) 462-7924

A magazine that covers gay and lesbian literature. Published six times per year.

Lana's World/How Do You Spell It Productions
P.O. Box 3633
Eugene, OR 97403

A quarterly magazine that publishes lesbian and feminist cartoons.

Lavender Morning
P.O. Box 50729
Kalamazoo, MI 49005

A lesbian newsletter for women by women. Offers local, regional, state, and national articles and stories.

Leader in Action
American Assoc. of University Women
1111 16th St. NW
Washington, DC 20036
(202) 785-7735

Covers issues for women in leadership positions. Published three times per year.

Lear's
655 Madison Ave.
New York, NY 10021-8043
(212) 888-0007.

A monthly feature and general interest magazine for mature women.

Legacy
Pennsylvania State Press
Barbara Bldg., Ste. C
University Park, PA 16802
(814) 865-1327

A biannual journal of seventeenth, eighteenth, nineteenth, and early twentieth century American women writers.

Lesbian Connection
Elsie Publishing Inst.
P.O. Box 811
East Lansing, MI 48826
(517) 371-5257

A national magazine for, by, and about lesbians. Published six times per year. Composed of reader-generated articles and responses.

Lesbian Contradiction
1007 N 47th St.
Seattle, WA 98103

A quarterly magazine of essays, humor, drawings, and cartoons for lesbians.

Lesbian Ethics
LE Publications
P.O. Box 4723
Albuquerque, NM 87106

A journal of lesbian feminist ethics, philosophy, and sociology.

Lesbian News
P.O. Box 1430
29 Palms, CA 92272
(619) 367-3386;
Fax: (619) 367-3386

A lesbian periodical including news, articles, features, columns, and personal advertisements.

Letras Femininas
Asociacion de Literatura Femenina Hispania
Univ. of Nebraska,
Dept. of Modern Languages
Lincoln, NE 68688-0315
(402) 472-3745

A biannual journal of contemporary Hispanic literature by women.

Lilith Magazine
250 W 57th St., Rm. 2432
New York, NY 10107
(212) 757-0818;
Fax: (212) 757-5705

A quarterly magazine for Jewish women. Addresses Jewish identity, politics, culture, and women's issues.

Madre
121 W 27th St., Rm. 301
New York, NY 10001
(212) 627-0444;
Fax: (212) 675-3704

A quarterly magazine that offers news, information, and essays on political and social issues affecting women and children in the United States and the Middle East.

Maize: A Lesbian Country Magazine
P.O. Box 130
Serafina, NM 87569

Offers news and information about lesbian country communities. Features how-to articles as well as articles discussing values, community building, and economic survival.

Mama Bears News and Notes
6536 Telegraph Ave.
Oakland, CA 94609
(510) 428-9684

Reviews of women's books from both the mainstream and feminist presses. Newspaper format, published monthly and very readable.

Matrix Women's Newsmagazine
108 Locust St., No. 14
Santa Cruz, CA 95060
(408) 429-1238

A monthly feminist magazine for women in the central coast and Bay area regions of California. Offers news, poetry, fiction, and book reviews for and by women.

Medical Digest
Planned Parenthood Federation of America
810 7th Ave.
New York, NY 10019
(212) 261-4660

A semiannual journal for individuals, the media, and health care professionals. Offers articles on family planning and reproductive health care.

Melpomene: A Journal for Women's Health Research
1010 University Ave. W
St. Paul, MN 55104-4706
(612) 642-1951

A magazine that includes articles and research on linking women's health and physical activity. Stresses research, publication, and education.

Michigan Woman Magazine
30400 Telegraph, Ste. 370
Birmingham, MI 48010
(313) 646-5575

A magazine for professional Michigan women. Published six times per year.

Midlife Woman
5129 Logan Ave. S
Minneapolis, MN 55419-1019
(612) 925-0020;
Fax: (612) 925-5430

A newsletter that offers research, book reviews, and items of interest to midlife women.

Midwifery Today
Box 2672
Eugene, OR 97402
(503) 344-7438

A quarterly magazine for midwives and childbirth educators.

Military Lifestyle Magazine
4800 Montgomery Ln., No. 710
Bethesda, MD 20814
(301) 718-7623;
Fax: (301) 718-7652

Offers articles on military marriages, parenting, finance, health, and travel. Published ten times per year.

Minerva
1101 S Arlington Ridge Rd.,
Rm. 210
Arlington, VA 22202
(703) 892-4388

A quarterly report for women in or involved in the military. Offers articles, reviews, fiction, and poetry.

Minnesota Clubwoman
5701 Normandale Rd., Ste. 315
Minneapolis, MN 55424
(612) 920-2057

A quarterly magazine that reports on club activities for women in Minnesota.

Minorities and Women in Business
Venture X, Inc.
P.O. Drawer 210
Burlington, NC 27216
(919) 229-1462

A magazine for women working in major corporations and small businesses owned and operated by minority and female entrepreneurs. Published six times per year.

MoneyWorks for Women
217 E 85th St.
Box 144
New York, NY 10028-1044
(212) 288-5271

A personal finance newsletter for women.

Morena
P.O. Box 12964
Berkeley, CA 94701
(510) 549-4710

A bilingual newspaper published six times per year. Also issues a bilingual women of color datebook calendar annually.

Mothering Magazine
P.O. Box 1690
Santa Fe, NM 87504
(505) 984-8116;
Fax: (505) 986-8335

Celebrates the experience of mothering and fathering. Through articles on parenting, seeks to inspire a recognition of the importance and value of parenting.

Mothers Today
24 Colonia Pkwy.
Bronx, NY 10708

A magazine for new mothers. Published six times per year.

Moving Out: A Feminist Literary and Arts Journal
P.O. Box 21249
Detroit, MI 48221

A literature and art magazine for feminists.

Moxie
Weider Publications
21100 Erwin St.
Woodland Hills, CA 91367
(818) 595-0450

A monthly magazine for women over forty.

Ms. Magazine
230 Park Ave., #7
New York, NY 10169
(212) 551-9595;
Fax: (212) 551-9384

A feminist bimonthly magazine. Focuses on national and international women's issues.

National Business Woman
2012 Massachusetts Ave. NW
Washington, DC 20036
(202) 293-1100;
Fax: (202) 861-0298

A quarterly magazine for working and business women.

National NOW Times
1000 16th St. NW, Ste. 700
Washington, DC 20036
(202) 785-8576

A feminist magazine that focuses on issues and concerns of the National Organization of Women. Published six times per year.

National Voter
League of Women Voters
1730 M St. NW
Washington, DC 20036
(202) 429-1965;
Fax: (202) 429-0854

Articles address public policy, energy, the environment, and international relations and issues.

National Women's Health Report
2440 M St. NW, Ste. 325
Washington, DC 20037
(202) 293-6045;
Fax: (202) 293-7256

A quarterly magazine covering women's health issues.

Network Magazine
1555 E 4905 S
Murray, UT 84107
(801) 262-8091;
Fax: (801) 261-5623

A monthly publication geared for progressive women and the men with whom they live and work.

New Directions for Women
108 West Palisade Ave.
Englewood, NJ 07631
(201) 568-0226

A women's newsmagazine covering politics, health, grass-roots activism, racism, homophobia, and sexism as they relate to women. The magazine, published six times per year, also reviews books, movies, theater, art, and music from a feminist perspective.

New Jersey Woman Magazine
27 McDermott Pl.
Bergenfield, NJ 07621
(201) 384-0201

A feminist magazine that promotes and documents the accomplish-

ments of women in New Jersey. Includes news and essays.

The Newsletter
P.O. Box 2272
Durham, NC 27702
(919) 490-6112

A monthly newsletter for lesbians and feminist women, especially those from Durham, Raleigh, and Chapel Hill.

New Vision Newsjournal
Lesbian Visionaries
P.O. Box 191443
Dallas, TX 75219
(214) 528-2426

A monthly journal featuring articles of interest to lesbians. Includes news, poetry, book and music reviews, cartoons, and classified and personal ads.

New Voice Women's Newspaper
45 Dream Ln.
Cohasset, CA 95926
(916) 345-7532

A monthly free newspaper for professional women. Publishes articles and reviews on politics, business, health books, and food, as well as a monthly calendar.

Ninety-Nine News
International Women Pilots Assoc.
Will Rogers Airport
P.O. Box 59965
Oklahoma City, OK 73159
(405) 685-7969

A monthly magazine for women pilots.

North Shore Woman's Newspaper
P.O. Box 1056
Huntington, NY 11743
(516) 271-0832

A feminist monthly publication. Material includes book reviews, film reviews, health information, letters, poetry, and prose of particular interest to women.

Nursing and Health Care
National League for Nursing
350 Hudson St.
New York, NY 10014
(212) 989-9393;
Fax: (212) 989-3710

Monthly journal for members of the NLN. Includes articles on trends, the quality of health care, and so on.

NWSA Journal
National Women's Studies Assoc.
Univ. of Hampshire,
Dept. of English
Durham, NH 03824
(603) 862-1313;
Fax: (603) 862-2030

A quarterly magazine that publishes articles and analysis of feminist scholarship and the feminist movement.

Of A Like Mind
Box 6021
Madison, WI 53716
(608) 255-5092

A women's spiritual newspaper and network. Focuses on women's spirituality, Goddess religions, paganism, and earth connections from a feminist perspective.

Off Our Backs: A Women's Newsjournal
2423 18th St. NW
Washington, DC 20009
(202) 234-8072

A national monthly newsjournal featuring strong feminist analysis, critiques, and reviews. Covers international, national, and regional news that affects women's rights, culture, health, etc. Chronicles the women's movement in all its diversity.

On Our Backs
526 Castro St.
San Francisco, CA 94114
(415) 861-4723

Celebrates lesbian sexuality by publishing fiction, sexy pictorials, columns, and reviews.

On Our Minds
Towson State Univ., Women's Studies Program
Baltimore, MD 21204
(301) 830-2334

An annual journal that focuses on campus, community, and regional activity on women and education.

On the Issues
97-77 Queens Blvd.
Forest Hills, NY 11374
(718) 275-6020;
Fax: (718) 997-1206

A feminist magazine of critical thinking dedicated to fostering collective responsibility for positive social change. Published quarterly as an informational and educational service of Choices Women's Medical Center, Inc.

Our Special
National Braille Press, Inc.
88 Stephen St.
Boston, MA 02115
(617) 266-6160

A monthly general interest magazine for blind women printed in Braille.

Ozark Feminist Review
P.O. Box 1662
Fayetteville, AR 72702

A bimonthly publication featuring news, book reviews, calendars of events, and creative writing by and for women.

Pen Woman
National League of American Pen Women, Inc.
Pen Arts Bldg.
1300 17th St. NW
Washington, DC 20036
(202) 785-1997

Emphasizes a how-to approach to music, art, and letters. Contains book reviews. Published nine times per year.

Perceptions
1530 Phillips
Missoula, MT 59802
(406) 543-5875
Contact: Temi Rose

A magazine of poetry for and by women.

Plainswoman
P.O. Box 8027
Grand Forks, ND 58202
(701) 777-8043

A monthly feminist journal that contains fiction, poetry, articles, and essays for women in the Great Plains area.

Political Woman Newsletter
276 Chatterton Pky.
White Plains, NY 10606
(914) 285-9761;
Fax: (914) 285-9763

An independent, progressive, pro-choice publication on women and national politics. Covers women candidates, women elected officials and women in the federal government. Also includes news and information on reproductive rights, child care, and sexual harassment.

Press Woman Magazine
Box 99
Blue Springs, MO 64013
(816) 229-1666

A monthly magazine for women in the fields of journalism and communications.

Primavera
Box 37-7547
Chicago, IL 60637

An annual publication that features original fiction, poetry, and art that reflects the experiences of women. Works to address the lives of women of different ages, races, sexual orientation, classes, and locations.

Professional Communicator
2101 Wilson Blvd., Ste. 417
Arlington, VA 22201
(703) 528-4200

Offers articles and information about women and communication issues. Published five times per year.

ProWoman Magazine
MatriMedia, Inc.
P.O. Box 6957
Portland, OR 97228-6957
(503) 221-1298

A magazine for professional women in the Northwest. Published six times per year.

Psychological Perspectives
10349 W Pico Blvd.
Los Angeles, CA 90064
(213) 556-1193;
Fax: (213) 556-2290

Contains essays and information on gender as a social construct and as a category of analysis. Covers issues such as family, sexual identity, and health.

Psychology of Women Quarterly
237 Dickey Hall, Univ. of Kentucky
Lexington, KY 40506-0017

A feminist journal that aims to encourage and develop a body of knowledge about the psychology of women. Publishes empirical research, critical reviews, theoretical articles, and invited book reviews.

Quarante
1600 S Eads St.
P.O. Box 2875
Arlington, VA 22202
(703) 920-3333

A quarterly magazine for affluent women over forty.

Radiance
P.O. Box 30246
Oakland, CA 94604
(510) 482-0680

A quarterly magazine for large women. Features articles on health, fashion, politics, and media images.

Radical America
1 Summer St.
Somerville, MA 02143
(617) 628-6585

A quarterly socialist-feminist journal. Articles on feminist politics, culture, and history.

Rainbow City Express
P.O. Box 8447
Berkeley, CA 94707

A semiannual journal about spiritual awakening, women's spiritual

*ity, evolution of consciousness, and
ecological and healing concerns.*

Reproductive and Genetic Engineering

Pergamon Press/Maxwell House
Farfield Park
Elmsford, NY 10523
(914) 345-6425;
Fax: (914) 592-3625

*A magazine offering articles that
analyze and promote reproductive
technology and genetic engineering
and their impact on women.*

Response to the Victimization of Women and Children

72 Spring St.
New York, NY 10012
(212) 431-9800

*A quarterly journal focusing on is-
sues of child and wife abuse, sexual
abuse, and pornography. Offers
new research studies and legislative information.*

Review of Law and Women's Studies

USC Law Center
University Park
Los Angeles, CA 90089-0071
(213) 740-5696;
Fax: (213) 740-5502

*A biannual journal serving as a fo-
rum for those in legal and other
fields to unite women's experiences
with current concepts of law.*

Re-Vision

College of St. Catherine
Abigail Quigley McCarthy Center
for Women
2004 Randolph Ave., Mail No. 4150
St. Paul, MN 55105
(612) 690-6736;
Fax: (612) 690-6024

*Offers articles on feminist issues
and programs. Publishes three
times per year.*

Sacred River: A Women's Peace Journal

P.O. Box 5131
Berkeley, CA 94705

*A magazine for women in the
Berkeley area. Also offers articles
on women's national issues.*

Sage: A Scholarly Journal on Black Women

P.O. Box 42741
Atlanta, GA 30311-0741
(404) 223-7528;
Fax: (404) 753-8383

*A biannual magazine that offers
features, interviews, book reviews,
and bibliographies for African
American women.*

Sage Woman

P.O. Box 641
Point Arena, CA 95468
(707) 882-2052;
Fax: (707) 882-2793

*A quarterly magazine of women's
spirituality. Features rituals, medi-
tations, and articles on women's
experiences.*

San Diego Woman Magazine
4186 Sorrento Valley Blvd., Ste. M
San Diego, CA 92121
(619) 452-2900

A monthly magazine that contains articles and information on issues of professional and personal growth for women in the San Diego area.

Santa Fe Women's Resource Directory
2966 Plaza Blanca
Santa Fe, NM 87505
(505) 473-0097

An annual guide to businesses, services, and resources for women in the Santa Fe area.

Sappho's Isle
960 Willis Ave.
Albertson, NY 11507
(516) 747-5417

A newspaper designed for lesbians in New York, New Jersey, and Connecticut.

Seattle Gay News
JT and A
704 E Pike St.
Seattle, WA 98122
(206) 324-4297

A weekly magazine in Seattle.

Sex Roles: A Journal of Research
520 Pearl St.
Boulder, CO 80302
(303) 449-7882;
Fax: (303) 449-6694

A monthly magazine that offers research on gender roles, as well as book reviews.

Short Fiction By Women
P.O. Box 1276 Stuyvesant Sta.
New York, NY 10009
(212) 255-0276

A women's magazine published three times per year. Contents include novel excerpts, short stories, stories in translation, and plays.

Signals: Women's News, Culture, and Politics
P.O. Box 1713
Santa Fe, NM 87504
(505) 438-8297

A publication of news, opinion, and creative work by and for women. Includes poetry, fiction, news, and reviews addressing women's issues.

Signs: Journal of Women in Culture and Society
Univ. of Chicago Press
5720 S Woodlawn Ave.
Chicago, IL 60637
(312) 702-7600

A quarterly journal on women's studies issues and education.

Sing Heavenly Muse!
P.O. Box 13320
Minneapolis, MN 55414

A women's literary magazine including short stories and poems by and for women.

SingleMother Magazine
P.O. Box 68
Midland, NC 28107
(704) 888-2337

Addresses the unique pressures, concerns, rewards and challenges facing single mothers today.

Sinister Wisdom
P.O. Box 3252
Berkeley, CA 94703
(415) 534-2335

A quarterly journal for lesbians. Addresses lesbians' roles in arts and politics.

Sisters
National Council of Negro Women, Inc.
1211 Connecticut Ave. NW, Ste. 702
Washington, DC 20036
(202) 659-0006

A quarterly magazine for African American women. Offers news, feature, and event information.

Sojourner
42 Seaverns Ave.
Jamaica Plain, MA 02130-2355
(617) 524-0415

A monthly feminist magazine.

Sonoma County Women's Voices
P.O. Box 4448
Santa Rosa, CA 95402

Publishes a monthly feminist newspaper containing articles of local, national, and international scope.

Spokane Woman
Northwest Business Press, Inc.
S 104 Division
Spokane, WA 99202
(509) 456-0203

A monthly life-style magazine for women living in metropolitan Spokane.

Successful Women in Business
1429 Walnut St.
Philadelphia, PA 19102
(215) 563-6005

A quarterly magazine for professional and executive women. Articles focus on management, finance, career, and personal issues.

Teen Voices Magazine
Women Express, Inc.
P.O. Box 6009 JFK
Boston, MA 02114
(617) 350-5030;
Fax: (617) 451-0496

A national magazine written for and by teenage girls. Topics include sexual pressure, career information, and features about other cultures. Does not use glamorous models pushing sex or makeup.

Texas Woman's News
RR 5, Box 574-46
Kerrville, TX 78028

A monthly tabloid for working and professional women in Texas.

13th Moon: A Feminist Literary Magazine
1400 Washington Ave.,
SUNY/Eng.
Albany, NY 12222
(518) 442-4181

A literary and scholarly publication specializing in literature by women. *Works include poetry, fiction, drama, criticism, and translations.*

Together
Univ. of California
112 Kerckhoff Hall
Los Angeles, CA 90024
(213) 206-6168

A news magazine for women and feminist students and the surrounding community. Published six times per year.

Tradeswomen
P.O. Box 40664
San Francisco, CA 94140
(415) 821-7334

A quarterly magazine written for and by women in blue-collar work.

Trivia: A Journal of Ideas
P.O. Box 9606
N Amherst, MA 01059-9606
(413) 367-0168

A radical feminist literary journal. Includes critical essays, reviews, translations, and experimental prose.

Tulsa Studies in Women's Literature
Univ. of Tulsa
600 S College
Tulsa, OK 74104-3189
(918) 631-2503;
Fax: (918) 631-2033

A biannual scholarly journal devoted to women's literature. In-

cludes articles, reviews, and forums on all forms of women's writing.

Union Signal
National Women's Christian
Temperance Union
1730 Chicago Ave.
Evanston, IL 60201
(708) 864-1396

A monthly journal offering features on alcohol, tobacco, and narcotics. Also offers legislative and political updates on these subjects.

U.S.-Japan Women's Journal: A Journal for the International Exchange of Gender Studies
926 Bautista
Palo Alto, CA 94303
(415) 857-9049;
Fax: (415) 494-8160

A journal with an English-language supplement that promotes the exchange of scholarship on women and gender.

U.S. Woman Engineer
345 E 47th St.
New York, NY 10017
(212) 705-7855;
Fax: (212) 319-0947

A magazine for women engineering students, engineering and technology professionals. Articles on career and political issues. Published six times per year.

Up Against the Wall, Mother
9114 Wood Spice Ln.
Lorton, VA 22079-3240
(703) 690-2246

A quarterly journal that offers poetry as mental health therapy for women in crisis.

Valley Women's Voice
321 Student Union Bldg.
UMASS Amherst, MA 01003
(413) 545-2436;
Fax: (413) 545-4751

A bimonthly newspaper on feminist thoughts and action. Publishes articles, poems, and artwork from local women sources.

Visibilities
P.O. Box 1169
Olney, MD 20830-1169
(301) 774-8591

An international publication by and for lesbians.

Visible
P.O. Box 1494
Mendocino, CA 95460
(707) 964-2756

A publication addressing the issues of older women. Published three times per year.

Voices, Hawaii Women's News Journal
Univ. of Hawaii, Kuyjebdakk 402
1733 Donaghho Rd.
Honolulu, HI 96822
(808) 956-8805

A feminist publication for women in Hawaii. Offers news, art, poetry, fiction, essays, and reviews. Published three times per year.

Well-Woman Journal
1325 S Wabash, #305
Chicago, IL 60605
(312) 939-3636;
Fax: (312) 939-4187

A quarterly publication devoted to women's health issues primarily in Chicago and Cook County.

Wichita Women
400 N Woodlawn, No. 28
Wichita, KS 67208
(316) 684-3620

A monthly tabloid for women in the Wichita area. Offers news, information, and fiction.

WIF News Magazine
Women in Film
6464 Sunset Blvd., Ste. 900
Los Angeles, CA 90028
(213) 463-6040;
Fax: (213) 463-0963

A monthly report for women working in the film industry or interested in film.

WIN News
Women's International Network
187 Grant St.
Lexington, MA 02173
(617) 862-9431

A quarterly journal that reports on women's issues and political concerns worldwide.

Wisconsin Woman
P.O. Box 10
Menomonee Falls, WI 53052-0010
(414) 273-1234

A monthly tabloid offering articles of interest to professional, affluent women in Wisconsin.

Wisconsin Women's Law Journal
Univ. of Wisconsin Law School
975 Bascom Hall
Madison, WI 53706
(608) 262-8294

An annual journal that offers updates and analysis of women's legal issues.

Wise Woman
2441 Cordova St.
Oakland, CA 94602
(510) 536-3174

A national quarterly journal. Focuses on feminist issues, Goddess lore, spirituality, and witchcraft. Includes women's history, news, analysis, reviews, art, poetry, cartoons, and research.

WLW Journal
Women Library Workers
2027 Parker St.
Berkeley, CA 94704
(510) 540-5322

A quarterly journal for women librarians. Contains articles on women and libraries, career equity, feminism, and networking.

Woman
350 Madison Ave.
New York, NY 10017
(212) 880-8800

A women's general interest magazine. Published ten times per year.

Woman Activist
2310 Barbour Rd.
Falls Church, VA 22043
(703) 573-8716

A national action bulletin that records events in the women's movement. Reports on issues affecting women and gives strategies for passage and ratification of the Equal Rights Amendment.

Woman Bowler
5301 S 76th St.
Greendale, WI 53129-1191
(414) 421-9000

A newsmagazine for women bowlers. Published eight times per year.

Woman Conductor
344 Overlook Dr.
West Lafayette, IN 47906
(317) 463-1738

A quarterly journal for women conductors and women interested in conducting. Focuses on career development and industry news.

Woman Entrepreneur
641 Lexington Ave., 9th Fl.
New York, NY 10022
(212) 688-1900;
Fax: (212) 688-2718

A monthly magazine for women in business.

Woman of Power
P.O. Box 827
Cambridge, MA 02238
(617) 625-7885

A quarterly feminist magazine on spirituality and politics. Features interviews, art, poetry, and fiction.

Woman's Art Journal
1711 Harris Rd.
Laverock, PA 19118
(215) 233-0639

A semiannual scholarly publication featuring women in all areas of visual arts.

Woman's Enterprise
28210 Dorothy Dr.
Box 3000
Agoura Hills, CA 91301
(818) 889-8740

A magazine for women who own or who would like to own their own small business. Published six times per year.

Woman's National Farm & Garden Magazine
2230 Quail Lake Rd.
Findlay, OH 45840
(419) 422-2466

Offers information on agriculture and horticulture for women.

Woman's Weal
P.O. Box 264
Lynden, WA 98264-0264
(604) 922-5891

A monthly women's general interest magazine.

Woman's World
P.O. Box 1648
Englewood Cliffs, NJ 07632
(201) 569-6699

A weekly women's general interest and entertainment magazine.

Women and Criminal Justice
Trenton State College, Dept. of Law and Justice
CN 4700
Trenton, NJ 08650
(609) 771-2644;
Fax: (609) 530-7884

A biannual journal offering articles on international feminist scholarship and information dealing with criminal justice.

Women and Health
117 St. John's Pl.
Brooklyn, NY 11217
(718) 305-3724;
Fax: (718) 305-6832

A quarterly magazine that features articles, research, reviews, and news on women's health.

Women and Language
4400 University Dr./
George Mason Univ.
Fairfax, VA 22030
(703) 993-1090;
Fax: (703) 993-1096

A feminist journal for women interested in communication, language, and gender. Provides an outlet for descriptive research and theoretical speculation, including essays, personal narratives, poetry, information, and news.

**Women and Performance:
A Journal of Feminist Theory**
New York Univ.
721 Broadway, 6th Fl.
New York, NY 10003
(212) 998-1625

A biannual feminist journal featuring articles on ritual and performance art, especially theater, dance, music, and film.

Women and Politics
The Haworth Press
10 Alice St.
Binghamton, NY 13904-1580
(307) 766-2983;
Fax: (307) 766-2697

A quarterly publication offering articles, features, research, reviews, and political news for women.

Women and Therapy
Univ. of Vermont,
Dept. of Psychology
John Dewey Hall
Burlington, VT 05405
(802) 656-2680

A quarterly feminist journal for therapists, consumers, and researchers. Articles address trends in the psychotherapy, research, and professional fields.

Women and Work
U.S. Dept. of Labor, Office of Information and Public Affairs
200 Constitution Ave. NW
Washington, DC 20210
(202) 523-7323

A monthly publication addressing legal, educational, and employment concerns of women.

Women Artists News
Midmarch Arts
300 Riverside Dr.
New York, NY 10025
(212) 666-6990

A periodical containing news and book information on the arts and women's issues.

Women in Business
9100 Ward Pkwy.
P.O. Box 8728
Kansas City, MO 64114-0728
(816) 361-6621

A women's business magazine. Published six times per year.

Women in Natural Resources
Univ. of Idaho, Bowers Laboratory
Moscow, ID 83843
(208) 885-6754

A quarterly journal for women in the wildlife and recreation professions.

Women Outdoors
55 Talbot Ave.
Medford, MA 02155
(508) 892-9515

Offers articles on outdoor issues and the environment.

Women's Alert Newsletter
c/o Cal Poly Economics Dept.
3801 W Temple Ave.
Pomona, CA 91768
(909) 869-3857;
Fax: (909) 869-3845

A bipartisan publication that examines politics and politicians from a woman's perspective.

Women's Almanac
RR 3 Box 786
Havana, FL 32333-9524
(904) 539-9955;
Fax: (904) 539-0580

A newspaper of mildly judgmental reflections on women's lives and times in Florida.

Women's Circle
306 E Parr Rd.
Berne, IN 46711
(219) 589-8741

Offers articles on women who work in the home. Features patterns and handicrafts articles. Published six times per year.

Women's Health Issues
409 12th St. SW
Washington, DC 20024-2188
(202) 863-4990;
Fax: (202) 863-2499

A quarterly health magazine. Deals with issues of health from a medical, social, legal, and political perspective.

Women's Network News
5804 Carey Dr.
Austin, TX 78757
(512) 459-0309

A Christian feminist newsletter containing health, education, humor, cartoon quotes, sexuality is-
sues, religion, and gender issues. Published six times per year.

Women's Record
55 Northern Blvd.
Greenvale, NY 11548
(516) 625-3033;
Fax: (516) 625-3411

A monthly newspaper serving Long Island women that provides information about health, law, careers, education, parenting, and lifestyles. Helps women make better business and financial decisions.

Women's Review of Books
Wellesley College
Wellesley, MA 02181
(617) 431-1453;
Fax: (617) 239-1150

A monthly journal that contains detailed reviews of current books written by or about women.

Women's Rights Law Reporter
15 Washington St.
Newark, NJ 07102
(201) 648-5320

A feminist law report dedicated to the needs and issues of women.

Women's Sports and Fitness
1919 14th St., Ste. 421
Boulder, CO 80302
(303) 440-5111;
Fax: (303) 440-3313

Covers women's fitness and health. Articles on sports activities, nutrition, and athletic training. Published eight times per year.

Women's Studies Abstracts
Transaction Periodicals and
Consortium
Rutgers Univ.
New Brunswick, NJ 08903
(908) 932-2280;
Fax: (908) 932-3138

A quarterly listing of feminist articles and book reviews. Lists articles on such subjects as education, prejudice, relationships, and politics as related to women.

**Women's Studies: An
Interdisciplinary Journal**
English Dept., Claremont Graduate
School
170 E 10th St.
Claremont, CA 91711-6163
(909) 621-8555, Ext. 2974

Provides a forum for the presentation of scholarship and criticism about women in the fields of literature, history, art, sociology, law, political science, economics, anthropology, and the sciences. Also publishes poetry, short fiction, and film and book reviews.

Women's Studies Quarterly
The Feminist Press at the City
Univ. of New York
311 E 94th St.
New York, NY 10128-5603
(212) 360-5790

A biannual feminist journal. Articles address education issues.

Women's Work
602 Avenue A
Snohomish, WA 98290
(206) 568-5914

A bimonthly magazine of social commentary, literary expressions, news, profiles, and reviews. Explores the definitions of women's work.

WomenWise
38 S Main St.
Concord, NH 03301
(603) 2739

A quarterly feminist health journal published by the Concord Feminist Health Center.

Womyn's Press
P.O. Box 562
Eugene, OR 97440
(503) 689-3974

An eclectic feminist newspaper that publishes news, reviews of books, films, and music, personal experience pieces, fiction, nonfiction, poetry, and photographs pertaining to women.

Womyn's Words
Women's Energy Bank
P.O. Box 15524
St. Petersburg, FL 33733-5524
(813) 823-5353

A monthly lesbian feminist magazine.

Woodswomen News
25 W Diamond Lake Rd.
Minneapolis, MN 55419
(612) 822-3809;
Fax: (612) 822-3814

Provides interesting information about women's achievements in the outdoors, such as expeditions, women as outdoor leaders, and so on. Also shares information on the environment, provides how-to advice, and book reviews.

WREE-View
Women for Racial and Economic Equality
198 Broadway, No. 606
New York, NY 10036
(212) 385-1103

A quarterly journal for working women.

Yale Journal of Law and Feminism
Box 401A Yale Sta.
New Haven, CT 06520
(203) 432-4056

A biannual journal that provides articles on women, society, and the law.

❑ Organizations Representing Women of Color

Alliance of Minority Women for Business and Political Development
Brasman Research
P.O. Box 13933
Silver Spring, MD 20911-3933
(301) 565-0258

A coalition of organizations that stresses the connection between business and politics and seeks to advance the participation of minority women in these two fields. Promotes networking between member organizations and provides information to individuals.

BIHA: Black Indian Hispanic Asian Women in Action
122 W Franklin Ave., #306
Minneapolis, MN 55404
(612) 870-1193

A long-standing organization of women of color active in the struggle against racism.

Coalition Against Racism and Sexism
8 E 48th St., #3C
New York, NY 10017

Recognizes the links between racism and sexism and organizes for equality.

Drifters, Incorporated
c/o Constance Brown
3000 Bickneel Rd.
Richmond, VA 23235

An organization of thirty chapters nationwide comprised of African American women of diverse backgrounds and professions who try to promote the universal image of womanhood. Local chapters sponsor fund raisers for a variety of social, civic, charitable, and educational causes. The Drifters is a family-oriented group. Members' spouses and escorts are known as "driftwood," children as "kindling," and grandchildren as "splinters."

See also Special Interests: Social and Volunteer Clubs.

Fannie Lou Hamer Educational Organization, Incorporated
198 Broadway, Rm. 606
New York, NY 10038
(212) 385-1103

Works to create and make available in schools, churches, unions, and other organizations information and educational programs on the effects of racism and discrimination against women of color. Funds research on issues such as child care, education, health care, housing, employment, and the environment.

Kitchen Table: Women of Color Press.

See Presses and Publishers.

National Institute for Women of Color
624 9th St NW
Washington, DC 20001
(202) 296-2661;
Fax: (202) 296-8140

Actively opposes discrimination and advocates full equity for all women of color. Supports contact among its members and the interchange of ideas. Its goal is to foster opportunities for the education, employment, and advancement of women of color. Provides materials and workshops.

National Women of Color Association
Dept. of Women's Studies, 336 North Hall
Univ. of Wisconsin
LaCrosse, WI 54601
(608) 785-8357

A membership organization that exchanges new findings about women of color. Also offers educational materials to the public.

Revolutionary Sisters of Color
P.O. Box 191021
Roxbury, MA 02119
(617) 445-3432

A socialist feminist organization of women of color with an internationalist, multi-issue, activist agenda. Holds four national meetings per year, in addition to local chapter meetings. See also Global Feminism and World Peace; Women's Rights.

Women of Color National Network
1611 Town Gate Pl.
Charleston, SC 29414
(800) 235-9706

Serves the national interests of women of color.

Women of Color Partnership Program, Religious Coalition for Abortion Rights.

See Health Organizations: Family Planning and Reproductive Rights.

Women of Color Resource Center
2288 Fulton St., #103
Berkeley, CA 94704
(510) 848-9272;
Fax: (510) 548-3474

An organization committed to strengthening the work of organiz- ers, advocates, and scholars who are working to improve the condition of women of color. Developing a library and nationally accessible database on women of color issues.

Women for Racial and Economic Equality.
See Women's Rights.

AFRICAN AMERICAN WOMEN

ACHE: A Journal for Black Lesbians.
See Newspapers, Newsletters, and Magazines.

African American Women's Conference
2415 56th St.
San Diego, CA 92105-5011
(619) 560-2770

A four-day women's conference that tours throughout the country. Speakers, seminars, and workshops are offered to help African American women affirm self, family, and community.

African American Women's Institute
2224 Main St.
Little Rock, AR 72206
(501) 372-5113;
Fax: (501) 372-0009

Offers activities around the state that provide opportunities for African American women to develop organizing skills and provide support for women working on social change and economic justice issues in their communities.

African Studies Association, Women's Caucus
Credit Union Bldg.
Emory Univ.
Atlanta, GA 30322
(404) 329-6410

Promotes scholarship and interest in all disciplines of African studies. Primarily an academic organization but all interested individuals are welcome. See also Research Centers and Organizations.

Afro Caribee Women's Association
3257 Martin Luther King Jr. Way
Oakland, CA 94609
(510) 658-1181

An organization of women who were born in Africa or the Caribbean. Encourages and promotes ways to communicate for better business, political, and personal interaction and support.

Association of Black Secretaries.

See Professional and Business Associations and Networks.

Association of Black Women Entrepreneurs.

See Professional and Business Associations and Networks.

Association of Black Women Historians.

See Professional and Business Associations and Networks.

Association of Black Women in Higher Education.

See Professional and Business Associations and Networks.

Bethune Museum and Archives of Black Women's History.

See Women's History.

Black Professional Women's Network.

See Professional and Business Associations and Networks.

Black Women in Sisterhood for Action, Incorporated
P.O. Box 1592
Washington, DC 20013
(301) 460-1565

Works to advance educational and employment opportunities for black women, offers scholarships, and

provides social assistance. Develops an annual calendar of distinguished black women, publishes books on black women, and offers seminars and meetings.

Black Women's Agenda, Incorporated
208 Auburn Ave. NE
Atlanta, GA 30303
(404) 524-8279

Works to initiate programs that promote black women's equity. Offers public education workshops that cover such issues as economic self-sufficiency, civil rights, educational priorities, and the general status of black women. BWA is a volunteer organization. See also Newspapers, Newsletters, and Magazines; Special Interests.

Black Women's Political Crusade
P.O. Box 625
Pittsburgh, PA 15230
(412) 243-9664

Works for political candidates to support women's rights.

Institute on Black Chemical Abuse.

See Health Organizations: Substance Abuse Services.

The Links, Incorporated
1200 Massachusetts Ave. NW
Washington, DC 20005
(202) 842-8686

A national organization with chapters in most cities. Offers educa-

tional and cultural activities to promote the status and education of African American women and men. See also Women's Centers; Special Interests.

National Association of Colored Women's Clubs
5808 16th St. NW
Washington, DC 20011
(202) 726-2044

A long-standing African American women's organization. Sponsors projects in employment and training, economic development, teenage pregnancy, education, and health. Has affiliates in most states. See also Special Interests.

National Association of Negro Business and Professional Women.

See Professional and Business Associations and Networks.

National Black Women's Health Project.

See Health Organizations: Advocacy, Education, and Research Organizations.

National Black Women's Political Leadership Caucus.

See Political Groups.

National Coalition of 100 Black Women
38 W 32nd St., 16th Fl.
New York, NY 10001
(212) 974-6140

A nonprofit organization of women interested in addressing social, economic, political, and cultural issues of concern to African American women. See also Women's Rights.

National Council of Negro Women
1211 Connecticut Ave. NW, Ste. 702
Washington, DC 20036
(202) 659-0006

A national economic and political advocacy organization with chapters in most states. It brings together African American women activists and organizations to strengthen black women's socioeconomic position. Also participates in the areas of international development, and joins litigation to achieve civil rights. See also Women's Rights.

National Hook-Up of Black Women
5117 S University Ave.
Chicago, IL 60615
(312) 643-5866

A support network that provides mentoring for African American women to aid in their career advancement. Sponsors seven annual scholarships for higher education. See also Educational Services and Organizations.

National Political Congress of Black Women
P.O. Box 411
Rancocas, NJ 08073
(609) 871-1500

Works to encourage, develop, and educate black women to participate in the political process at all levels. See also Political Groups; Women's Rights.

Sisterhood of Black Single Mothers
1504 Bedford Ave.
Brooklyn, NY 11216
(718) 638-0413

A support network for black single mothers.

ASIAN/PACIFIC WOMEN

Asian American Legal Defense and Education Fund
99 Hudson St.
New York, NY 10013
(212) 966-5932

Offers legal assistance and advice to Asian Americans on employment discrimination issues and back wage claims. See also Legal Services.

Asian Indian Women in America
RD 1, Box 98
Palisades, NY 10964
(914) 365-1066;
Fax: (914) 425-5804

Offers consulting and counseling to Asian Indian women in the U.S. Offers services for battered women and their families and provides financial information.

Asian Pacific American Women's Association, Incorporated
1503 Colorado Dr.
E Lansing, MI 48823
(517) 351-1823

Maintains a support system for Asian Pacific women in Michigan.

Promotes and supports professional development and represents the concerns of Asian Pacific women. Networks with other individuals and organizations.

Asian Task Force Against Domestic Violence.

See Violence Against Women: Antiviolence Coalitions, Associations, and Special Services.

Asian Women's Resource Center
940 Washington St.
San Francisco, CA 94108
(415) 421-8827

Provides a full range of services to immigrant women, including classes in English, parenting skills, citizenship, and more.

Asian Women United
P.O. Box 640478
San Francisco, CA 94164

An advocacy and support group.

Association of Asian Studies, Committee of Women in Asian Studies
State Univ. of New York,
Dept. of History
Albany, NY 12222
(518) 442-4800;
Fax: (518) 442-4936

Networks women interested in Asian women's issues and those involved in research on gender. Publishes a newsletter. See also Research Centers and Organizations.

Cambodian Women for Progress
8102 Bonair Ct.
Silver Spring, MD 20910
(301) 386-0202

Provides numerous support services to Cambodian women immigrants.

Chinese Women's Benevolent Association
22 Pell St., No. 3
New York, NY 10013
(212) 267-4764

An organization of Chinese women who engage in philanthropic activities such as volunteering and fundraising. Offers interpreting and translating services. See also Foundations and Funding Sources.

Committee on South Asian Women.
See Global Feminism and World Peace.

Council of Asian American Women
232 E Capitol St. NE
Washington, DC 20003
(202) 544-3181

Promotes, supports, and networks Asian American women. Works in areas of politics, education, career development, and legislation. See also Women's Rights.

KAWA: Korean American Women with Attitude
c/o Women's Resource Center
250 Golden Bear Center
UC Berkeley,
Berkeley, CA 94720

A collective of progressive Korean and Korean American women composed primarily of UC Berkeley undergraduate students. Provides a forum to address community issues and needs, acts as a means for political mobilization, and develops a support network to fight, survive, and celebrate a radical collective. See also Women's Rights.

Korean American Women Artists and Writers Association
447 7th Ave., No. 4
San Francisco, CA 94118-3011

Offers services and support to Korean American writers. Conducts networking, educational, and literacy activities. See also Art and Media.

Korean American Women in Need
P.O. Box 25139
Chicago, IL 60603
(213) 583-0880

Offers services, counseling, and referrals to Korean American women in crisis.

Manavi
P.O. Box 614
Bloomfield, NJ 07003
(908) 687-2662

An organization for South Asian women in the United States. Focuses on stopping violence against these women. See also Special Interests.

Minnesota Korean Women's Association
5126 Minnaqua Dr.
Golden Valley, MN 55422-4014

Networking organization for Korean American women in the Minnesota area.

National Association of Professional Asian American Women
P.O. Box 494
Washington Grove, MD 20880

Supports and offers services and activities to Asian American women. Conducts educational programs and promotes personal and professional development. See also Professional and Business Associations and Networks.

New York Asian Women's Center.

See Violence Against Women: Antiviolence Coalitions, Associations, and Special Services.

Organization of Asian Women
P.O. Box 20502 Park West Sta.
New York, NY 10025

Supports the interests of Asian women, particularly those who are economically disadvantaged.

Organization of Chinese American Women
1300 N Street NW, Ste. 100
Washington, DC 20005
(202) 638-0330;
Fax: (202) 638-2196

Provides leadership, integration programs, and networking for Chinese American women. Conducts seminars on management, self-realization, career development, and job training.

Organization of Pan Asian Women, Incorporated
P.O. Box 39218
Washington, DC 20016
(202) 659-9370

Works to change stereotypes of Asian and Pacific Islander women, as well as to network, educate, and support these women. Advocates for national public policy and programs to meet Pan Asian women's needs. See also Special Interests.

Refugee Women's Project
P.O. Box 5107
Tacoma, WA 98415
(206) 471-9582

A family literacy program with English as a Second Language instruction and on-site child care. Provides outreach and support services for Southeast Asian women and their families. See also Special Interests.

Sakhi for South Asian Women.

See Violence Against Women: Antiviolence Coalitions, Associations, and Special Services.

INDIAN/NATIVE AMERICAN WOMEN

Indian Sisterhood Project
P.O. Box 3316
Lame Deer, MT 59043
(406) 477-6390

Sponsors conferences and works for the empowerment of Native American women.

Indigenous Women's Network
P.O. Box 174
Lake Elmo, MN 55042
(612) 770-3861;
Fax: (612) 770-3976

An organization to improve the visibility of indigenous women. Goals include applying traditional values to modern situations, promoting and empowering Native women by regaining self-esteem and well-being, and promoting the practice of traditional ceremonies and rituals. See also Special Interests.

Minnesota Indian Women's Resource Center
2300 15th Ave. S
Minneapolis, MN 55404
(612) 728-2000

Offers a wide range of services including those for alcoholism, battered women, and parenting skills support.

Native American Women's Health Education Resource Center.

See Health Organizations: Advocacy, Education, and Research Organizations.

Ramah Navajo Weavers Association
Box 153
Pine Hill, NM 87357
(505) 775-3253

A grass-roots cooperative group of traditional women weavers who live on the Ramah Navajo Reservation in New Mexico. Works to increase family self-reliance from indigenous resources and native skills and works to strengthen land-based traditions, values, and spirituality. See also Special Interests.

Sovereign Indigenous Women of the Arctic
P.O. Box 143
Sterling, AK 99672
(907) 262-5403

A grass-roots organization involved in a variety of self-help projects.

United Indian Women
5632 NW Willbridge Ave.
Portland, OR 97210
(503) 274-2320

Unites American Indian women in order to promote and better their lives, homes, families, and communities. Offers services to improve health, education, and welfare, and to preserve Indian culture.

White Buffalo Calf Women's Society and Shelter.

See Violence Against Women: Antiviolence Coalitions, Associations, and Special Services.

Women of Nations
Eagle Nest Shelter
P.O. Box 40309
St. Paul, MN 55104
(612) 222-5830;
Fax: (612) 222-1207

A nonprofit organization formed by volunteer Indian advocates concerned with the issue of battered Indian women. Provides advocacy, support, and shelter to battered women and their children, community education, training, and networking opportunities. See also Special Interests; Violence Against Women.

LATINA/HISPANIC WOMEN

Chicana Foundation of Northern California
P.O. Box 27083
Oakland, CA 94602
Fax: (510) 531-2609

An organization of professional Hispanic women who are interested in personal and career development, leadership enhancement, and involvement within the Hispanic community. Sponsors an annual scholarship competition for continuing Latina college students. See also Educational Services and Or-ganizations; Foundations and Funding Sources.

Chicana/Latina Research Project
Dept. of Chicano Studies
UC Davis
Davis, CA 95616
(916) 752-8882;
Fax: (916) 752-8814

Conducts research and teaches courses on Chicana/Latina and Native American women's writings, history, issues, and concerns.

CoMadres, USA
945 G St. NW
Washington, DC 20001
(202) 393-0126

Advocates for the rights of His-
panic women.

Comision Feminil Mexicana
Nacional, Incorporated
P.O. Box 86013
Los Angeles, CA 90006
(213) 244-6448

Seeks to educate and advocate pro-
grams in the interests of Latina
women's equity. Also offers direct
service programs to local organiza-
tions in child care and other social
services. See also Women's Centers.

Esto No Tiene Nombre.
See Newspapers, Newsletters, and
Magazines.

Fuerza Unido.
See Work, Union, and Career Services.

HACER: Hispanic Women's
Center.
See Work, Union, and Career Ser-
vices.

Hispanic Women's Council
5803 E Beverly Blvd.
Los Angeles, CA 90022
(213) 725-1657

Provides seminars and workshops
to advance Hispanic women's edu-
cational goals, careers, and leader-

ship abilities. Targets high school
students, women who are reenter-
ing the job market, and others who
are already employed. See also Educational Services and Organizations.

La Mujer Obrera.
See Work, Union, and Career Services.

Las Hermanas
P.O. Box 15792
San Antonio, TX 78212
(210) 434-0947

Promotes solidarity within the His-
panic community in its struggle for
justice and liberation. Instigates
necessary change in the church and
in society. See also History of
Women; Religious and Spiritual
Groups; Rights of Women.

Latin American Professional
Women's Associations
3516 N Broadway
Los Angeles, CA 90031
(213) 227-9060

A vocational, educational, and cul-
tural support group for Latina wom-
en. Provides career enhancement
seminars, Little Sisters programs,
scholarship programs, and confer-
ences. See also Professional and
Business Associations and Networks.

Mexican American Women's
National Association
1101 17th St. NW, #803
Washington, DC 20036
(202) 833-0060

Seeks to enrich the lives of Mexican American women economically, socially, and culturally. Sponsors youth outreach programs, offers scholarships, and conducts leadership workshops to advance careers. See also Educational Services and Organizations.

Mujeres Latinas en Accion
1823 W 17th St.
Chicago, IL 60608
(312) 226-1544

Multiservice agency serving battered women, offering substance abuse services, and training programs. Publishes a newsletter.

Mujeres Unidas en Accion
1534 Dorchester Ave.
Dorchester, MA 02122
(617) 265-3015

A community-based school for economically disadvantaged Latina women and their children. See also Special Interests.

National Association of Cuban-American Women
2119 Webster St.
Fort Wayne, IN 46802
(219) 745-5421;
Fax: (219) 744-1363

A national organization that provides services to Cuban-American and other Spanish-speaking women. Sponsors desegregation efforts, women's equity, educational opportunities for minority women, and holds language classes and provides bilingual materials. See also Women's Centers.

National Association of Hispanic Nurses.

See Professional and Business Associations and Networks.

National Conference of Puerto Rican Women, Incorporated
5 Thomas Cir. NW
Washington, DC 20005
(202) 387-4716

Offers information and activities on the economic, social, and political roles of Puerto Rican and other Hispanic women. Sponsors awards and conferences. See also Special Interests.

National Network of Hispanic Women
12021 Wilshire Blvd., Ste. 353
Los Angeles, CA 90025
(213) 225-9895

Seeks to foster the career and business potential of Hispanic women. Supports programs in job training and leadership development. Works to increase the participation of Hispanic women in all professions. See also Professional and Business Associations and Networks.

Organizacion Nacional de la Salud.

See Health Organizations: Advocacy, Education, and Research Organizations.

❏ **Political Groups**

Alabama Women's Agenda
3414 7th Ct. S
Birmingham, AL 35222
(205) 324-6947

A statewide network that organizes public hearings about issues that affect women and their families, supports political candidates that support women's issues, and lobbies for and monitors legislation on the state and federal levels. See also Women's Rights.

Always Causing Legal Unrest
P.O. Box 2085
Rancho Cordova, CA 95741-2085
(408) 427-2858

A radical feminist activist organization working to challenge First Amendment fundamentalism and expand political expression. Organizes demonstrations and offers publications. See also Legal Services; Special Interests.

American Political Science Association
Committee of the Status of Women in Political Science
1527 New Hampshire Ave. NW
Washington, DC 20036
(202) 483-2512

An organization of academic political scientists. Works to improve the status of women in political science. See also Women's Rights.

Arkansas Women's Political Caucus
P.O. Box 2494
Little Rock, AR 72203
(501) 376-7913

A multilevel, grass-roots organization devoted to getting women elected to public office.

Black Women's Agenda
See Organizations Representing Women of Color: African American Women.

Black Women's Roundtable on Voter Participation
1430 K St. NW, Ste. 401
Washington, DC 20011
(202) 898-2220

A coalition of African American women's organizations promoting voter participation and increased awareness of the political process. Organizes voter registration and sponsors social and political education programs and leadership seminars. See also Organizations Representing Women of Color.

**Campaign California/
Women's Equity Fund**
40 N 1st St., Ste. 204
San Jose, CA 95113
(408) 286-6113

*A nonprofit research and education
organization focusing on campaign
finance reform. Also deals with
other issues from affordable housing and health care to nuclear energy.*

**Capital Hill Women's Political
Caucus**
Longworth House Office Bldg.
P.O. Box 599
Washington, DC 20515
(202) 986-0994

*Supports and promotes women in
politics at all levels. Sponsors job
seminars and educational and informational programs on career
development, political processes,
and women's issues. See also* Work,
Union, and Career Services.

**Center for the American Woman
and Politics**
Eagleton Inst. of Politics
Rutgers Univ.
New Brunswick, NJ 08901
(908) 828-2210;
Fax: (908) 932-6778

*Sponsors research and education
projects dealing with women's role
in the political process. Offers information and materials. Sponsors
activities to encourage women's involvement in politics. See also* Research Centers and Organizations.

**Coalition for Women's
Appointments**
c/o Natl. Women's Political Caucus
1275 K St. NW, Ste. 750
Washington, DC 20005-4051
(202) 898-1100;
Fax: (202) 898-0458

*Promotes and assists women seek-
ing appointment or election to government positions. Provides information and resource materials.*

Congressional Club
2001 New Hampshire Ave. NW
Washington, DC 20009
(202) 332-1155

*A coalition of women's organiza-
tions made up of wives of present
and former U.S. representatives,
senators, cabinet members, and Supreme Court justices. Holds weekly
luncheons.*

Emily's List
1112 16th St. NW, Ste. 750
Washington, DC 20036
(202) 887-1957;
Fax: (202) 452-1997

*A donor network for Democratic
pro-choice women candidates.
Contributes millions of dollars to
these women on the national level.*

Fifty/Fifty by 2000
P.O. Box 34
Fairfield, CT 06430
(203) 259-1446

*A political action committee dedi-
cated to equal representation of*

women in the United States Congress.

Florida Women's Political Caucus
9349 Abbott Ave.
Surfside, FL 33154
(305) 866-1384

A nonpartisan organization seeking to have qualified women appointed and elected to office. Conducts training programs.

Freedom Socialist Party
5018 Rainier Ave. S
Seattle, WA 98118
(206) 722-2453

An organization of socialist feminists. Sponsors activities on revolutionary social change, Marxist theory, international politics, and feminist history.

GFWC-W Progressive Women's Club
P.O. Box 1373
Riverton, WY 82501
(307) 856-1128

A feminist women's club that sponsors activities to enhance the status and role of women. Conducts charitable activities and political events. See also Women's Rights.

Girls' Nation
777 N Meridian St.
Indianapolis, IN 46204
(317) 635-6291;
Fax: (317) 636-5590

A youth citizenship training program conducted annually to give high school juniors practical experience in the processes of government. Girls' state sessions are held in state capitals or on campuses in June or July.

Indiana Women's Political Caucus
557 E Washington
Indianapolis, IN 46041
(317) 659-4535

Supports women and men candidates for public office who are dedicated to women's rights and women's issues. Presents awards and offers funding.

International Institute for Women's Political Leadership
1511 K St. NW, Ste. 410
Washington, DC 20005
(202) 842-1523;
Fax: (202) 347-1306

Works to get women involved and interested in the political process in countries worldwide. Sponsors workshops and training seminars.

League of Women Voters
1730 M St. NW
Washington, DC 20036
(202) 429-1965;
Fax: (202) 429-0854

A large nonpartisan political organization founded in 1920 that is devoted to informing all individuals about government and public policy. Actively works to increase voter registration and encourages voter participation. Chapters exist in most states and larger cities.

Massachusetts Women's Political Caucus
145 Tremont St., Ste. 607
Boston, MA 02111
(617) 451-9294

A political organization of feminists in Massachusetts. Sponsors activities, educational programs, and fund-raising events to get women elected and appointed to office at all levels of government.

Michigan Women's Campaign Fund
P.O. Box 71626
Madison Heights, MI 48071
(313) 347-6669

A political action committee that raises funds to support feminist candidates.

Minnesota $$ Million
550 Rice St.
St. Paul, MN 55103
(612) 221-0441

A fund-raising committee to elect Democratic women to the U.S. Senate.

Minnesota Women's Campaign Fund
550 Rice
St. Paul, MN 55013
(612) 222-1603

A feminist political action committee dedicated to electing feminist candidates in Minnesota.

Montana Women's Lobby
Box 1099
Helena, MT 59624
(406) 549-4466

A statewide coalition of organizations working on development and advocacy for public policy of interest to women and their families.

National Association of Commissions for Women
2000 14th St. NW
Washington, DC 20009
(202) 628-5030

The national network for local commissions on the status of women. Most states, cities, and counties have a commission monitoring women's rights.

National Association of Minority Political Women
6120 Oregon Ave. NW
Washington, DC 20015
(202) 686-1216

An organization of minority women interested in learning about or being involved in the political process. Sponsors research and educational programs. See also Research Centers and Organizations.

National Black Women's Political Leadership Caucus
3005 Bladensburg Rd. NE, #217
Washington, DC 20018
(202) 529-2806

Works to educate and involve African American women and children in the political and economic pro-

cesses. Presents awards, trains speakers, conducts research, and holds legislative workshops. See also Organizations Representing Women of Color.

National Federation of Cuban-American Republican Women

2904 Shawnee Dr.
Ft. Wayne, IN 46807
(219) 456-8200

Helps Republican Cuban-American women to network and raise campaign funds. Encourages women to seek office and vote for Republican candidates.

National Federation of Democratic Women

828 Lemont Dr.
Nashville, TN 37216
(615) 244-4270;
Fax: (615) 244-4281

Helps democratic women network and raise campaign funds. Also coordinates the activities of local democratic women's groups.

National Federation of Republican Women

c/o Republican National Committee
310 1st St. SE
Washington, DC 20003
(202) 547-9341

Coordinates and supports the work of local Republican women's organizations.

National Order of Women Legislators

1300 Berkeley Rd.
Columbia, SC 29205
(803) 734-0480

A national organization of women legislators from all political parties. Provides information and works to elect and appoint women to public office.

National Political Caucus of Black Women

P.O. Box 411
Rancocas, NJ 08073
(609) 871-1500

Promotes and supports African American women candidates and works to involve African American women in the political process. See also Organizations Representing Women of Color.

National Women's Party

144 Constitution Ave. NE
Washington, DC 20002
(202) 546-1210;
Fax: (202) 543-2365

A woman's suffrage organization founded in 1913. Wrote and sponsors the Equal Rights Amendment. See also Women's History.

National Women's Political Caucus

1257 K Street NW, Ste. 750
Washington, DC 20005
(202) 898-1100;
Fax: (202) 898-0458

A multipartisan, grass-roots orga-

nization focused on getting women elected and appointed to public office. Supports women candidates who are pro-choice and who support and promote women and family issues. The organization has chapters in all states and most urban areas.

New Mexico Women's Agenda
P.O. Box 40183
Albuquerque, NM 87196
(505) 281-5603

A statewide coalition of organizations and individuals who lobby at the state level on a wide variety of women's issues.

Oregon Women's Political Caucus
534 SW 3rd, #716
Portland, OR 97204
(503) 224-2588

Promotes the election and appointment of women to local, state, and national levels of government.

Radical Women
523-A Valencia
San Francisco, CA 94110
(415) 864-1278;
Fax: (415) 864-0778

A multiracial, socialist, and feminist organization that works to empower people of color, lesbians and gays, and working women. Uses education and coalition-building to advance ideas. See also Lesbian and Gay Organizations; Women's Rights.

Women in Illinois Needed Now (WIINN)
P.O. Box 1555
Rockford, IL 61105

A political action committee actively involved in promoting and supporting women to run for political office.

Women in Service and Politics
25 11th Ct. W
Birmingham, AL 35204
(205) 251-5566

An organization for professional women interested in service and the political process in the Birmingham area. Conducts public education activities. See also Professional and Business Associations and Networks.

Women Organizing Women
P.O. Box 1652
New Haven, CT 06507
(203) 281-3400

A political action committee dedicated to organizing women to end social, political, and economic injustices against women.

Women's Action Coalition
P.O. Box 131148
Houston, TX 77219
(713) 867-9581

A feminist organization dedicated to working to end women's social inequity, homophobia, racism, prejudice, and violence against women. Stages demonstrations and circulates information.

Women's Action for Nuclear Disarmament
691 Massachusetts Ave.
Arlington, MA 02174
(617) 643-6740;
Fax: (617) 643-6744

A membership organization dedicated to increasing women's political power in military issues. Lobbies legislators, sponsors Mothers' Day for Peace, and offers public education.

Women's Campaign Fund
120 Maryland Ave. NE
Washington, DC 20002
(202) 544-4484

A bipartisan committee supporting women candidates who are pro-choice and pro-ERA. Contributes to candidates' political campaigns and offers guidance and hands-on assistance in getting elected to office.

Women's Caucus for Political Science
Emory Univ.
Dept. of Political Science
Atlanta, GA 30322
(404) 727-6572;
Fax: (404) 874-6925

An organization of women political scientists. Addresses career advancement and development for women and improvement in political science education. Conducts workshops and a program about women and politics.

Women's Legislators' Lobby (WILL)
110 Maryland Ave. NE
Washington, DC 20002
(202) 543-8505;
Fax: (202) 675-6469

A bipartisan national organization of women state legislators who work to influence federal policies with an emphasis on programs for women and children, the environment, health care, and jobs in a peacetime economy. See also Special Interests.

Women's Lobby Alliance
3101 Richmond Ave., #150
Houston, TX 77085

Advocates women's rights in Texas.

Women's National Democratic Club
1526 New Hampshire Ave. NW
Washington, DC 20036
(202) 232-7363

A private membership club. Provides a forum where Democrats come to be heard. Speakers are invited twice each week with a reception following the discussion.

Women's National Republican Club
3 W 51st St.
New York, NY 10019
(212) 582-5454;
Fax: (212) 977-8972

Conducts educational, cultural, social, and political programs for Republican women. Provides political training to Republicans and education on city, state, national, and international affairs.

Women's Political Action Committee of New Jersey
P.O. Box 170
Edison, NJ 08818
(201) 638-6784

Supports feminist political candidates in New Jersey.

Women's Political Fund
P.O. Box 421811
San Francisco, CA 94142-1811
(415) 474-6808

A bipartisan political action committee that provides funds to candidates and seeks to increase women's participation in government at all levels.

Women's Project
2224 S Main St.
Little Rock, AR 72206
(501) 372-5113;
Fax: (501) 372-0009

A community-based, nonprofit organization committed to the elimination of sexism, racism, and

homophobia. *Provides education and assistance with local organizing and services. Focuses on hate crimes, women in prison, women and AIDS, and African American women's community needs. See also* Organizations Representing Women of Color; Women's Rights.

Women's Statewide Legislative Network of Massachusetts
37 Temple Pl.
Boston, MA 02111
(617) 426-1878

A network to support feminist legislation in Massachusetts.

Women's Vote Project
1601 Connecticut Ave. NW,
Ste. 801
Washington, DC 20009
(202) 328-2312

A coalition of national women's organizations working to increase the number of women voters to enhance women's voice in public affairs. Provides day-care services and transportation on Election Day, and maintains phone banks to remind registered women to vote.

❏ Presses and Publishers

Most of the publishers listed in this section are owned and operated by women. Those that do not meet this criteria have a strong commitment to publishing women's titles. These publishers are indicated with an asterisk (*).

Acacia Books
P.O. Box 3630
Berkeley, CA 94703
(510) 451-9559

An independent feminist publisher. Publications include essays for women's studies, journals, and women's biographies.

Advocacy Press.

See Family, Children, and Youth Services.

Alleluia Press
Box 103
Allendale, NJ 07401

Publishes feminist religious books.

*Arte Publico Press
The Americas Review
Univ. of Houston
Houston, TX 77204
(713) 749-4768

Publishes literature by Hispanic authors, with an emphasis on works by Hispanic women. Offers poetry, plays, essays, short stories, and novels.

Ash Tree Publishing Company
P.O. Box 64
Woodstock, NY 12498
(914) 246-8081

Provides alternative medical information to women. Publishes books on herbal medicine and natural remedies for excess fertility, infertility, healthy pregnancy, menopause without drugs, and menstruation.

Astarte Shell Press
P.O. Box 10453
Portland, ME 04104
(207) 828-1992

Publishes books reflecting feminist

perspectives on spirituality, justice, and issues of personal and social life. Books are for courses in Women's Studies and Religion in colleges, universities, and divinity schools, as well as for a general audience.

Aunt Lute Book Company
223 Mississippi
San Francisco, CA 94107
(415) 558-8116

Publishes fiction and nonfiction by women, especially by women of color and lesbians.

Baby Steps Press
P.O. Box 1917
Beaverton, OR 97075

Publishes feminist fiction.

Banned Books
P.O. Box 33280, #292
Austin, TX 78764
(512) 282-8044

Offers books for gays and lesbians. Publishes erotic titles, fiction, humor, and mystery.

B.A. Press
1269 North E St.
San Bernardino, CA 92405
(714) 355-1100

Publishes information on domestic violence education, prevention, and intervention services and techniques.

Barn Owl Books
1101 Keeler Ave.
Berkeley, CA 94705

Feminist publisher of fiction.

Bergamot Books
P.O. Box 7413
Minneapolis, MN 55407
(612) 722-6058

Publishes books on environmental issues written by women.

Biblio Press
1140 Broadway, Rm. 1507
New York, NY 10001
(212) 684-1257;
Fax: (212) 545-9530

A specialized Women's Studies publisher, with books specifically about Jewish women. Offers research resources, nonfiction, and specialty books.

Black Widow Publications
1044 53rd St.
Oakland, CA 94608

Publisher of feminist and lesbian fiction.

Booklegger Press
555 29th St.
San Francisco, CA 74131
(415) 647-9074

Publishes primarily feminist nonfiction.

Bookweaver Publishing
P.O. Box 113
Hayward, WI 54843
(317) 257-0476

Publishes the fiction and nonfiction works of Audrey Savage.

Boston Women's Health Book Collective.

See Health Organizations: Advocacy, Education, and Research Organizations.

* Branden Publishing Co., Incorporated
17 Station St.
P.O. Box 8
Brookline Village
Boston, MA 02147
(617) 734-2045

Publishes fiction, nonfiction, biographies, and autobiographies by or about women.

Brighton Street Press
53 Falstaff Rd.
Rochester, NY 14609

Publishes women's fiction.

Brush Hill Press
P.O. Box 96
Boston, MA 02137

Feminist publisher of fiction.

Caillech Press
482 Michigan St.
St. Paul, MN 55102
(612) 225-9647

A feminist publisher that focuses on multicultural materials of interest to audiences of all ages.

Calyx Books
P.O. Box B
Corvallis, OR 97339
(503) 753-9384;
Fax: (503) 753-0515

Publishes books written by women, with a particular emphasis on those by women of color, lesbians, working class women, and older women. Work includes fiction, nonfiction, and poetry.

Carolina Wren Press
P.O. Box 277
Carrboro, NC 27510
(919) 560-2738

Publishes works of fiction, poetry, and drama by women and African American writers.

Cassiopeia Press
P.O. Box 2
Morrison, CO 80465-0208
(303) 986-4370

Publishes materials and books on women's history.

Chicory Blue Press
795 East St. N
Goshen, CT 06756
(203) 491-2271

Publishes materials and books written by women. Genres include memoirs and poetry.

Cleis Press
P.O. Box 8933
Pittsburgh, PA 15221
(412) 937-1555;
Fax: (412) 937-1567

Publishes books by and about women. Book topics include women's adventure and fiction, as well as resource books on women on issues such as incest, disability,

AIDS, and cancer. Also publishes translations of women's literature from Latin America and Europe.

Clothespin Fever Press
655 4th Ave., #34
San Diego, CA 92101
(619) 234-2656

Exclusively publishes feminist books on a variety of fiction and nonfiction subjects. Specializes in books for lesbians.

* Cottonwood Press
P.O. Box 1947
Boulder, CO 80306
(303) 433-4166

Publishes books on women and minorities in the United States.

Crones' Own Press
P.O. Box 488
Durham, NC 27702
(919) 688-3521

Publishes feminist work by mature women.

Daughter Culture Publications
1840 41st Ave., Ste. 102-301
Capitola, CA 95010

Lesbian and feminist publishers.

Delphi Press
P.O. Box 1538
Oak Park, IL 60304
(708) 524-7900;
Fax: (708) 524-7902

A publisher that prints primarily nonfiction books on women's spiri-

tuality, pagan theology, and contemporary Wiccan practice.

Down There Press
938 Howard St., Ste. 101
San Francisco, CA 94103
(415) 974-8985;
Fax: (415) 974-8989

Publishes sexual health books for children and adults. Concentrates on books that provide basic physiological information along with realistic and nonjudgmental techniques for developing good sexual communication.

Earth Books
P.O. Box 7
Redwood Valley, CA 95470
(707) 485-5684

Publishes fiction, nonfiction, and poetry by women. Also offers audiocassettes and cards.

Eighth Mountain Press
624 SE 29th Ave.
Portland, OR 97214
(503) 233-3936

Publishes fiction by and about women, books on women's sexuality, poetry, and feminist essays. Sponsors the Eighth Mountain Poetry Prize, a biennial contest in which winners get their works published.

Feminist Press at the City University of New York
311 E 94th St.
New York, NY 10128
(212) 360-5790

A nonprofit publisher that seeks to redefine the teaching of the social sciences, history, and literature by publishing specific works of fiction and nonfiction. Write for their publications list.

Ferrari Publications
P.O. Box 37887
Phoenix, AZ 85069
(602) 863-2408

Publishes Places of Interest to Women, *an international guidebook.*

Firebrand Books
141 The Commons
Ithaca, NY 14850
(607) 272-0000

A feminist and lesbian publishing house committed to producing quality literature in a wide variety of genres by ethnically and racially diverse authors.

Flower Press
10332 Sharer Rd.
Kalamazoo, MI 49002

Publisher of books by and for women.

Free Women Press
398 Columbus Ave., #306
Boston, MA 02116

A feminist publisher, primarily of fiction.

Frog in the Well
P.O. Box 170052
San Francisco, CA 94117
(415) 431-2113

A feminist publishing company. Offers literature and nonfiction books for women.

Granite Press
Box 7
Penobscot, ME 04476

A small feminist press.

Helicon Nine Editions
P.O. Box 22412
Kansas City, MO 64113
(913) 722-2999

A small literary press that publishes women's fiction. Also sponsors an annual literary contest.

Hen's Teeth Publishing
P.O. Box 689
Brookings, SD 57006

Publishes fiction by women.

HerBooks
P.O. Box 7467
Santa Cruz, CA 95061
(408) 425-7493

A lesbian and feminist book publisher. Emphasizes work by Jewish lesbians.

Heron Press
P.O. box 31539
San Francisco, CA 94131

A small feminist press.

Her Own Words
P.O. Box 52
Madison, WI 53705
(608) 271-7083

Publishes women's literature and

history for general and academic audiences. Offers audiocassettes, videocassettes, and t-shirts.

Hot Flash Press
P.O. Box 21506
San Jose, CA 95151
(408) 292-1172

A small press publishing primarily on women and religion.

* Hughes Press
500 23rd St. NW, B203
Washington, DC 20037
(202) 293-2686

Publishes books dealing with issues of sex discrimination and gender inequity.

Ide House
4631 Harvey Dr.
Mesquite, TX 75150
(214) 686-5332

An independent feminist press that publishes feminist scholarly works, especially dealing with social, economic, and political aspects of feminism.

Ikesdatter Press
P.O. Box 45285
Seattle, WA 98145
(206) 363-7185

A small feminist press publishing women's fiction.

Imp Press
270 Potomac
Buffalo, NY 14213
A feminist press.

Jewels Graphics and Publishing
304 15th St.
Oakland, CA 94612
(510) 763-9671

Publishes feminist clip art that portrays feminist images of women.

Kelsey Street Press
P.O. Box 9235
Berkley, CA 94709
(510) 845-2260;
Fax: (510) 548-9185

A literary press that challenges the boundaries of language and identity. Includes women of color and lesbian authors and collaborations between writers and visual artists.

Kid's Project/Squeaky Wheels Anthology
P.O. Box 448
Berkeley, CA 94701
(415) 587-2885

Publishes the works of disabled women. See also Family, Children, and Youth Services.

Kitchen Table: Women of Color Press
P.O. Box 908
Latham, NY 12110
(518) 434-2057

Publishes books by women of color.

Knowledge, Ideas, and Trendsetting: The Positive Publisher
1131-0 Tolland Tpke., #175
Manchester, CT 06040
(203) 646-0745;
Fax: (203) 646-3931

Publishes books that explore ways to improve women's lives and the world in general. Offers books about social and personal change.

* Lake Press
P.O. Box 7934, Avondale St.
Paducah, KY 42002
(502) 575-2200

Publishes books on women's health, emphasizing prevention, self-help, and education.

Left-Hand Lighthouse Press
P.O. Box 19250
San Diego, CA 92119

Publishes books by and for women.

Liaud: A Women's Press
P.O. Box 6793
Houston, TX 77265

A small feminist publisher.

Library B Books
584 Castro St.
San Francisco, CA 94114

A small lesbian/feminist press.

Light Cleaning Press
6600 Blvd. East
West New York, NJ 07093

A feminist press that publishes women's books, gay and lesbian poetry, and reviews. Publications have a feminist, spiritual, or astrological interest.

Lollipop Power Books
c/o Carolina Wren Press
120 Morris St.
Durham, NC 27701
(919) 560-2738

Publishes nonsexist, multicultural, and bilingual children's books. Also publishes a newsletter and offers a writing consultation service.

Luna Press
P.O. Box 511, Kenmore Sta.
Boston, MA 02215
(617) 427-9846

Annually publishes The Lunar Calendar, a moon calendar dedicated to the Goddess. Shows moon's phases, rising and setting times, earth festivals, and more.

LuraMedia Publishing
7060 Miramar Rd., #104
San Diego, CA 92121
(619) 578-1948;
Fax: (619) 578-7560

Publishes books on women's issues, spirituality, religion, self-discovery, psychology, feminism, and health.

Madwoman Press
P.O. Box 690
Northboro, MA 01532
(508) 393-3447;
Fax: (508) 393-8305

Publishes fiction and nonfiction books by and about lesbians and about lesbian experience.

Magic Circle Press
10 Hyde Ridge Rd.
Weston, CT 06883
(203) 226-1903

Publishes books for women and children.

Martha Rosier
143 McGuinness Blvd.
Brooklyn, NY 11222
(212) 834-1466

Publishes books for women dealing with women's perspectives on food, class, and politics.

Merging Media
516 Gallows Hill Rd.
Cranford, NJ 07016

Publishes literature and fine art.

Midmarch Associates
300 Riverside Dr.
New York, NY 10025
(212) 666-6990

Provides nonfiction publications, including directories on women in the arts.

Morning Glory Collective
P.O. Box 1631
Tallahassee, FL 32302
(904) 222-8115

Publishes a lunar/menstrual chart.

Mother Courage Press
1667 Douglas Ave.
Racine, WI 53404
(414) 637-2227;
Fax: (414) 637-8242

Publishes books of interest to women, by women. Book topics include sexual abuse, prevention of abuse, adventure, humor, and lesbian issues.

Moving Parts Press
70 Cathedral Dr.
Santa Cruz, CA 95060

A small feminist press.

Naiad Press, Incorporated
P.O. Box 10543
Tallahassee, FL 32302
(904) 539-5965

Publishes lesbian literature. Offers videocassettes.

Nanny Goat Publications
P.O. Box 8
Laguna Beach, CA 92652
(714) 494-7930

Publishes materials focusing on feminist humor and outlook. Publishes underground-style comic books. Much of subject matter is sexual satire from a woman's point of view.

National Radical Women Publications
608 22nd Ave.
Seattle, WA 98122
(202) 722-6057

Publishes books and materials on the feminist movement, feminist theory, racism, sexism, bigotry, and labor inequities.

New Pages Press
4426 S Belsay Rd.
Grand Blanc, MI 48439

A small press publishing the works of women.

New Seed Press
P.O. Box 9488
Berkeley, CA 94709
(510) 540-7576

Publishes multicultural children's books free from stereotyping and books that encourage thinking about how the world could be different and how to change it.

New Victoria Publishers, Incorporated
P.O. Box 27
Norwich, VT 05055
(802) 649-5297;
Fax: (802) 649-5297

A nonprofit, feminist literary and cultural organization that publishes lesbian fiction and nonfiction.

Omnicorn Productions, Incorporated
P.O. Box 15
Sedona, AZ 86336
(602) 282-3666

Publishes self-help books on abused women.

Our Power Press
P.O. Box 6680
Denver, CO 80206

A women's press.

Paper-Mache Press
795 Via Manzana
Watsonville, CA 95076
(408) 726-2933

Publishes poetry and fiction by, for, and about women. Offers t-shirts, posters, and audiocassettes.

Paradigm Publishing
P.O. Box 3877
San Diego, CA 92163
(619) 234-7115;
Fax: (619) 234-2607

A woman-owned small press that publishes trade paperback books from the lesbian and gay women's communities.

Pennypress, Incorporated
1100 23rd Ave. E
Seattle, WA 98112
(206) 325-1419;
Fax: (206) 325-0472

A woman-owned, woman-run publishing company that produces materials on childbirth and parenting. Topics include breastfeeding, obstetric tests and technology, and teen pregnancy.

Pocahonas Press, Incorporated
2805 Wellesley Ct.
P.O. Drawer F
Blacksburg, VA 24063-1020

Feminist publisher. Offers fiction, poetry, memoirs, and books on women's history.

Red Alder Books
P.O. Box 29
Santa Cruz, CA 95063
(408) 426-7082

Publishes books of erotica, poetry, photographs, and drawings dealing with the sexual experiences of women.

Rhiannon Press
1105 Bradley Ave.
Eau Claire, WI 54701
(715) 835-0598

Publisher of midwest women's poetry.

Rising Tide Press
5 Kivy St.
Huntington Station, NY 11746

Publishes feminist fiction.

Rose Shell Press
516 Gallows Hill Rd.
Cranford, NJ 07016
(908) 276-9479

Publishes books by and for women. Publications focus on women's poetry.

Saturday Press, Incorporated
P.O. Box 884
Upper Montclair, NJ 07043
(201) 256-5053

Publishes the work of women poets over forty.

Sea Horse Press
52 Liberty St.
Metuchen, NJ 08840
(201) 548-8600

Publishes fiction, poetry, drama, and selected nonfiction written by and about lesbians and gays.

Seal Press
3131 Western Ave., Ste. 410
Seattle, WA 98121
(206) 283-7844

Publishes women writers in fiction and nonfiction, including mysteries, contemporary stories, books on domestic violence and recovery, and other women's studies issues.

Sidewalk Revolution Press
P.O. Box 9062
Pittsburgh, PA 15224
(412) 241-6135

Publishes lesbian feminist poetry.

Silverleaf Press
P.O. Box 70189
Seattle, WA 98107

Offers fiction by feminist writers.

Smith Publishers
69 Joralemon St.
Brooklyn, NY 11201
(718) 522-0623

Publishes books on women's issues and collections of women's poetry. Also publishes a newsletter.

Smooth Stone Press, Incorporated
P.O. Box 198
St. Louis, MO 63144
(314) 968-2596

Publishes books and materials on women's health.

Spinsters Ink
P.O. Box 300170
Minneapolis, MN 55403
(612) 377-0287;
Fax: (612) 377-1759

A publisher of feminist and lesbian books. Publishes fiction and nonfiction that deals with women's issues.

Steppingstone Press
3113 Falling Brook Ln.
Boise, ID 83706
(208) 384-1577

Publishes self-help books for women.

Tabor Sarah Books
2419 Jefferson Ave.
Berkeley, CA 94703
(510) 843-2779

Publishes books for children that are nonsexist, nonracist, and multicultural stories.

Third Side Press
2250 W Farragut
Chicago, IL 60625
(312) 271-3029;
Fax: (312) 271-0459

Publishes feminist literature, lesbian fiction, and women's nonfiction. Specializes in books on women's health and recovery.

Third Woman Press
c/o Ethnic Studies
Dwinelle Hall 3412
Berkeley, CA 94720
(510) 642-0240;
Fax: (510) 642-6456

Publishes the literature of women of color.

Timely Books
P.O. Box 267
New Milford, CT 06776
(615) 875-9447

Publishes feminist and lesbian/feminist fiction.

Tough Dove Books
P.O. Box 1999
Redway, CA 95560

Publishes feminist and lesbian fiction.

Vanessa Press
P.O. Box 82761
Fairbanks, AK 99708
(907) 479-0172

Publishes works by Alaskan women. Works reveal the courage, humor, humanity, and insights of women living in the physical, cultural, and social environment of Alaska.

Venus Press
7100 Blvd. E
Guttenberg, NJ 07093

Publishes books by and for women.

Vintage '45 Press
P.O. Box 266
Orinda, CA 94563
(510) 254-7266

Specializes in books for midlife and older women. Sells books through an annual catalog.

Violet Ink
307 W State St.
Ithaca, NY 14850

A lesbian-feminist publisher.

Volcano Press
P.O. Box 270
Volcano, CA 95689
(209) 296-3445;
Fax: (209) 296-4515

Publishes women-oriented books on women's health, social issues, and domestic violence. Also has a line of multicultural children's books.

Wildfire Books
P.O. Box 105
Albuquerque, NM 87184
(505) 344-4790

Publishes books on feminist theory by Sonia Johnson. Also offers audiocassettes and videocassettes.

Wild Trees Press
P.O. Box 378
Navarro, CA 95463

Publishes fiction, primarily by women of color.

Wild Violet Publishing
P.O. Box 1311
Hamilton, MT 59840
(406) 363-2696

Publishes books on women's spirituality.

Wind River Publications, Incorporated
2359 Henderson Mill Ct.
Atlanta, GA 30345
(404) 496-4986

Publishes a national directory of women-owned businesses.

Women in Literature, Incorporated
P.O. Box 60550
Reno, NV 89506
(702) 972-1671

Publishes regional anthologies of poetry by women. Anthologies include criticism, interviews, and biographies of featured poets.

Women in the Moon Publications
P.O. Box 2087
10203 Parkwood Dr., No. 7
Cupertino, CA 95015-2087
(408) 253-3329;
Fax: (408) 253-3329

A woman-owned, black-owned poetry book publisher that publishes books by minority and nonmainstream writers. Also publishes reference and business titles.

Women in Translation
3131 Western Ave., Ste. 410
Seattle, WA 98121

Publishes books by international women writers.

Women's Education Equity Act Publishing Center
55 Chapel St.
Newton, MA 02160
(800) 225-3088;
Fax: (617) 332-4318

A national resource center for gender equity. Publishes nonsexist, multicultural materials for teachers, counselors, administrators, parents, business leaders, and community members committed to encouraging equal education opportunity.

Women's Times Publishing
P.O. Box 2
Grand Marais, MN 55604
(707) 829-0558

Publishes literature by and for women of northeastern Minnesota.

Womontyme Distribution Company
P.O. Box 50145
Long Beach, CA 90815
(800) 247-8903;
Fax: (310) 425-6494

National distributor specializing in books and tapes regarding sexual assault, incest, domestic violence, parenting, self-esteem, drug abuse, and codependency.

Womyn's Braille Press.

See Special Interests: Physically Challenged Services.

❏ Professional and Business Associations and Networks

African-American Women's Clergy
P.O. Box 1493
Washington, DC 20013
(202) 797-7460

An association of inner-city women preachers. Publishes a newsletter.

American Anthropology Association
Assoc. for Feminist Anthropology
1703 New Hampshire Ave. NW
Washington, DC 20009
(202) 232-8800

Advances feminist approaches to the study of anthropology and proposes curriculum changes that incorporate feminist perspectives.

American Association for Women Podiatrists
1300 State Hwy.
Ocean Township, NJ 07712
(201) 531-0490

A networking organization for women in the practice of podiatric medicine. Provides guidance, consultation, and financial assistance to women students in the field of podiatry.

American Association of Black Women Entrepreneurs
P.O. Box 13911
Silver Spring, MD 20911
(301) 565-0258

Fosters companies owned by African American women to increase their financial success. Offers business development information, sponsors training programs, provides discounts on business supplies, and has a networking service. Publishes Chronicle of Minority Business, *a national newsletter. See also* Organizations Representing Women of Color.

American Association of Women Dentists
111 E Wacker Dr., Ste. 600
Chicago, IL 60601
(312) 644-6610;
Fax: (312) 565-4658

An organization of women dentists and dental students. Its goal is to help women advance in the profession and provide networking opportunities and cooperation among its members. Offers scholarships and holds annual meetings.

American Association of Women Radiologists
1891 Preston White Dr.
Reston, VA 22091
(703) 648-8939

An organization of women physicians in diagnostic or therapeutic radiology, nuclear medicine, or radiologic physics. Conducts seminars and workshops.

American Business Women's Association
9100 Ward Pkwy.
P.O. Box 8728
Kansas City, MO 64114-0728
(816) 361-6621;
Fax: (816) 361-4991

A national association that provides education and business training for women of diverse backgrounds to help them gain career advancement and personal development. Education is fostered through national and local business training programs; a national leadership development program; educational speakers at chapter, regional, and national meetings; a national magazine, and seminars.

American Library Association Feminist Task Force
50 E Huron St.
Chicago, IL 60611
(312) 944-6780

A professional caucus for feminist library workers and the official voice for women's issues within the ALA.

American Medical Women's Association
801 N Fairfax St., Ste. 400
Alexandria, VA 22314
(703) 838-0500;
Fax: (703) 549-3864

A national organization of women physicians and medical students working together to advance women's health on all levels. Members are encouraged to network and to communicate with each other on new developments. Furthers career opportunities for women in the medical profession, increases women's influence in health care initiatives, and takes a stand on issues as they emerge.

American Musicological Society.
See Art and Media.

American News Women's Club
1607 22nd St. NW
Washington, DC 20008
(202) 332-6770

A professional association for women who write news for all media. Sponsors social events, main-

tains a club house, and offers publications.

American Nurses' Association
600 Maryland Ave.
Washington, DC 20024
(202) 554-4444

An organization of registered nurses. Seeks to advance the nursing profession by promoting high standards, increasing opportunities, advocating better economic and working conditions, and lobbying for issues affecting not only nurses, but all women in health care. Also monitors employment practices and trends.

American Psychiatric Association Association of Women Psychiatrists
c/o Marion Z. Goldstein
462 Grider St.
Department of Psychiatry
Buffalo, NY 14215

An international network of women psychiatrists. Designed to improve communications among and provide support to women psychiatrists, to provide information on women's mental care issues, and to foster research in this field. See also Global Feminism and World Peace.

American Society of Professional and Executive Women
1429 Walnut St.
Philadelphia, PA 19102
(215) 563-4415

Promotes and supports career women involved in all areas of American enterprise. Conducts seminars and offers education.

American Sociological Association Committee on the Status of Women
1722 N Street NW
Washington, DC 20036
(202) 833-3410;
Fax: (202) 785-0146

A special committee of the American Sociological Association that is comprised of sociologists who oversee the status and participation of women in the profession. Includes both practitioners and teachers. Publishes several journals, a monthly newsletter, and holds an annual professional meeting.

American Women's Society of Certified Public Accountants
401 N Michigan Ave.
Chicago, IL 60611
(312) 644-6610

Provides networking opportunities, encouragement, and advice to further career opportunities. Conducts research on issues relevant to women CPAs.

American Women in Psychology Roster
c/o KNOW
Box 86301
Pittsburgh, PA 15221
(412) 241-4844

Publishes a comprehensive roster of feminist psychotherapists.

American Women in Radio and Television

1101 Connecticut Ave. NW,
Ste. 700
Washington, DC 20036
(202) 429-5102;
Fax: (202) 223-4579

Professionals in administrative, creative, or executive positions in the broadcasting industry. Sponsors educational programs, bestows awards, and holds competitions. See also Art and Media.

American Women's Clergy Association.

See Religious and Spiritual Groups.

American Women's Economic Development Corporation

71 Vanderbilt Ave., 3rd Fl.
New York, NY 10169
(212) 688-1900

Offers training to women who are starting their own businesses. Also helps women manage the businesses they now have. Provides networking opportunities where businesswomen can exchange services.

Association for Women in Architecture

7440 University Dr.
St. Louis, MO 63130
(314) 621-3484

A professional organization for women working in architecture or related fields.

Association for Women in Computing

41 Sutter St., Ste. 1006
San Francisco, CA 94104
(415) 908-4663

A coalition of women in computing. Promotes education, professional development, and career advancement. Sponsors seminars and maintains a speakers' bureau. Provides networking opportunities. Has chapters in many cities. See also Science and Technology.

Association for Women in Development

Virginia Polytechnic Institute and State Univ.
Blacksburg, VA 24061
(703) 231-3765

An organization of policymakers and scholars who seek to increase women's participation in international development issues.

Association for Women in Mathematics

4114 Computer and
Space Science Bldg.
Univ. of Maryland
College Park, MD 20742
(301) 405-7892

An educational and professional organization. Offers workshops, provides prizes for undergraduate women in mathematics and travel funds for graduate and postgradu-

ate students. Also publishes a bi-monthly newsletter to keep members abreast of issues.

Association for Women in Psychology
Haverford College
370 Lancaster Ave.
Haverford, PA 19041-1392

Supports and promotes women in psychology. Sponsors research, holds meetings and seminars, and maintains a hall of fame.

Association for Women in Science.
See Science and Technology.

Association for Women in Social Work
Colorado State Univ.
Dept. of Social Work
Fort Collins, CO 80523
(303) 491-0472

Established to provide "a room of our own" for feminist social workers. Publishes a newsletter.

Association for Women Soil Scientists
P.O. Box 115, Ancram
New York, NY 12502
(914) 677-3194

An organization of women soil scientists, soil conservationists, soil agriculturists, research scientists, professors, and students. Identifies women in the field and provides them with communication opportu-nities, technical and career infor-mation, and encouragement.

Association for Women Veterinarians
32205 Allison Dr.
Union City, CA 94587
(415) 471-8379

A professional association of women veterinarians and students of veterinary medicine. Bestows awards, provides networking opportunities, and offers publications.

Association of Black Secretaries
1212 Broadway, #830
Oakland, CA 94612
(510) 834-7897, (800) 228-8227;
Fax: (510) 238-6153

An organization that provides for the personal and professional development of office workers, including career advancement resources, job-related data, networking opportunities, and career counseling.

Association of Black Women Attorneys
134 W 32 St., Ste. 602
New York, NY 10001
(212) 244-4270

A professional association for black women lawyers. Publishes a newsletter.

Association of Black Women Entrepreneurs
909 Pershing Dr., Ste. 200
Silver Spring, MD 20910

Works to increase the success of companies owned by African American women, conducts research on the economic conditions related to black women in business, and offers business development services. Also sponsors training programs, offers discounts on business supplies, and has a networking service.

Association of Black Women Historians

P.O. Box 19753
Durham, NC 27707
(919) 493-1024

Works to promote black women historians and offers information on black women.

Association of Black Women in Higher Education

Fashion Institute of Technology
Office of V. Pres. of Academic Affairs
227 W 27th St., C-913
New York, NY 10001
(212) 760-7911

Promotes and supports black women in higher education. Conducts workshops and seminars.

Association of Executive and Professional Women

The International Alliance
8600 LaSalle Rd., Ste. 308
Baltimore, MD 21204
(410) 321-6699;
Fax: (410) 823-2410

Represents the interests of execu-
tive and professional women all over the world. Facilitates networking through its annual directory of members. Also offers a Directors Resource Database, and holds regional network meetings. See also Global Feminism and World Peace.

Association of Part-Time Professionals

Flow General Bldg.
7655 Old Springhouse Rd.
McLean, VA 22102
(703) 734-7975

A nonprofit organization that sponsors workshops, job referrals for its members, and information on alternative work options. Publishes a newsletter ten times each year that includes articles on part-time employment, listings of companies that are "family-friendly," and announcements of upcoming events.

Black Professional Women's Network

123 W 44th St., Ste. 2E
New York, NY 10036
(212) 302-2924

Provides information to black and Hispanic professionals, managers, and technical employers. Provides employment, health care, financial information, literature, and referrals.

Catalyst

250 Park Ave. S
New York, NY 10003
(212) 777-8900;
Fax: (212) 477-4252

A well-known national nonprofit educational, self-help, and research organization that addresses women in the work force. Advises on the changing role of women in business, including career opportunities, part-time and flexible work arrangements, and how women can break into the boardroom. See also Research Centers and Organizations.

Coalition for Women in International Development
c/o OEF International
1717 Massachusetts Ave. NW,
8th Fl.
Washington, DC 20036

An organization of professional women that promotes the participation of American women in U.S. foreign policy and of women throughout the world in the economic, social, and political development of their respective countries. Conducts research programs. See also Global Feminism and World Peace.

Council of Women Chiropractors
4002 Washington
Amarillo, TX 79110
(806) 355-7217

Promotes the practice of chiropractic medicine and the professional status of its members. Offers support and encouragement through the interchange of ideas.

Executive Women International
515 S 700 E, #2E
Salt Lake City, UT 84102
(801) 263-3296

Networks among businesswomen from different industries for professional development. Publishes a newsletter.

Federation of Organizations for Professional Women
2001 S Street NW, #500
Washington, DC 20009
(202) 328-1415;
Fax: (202) 328-1415

A national, nonprofit federation of affiliated organizations joined to enhance the status of professional women through education, exchange of information, and mutual support.

Feminist Business and Professional Network
P.O. Box 91214
Washington, DC 20090-1214

A coalition of companies and individuals that promotes increased visibility and opportunity for women in business. Provides technical assistance, networking support, information, and seminars.

Financial Women International
710 Woodmont, Ste. 1430
Bethesda, MD 20814
(301) 657-8288

Formerly called the National Association of Bank Women, this is a group of women in the financial in-

dustry. Provides education seminars, a national conference, and networking opportunities.

Home Economists in Business
5008 Pine Creek Dr.
Westerville, OH 43081
(614) 890-4342

A professional organization of graduate home economists and consumer specialists employed by businesses. Publishes a newsletter.

International Alliance
8600 LaSalle Rd., Ste. 617
Baltimore, MD 21286
(410) 472-4221

An organization of professional and executive women that serves as a resource to unite members in the corporate, public, and civic sectors worldwide. Sponsors an annual conference, meetings in Washington, DC and Europe, and a resource data bank, in addition to publishing a directory and bimonthly newsletter. See also Global Feminism *and* World Peace.

International Association for Personnel Women
P.O. Box 969
Andover, MA 01810-0017
(508) 474-0750;
Fax: (508) 474-0750

A professional association of personnel executives in business, industry, education, and government. Offers publications.

International League of Women Composers Journal
Abilene Christian Univ.
Box 8274
Abilene, TX 79699
(915) 674-2044;
Fax: (915) 674-2232

A quarterly report available on women composers and related issues. Also includes announcements of awards and competitions and opportunities for women composers.

International Network for Women in Enterprise and Trade
P.O. Box 6178
McLean, VA 22106
(703) 893-8541;
Fax: (703) 356-6655

Provides a global forum for businesswomen worldwide to exchange ideas and to develop and implement effective alternatives in the way business is conducted. Provides training seminars and financial support. Publishes a newsletter.

International Organization of Women in Telecommunications
2308 Oakwood Ln.
Arlington, TX 76012
(817) 275-0683

A professional organization for women in telecommunications and telecommunications students. Offers a forum for the exchange of information on job opportunities and education, sponsors seminars, and maintains a library in New York City.

International Society of Women Airline Pilots
P.O. Box 66268
Chicago, IL 60666-0268

A professional association for women airline pilots. Operates an information bank, maintains a speakers' bureau, and offers publications.

International Women Pilots Association
The Ninety-Nines, Inc.
P.O. Box 59965
Will Rogers Airport
Oklahoma City, OK 73159
(405) 685-7969;
Fax: (405) 584-7985

An organization formed to network and educate women pilots. Sponsors flying companion seminars and safety seminars. Offers an Amelia Earhart Memorial Scholarship Award. See also Educational Services and Organizations.

International Women's Writing Guild
P.O. Box 810
Gracie Sta.
New York, NY 10028-0013
(212) 737-7536

A networking organization for women writers. Offers networking publications and conferences.

Massachusetts Friends of Midwives.
See Health Organizations: Alternative Health Services.

Mothers' Home Business Network
P.O. Box 423
East Meadow, NY 11554
(516) 997-7394;
Fax: (516) 997-0839

A national organization for mothers who choose to work at home. Provides home business guidance for mothers, networks mothers across the United States, and publishes Homeworking Mothers and Kids *and* Career: New Ideas and Options for Mothers *newsletter.*

National Association for Female Executives
127 W 24th St., 4th Fl.
New York, NY 10011
(212) 645-0770;
Fax: (212) 633-6489

Provides women with networking tools and information to advance their careers. The organization has 300 chapters and 240,000 members nationwide, and publishes Executive Female *magazine. See also* Work, Union, and Career Services.

National Association for Professional Saleswomen
5520 Cherokee Ave., Ste. 200
Alexandria, VA 22312
(703) 256-9226;
Fax: (703) 658-8887

An organization for women in professional sales and marketing careers. Offers publications, maintains a library, and sponsors competitions.

National Association for Women in Careers
P.O. Box 81525
Chicago, IL 60681-0525
(312) 938-7662;
Fax: (312) 819-1220

A service organization for career women. Provides support, networking, and skill-development services. Conducts seminars, provides job referral, career planning, and lectures.

National Association for Women in Construction
P.O. Box 5312
Denver, CO 80217
(303) 669-0535

A networking organization whose members are women directly employed in construction or employed in firms that are construction related, such as attorneys. Publishes a newsletter.

National Association of Black Women Attorneys.
See Legal Services.

National Association of Collegiate Women Athletic Administrators
Univ. of Minnesota, Athletic Dept.
Minneapolis, MN 55455
(612) 624-8000;
Fax: (801) 750-2615

An organization of women working in athletic administration at U.S. colleges and universities. Serves as a forum for the exchange of information among members and as an advocate for opportunities for women in sport.

National Association of Hispanic Nurses
1501 16th St. NW
Washington, DC 20036
(202) 387-2477;
Fax: (202) 797-2477

Works for the improvement of health standards and availability of health care services for Hispanics. Fosters high standards of nursing. Promotes professional development of Hispanic nurses to advance their economic and general welfare.

National Association of Insurance Women
1847 E 15th
P.O. Box 4410
Tulsa, OK 74159
(918) 744-5195;
Fax: (918) 743-1968

A coalition of women in the insurance business. Sponsors educational programs, bestows awards, holds competitions, and offers publications.

National Association of M.B.A. Women
7701 Georgia Ave. NW
Washington, DC 20012

A professional organization that al-

lows women with M.B.A. degrees to network and exchange ideas. Its goal is to advance career opportunities and recognition in the field. Also offers scholarship opportunities and publications. See also Special Interests.

National Association of Media Women
1185 Niskey Lake Rd. SW
Atlanta, GA 30331
(404) 344-5862

A professional association for women in mass communications. Sponsors studies, research, and seminars. Grants scholarships and presents awards. See also Art and Media.

National Association of Negro Business and Professional Women
1806 New Hampshire Ave. NW
Washington, DC 20009
(202) 483-4206;
Fax: (202) 462-7253

An umbrella organization that links related national and international groups, provides scholarships and financial aid, and offers workshops. Local clubs work in the community to serve as role models and sponsor programs that inspire change.

National Association of Railway Business Women
2720 Mayfield Rd.
Cleveland Heights, OH 44106
(216) 321-0971, (800) 348-6272

Works to support and further the educational, social, and professional interests of women who work for railroads. Conducts charitable and social welfare projects, maintains a residence for retired members, bestows awards, and offers scholarships. See also Educational Services and Organizations.

National Association of Women Business Owners
600 S Federal St., Ste. 400
Chicago, IL 60605
(312) 922-0465

An international and national network for women who own their own businesses. Also provides political advocacy for small businesses. See also Global Feminism and World Peace.

National Association of Women Judges
300 Newport Ave.
Williamsburg, VA 23187-8798
(804) 253-2000;
Fax: (804) 220-1449

An association for women holding judicial positions and working to address legal, educational, social, and ethical problems encountered by women judges. Conducts research, educational, and referral services.

National Chamber of Commerce for Women
10 Waterside Pl., #6H
New York, NY 10010
(212) 685-3454

Provides women with information on how to efficiently manage their businesses. Helps women network and offers information and workshops on marketing, automating, business plan writing, accounting, billing, and strategic planning.

National Commission on Working Women
1325 G St. NW
Washington, DC 20005
(202) 737-5764

Advocates for the needs and concerns of women in the work force and conducts public education on issues such as pay equity, child care, economically disadvantaged working women, and the image of women in the media. Conducts research and offers publications. See also Women's Rights.

National Conference of Women's Bar Association
P.O. Box 77
Edenton, NC 27932
(919) 482-8202

Promotes the interests of women lawyers and promotes the advancement of women in the legal profession.

National Council of Career Women
3202 Gemstone Ct.
Oakton, VA 22124
(703) 591-4359

An organization of women interested in advancing their careers.

Works to enhance the image and role of women in the business and professional world through education and skill development.

National Education Association Women's Caucus
1202 16th St. NW
Washington, DC 20036
(202) 373-1800

A professional and advocacy organization for women in education. Works to eliminate sexism and racism regarding educational issues. Develops programs for teaching awareness of sex role stereotyping.

National Federation of Business and Professional Women's Clubs
2012 Massachusetts Ave. NW
Washington, DC 20036
(202) 293-1100;
Fax: (202) 861-0298

Mission is to advance equality in every area of business and throughout the professions. Has about three thousand locations in the U.S. and sponsors an annual convention. Supports such goals as pay equity, equal career opportunities, and economic self-sufficiency for all working women. Sponsors community awareness and research.

National Federation of Press Women
Box 99
Blue Springs, MO 64015
(816) 229-1666

A professional organization for women in communications. Sponsors seminars, conferences, research, and publications.

National League for Nursing
350 Hudson St.
New York, NY 10014
(212) 989-9393, (800) 669-1656;
Fax: (212) 989-3710

A coalition of nurses and health care professionals. Works to improve the quality of health care. Provides continuing education programs, research, publications, and lobbying efforts.

National Network of Women in Sales
710 E Ogden Ave., #113
Naperville, IL 60563
(708) 369-2406

A national organization that supports women in sales through networking and professional development.

Network for Professional Women
City Personnel
100 Committee Pl., Ste. 220
Hartford, CT 06103
(203) 727-1988;
Fax: (203) 727-9623

Works to educate and motivate professional women. Sponsors seminars and workshops on topics such as management of credit, employment networking, and reentering the work force. See also Work, Union, *and* Career Services.

Professional Women in Construction
342 Madison Ave., Rm. 451
New York, NY 10173
(212) 687-0610;
Fax: (212) 490-1213

An association for management-level women in construction, including owners, suppliers, architects, engineers, field personnel, and office personnel. Conducts lobbying efforts, offers networking opportunities, and sponsors educational and research projects.

Professional Women Photographers
c/o Photo Unlimited
17 W 17th St., No. 14
New York, NY 10011
(212) 255-9678

An organization that promotes and encourages women photographers. Conducts charitable, educational, and artistic activities. Publishes a newsletter. See also Art and Media.

Society of Women Engineers
120 Wall St.
New York, NY 10005
(212) 509-9577, (800) 666-1SWE;
Fax: (212) 509-0224

Supports and promotes women engineers. Offers professional workshops, information, scholarship programs, and career guidance. Publishes a newsletter. Chapters in many states and universities. See also Educational Services and Organizations.

Soroptimist International of the Americas
1616 Walnut St., #700
Philadelphia, PA 19103
(215) 732-0512;
Fax: (215) 732-7508

A community service organization comprised of executive and professional women. The largest organization of its kind in the world. Goals are attained through six programs of service: Environment, Economic Development, Health, Education, Human Rights/Status of Women, and International Goodwill and Understanding. Local clubs are found in many areas. Clubs also exist for college and high school students. Publishes a newsletter. See also Global Feminism and World Peace.

Women in Communications, Incorporated
2101 Wilson Blvd., Ste. 417
Arlington, VA 22201
(703) 528-4200;
Fax: (703) 528-4205

A networking and education organization for women in print journalism, broadcasting, marketing, communications education, photojournalism, publishing, film, and graphics. Offers a national job line, award programs, conferences, and loan and insurance programs. Publishes a newsletter. Chapters exist in many cities.

Women in Data Processing
P.O. Box 880866
San Diego, CA 92108
(619) 569-5615

An association for female technical personnel, managers, and students in data processing. Provides educational opportunities, workshops, and management seminars. Offers publications. See also Science and Technology.

Women in Design/Chicago
400 W Madison, Ste. 2400
Chicago, IL 60606
(312) 648-1874

A nationally recognized organization that promotes greater recognition of women's contributions to design and encourage designers' achievement of personal and professional goals. Publishes a newsletter.

Women in Film
6464 Sunset Blvd., Ste. 900
Los Angeles, CA 90028
(213) 463-6040; Fax: (213) 463-0963

A professional organization for women in film and television. Offers educational forums, conducts research, provides information, and offers financial assistance to women for education and research. See also Art and Media.

Women in Scholarly Publishing (WISP)
55 Hayward St., The MIT Press
Cambridge, MA 02142
(617) 253-5642

Devoted to the encouragement of educational and professional advancement for its members. Publishes a newsletter.

Women in the Fire Service
P.O. Box 5446
Madison, WI 53705
(608) 233-4768

A national network providing information and support to women in the fire and rescue services as well as to others seeking a smooth transition to a gender-integrated fire service work force. Holds conferences and publishes a newsletter.

Women's Alliance for Job Equity
1422 Chestnut St., Ste. 1100
Philadelphia, PA 19102
(215) 561-1873;
Fax: (215) 561-7112

A nonprofit organization dedicated to improving economic and workplace conditions for women in the Delaware Valley. Provides advice and support in dealing with age or sex discrimination, educates businesses on sexual harassment, offers workshops on pay equity, job rights, etc. and sponsors a mentor program for homeless or formerly homeless women trying to enter the job force.

Women's Economic Roundtable
866 United Nations Pl., #4052
New York, NY 10017
(212) 759-4360;
Fax: (212) 666-1625

A nonprofit organization of business women and men who question economic policymakers in a public forum. Serves to consolidate women's opinions in the formation of a national economic policy. Also provides round table discussions, activities, and programs to its members and the public. Also acts as a channel through which the nation's media and policymakers are accessible to members. Educates women on how to keep the economic power they now hold.

Women's Institute for Freedom of the Press
3306 Ross Pl. NW
Washington, DC 20008-3332
(202) 966-7783

A support and information network for women in media. Conducts research and offers information about women and the media. See also Work, Union, and Career Services.

Women's National Book Association
160 Fifth Ave.
New York, NY 10010
(212) 675-7805

A national networking association with eight chapters. Promotes recognition of women's achievements in the book industry. Publishes a newsletter, Bookwoman, *three times a year.*

❏ Recreation, Fitness, and Sports Groups

Adventure Associates
P.O. Box 16304
Seattle, WA 98116
(206) 932-8352;
Fax: (206) 938-2654

An adventure travel company that specializes in small-group international and stateside tours and treks. Offers both women-only and co-ed trips. Sea kayaking in Baja, Mexico; safari in East Africa; llama treks in the Pacific Northwest; hikes in the Canadian Rockies; Mexico treks; and skiing in Yellowstone are some of the available trips.

Adventures for Women in Outdoor Living, Incorporated
P.O. Box 515
Montvale, NJ 07645
(201) 930-0557

Offers skill-based and recreational experiences in hiking, canoeing, and cross-country skiing in New Jersey and New York.

Alaska Women of the Wilderness
Box 773556
Eagle River, AK 99577
(807) 688-2226

A year-round, nonprofit wilderness program for women designed to promote a sense of confidence and connection in the outdoors. Provides a safe, supportive, and noncompetitive approach to wilderness adventure travel. Activities include backpacking, hiking, sea kayaking, fishing, dog mushing, skiing, women's retreats, and workshops.

Alliance of Women Bikers
P.O. Box 484
Eau Claire, WI 54702

An international organization for women motorcyclists. Educates the public and media on sexist images of female bikers. Conducts lobbying efforts on issues affecting the rights of bikers. Holds motorcycle shows.

Blue Moon Explorations
P.O. Box 2568
Bellingham, WA 98227
(206) 966-8805

Women's and coed women-led adventures in nature. Offers trips in the Pacific Northwest, Hawaii, and the Southwest, including sea kayaking and cross-country skiing.

Camping Women
7623 Southbreeze Dr.
Sacramento, CA 95828
(916) 689-9326

An organization for women seeking to improve their camping skills and who are interested in outdoor activities such as backpacking, hiking, canoeing, rafting, and skiing. Provides skills-training workshops, materials, and leadership programs.

Earth Spirit Women's Wilderness Trips and Vision Quests
P.O. Box 283
San Geronimo, CA 94963

Leads women's outings in the wilderness that are geared toward spiritual and transformational experiences.

Earthwise Adventures for Women
23 Mount Nebo Rd.
Newton, CT 06470
(203) 426-6092

Offers noncompetitive, self-challenging trips that combine an appreciation of the outdoors with women's spirituality and self-knowledge. Offerings include yoga and meditation, canoeing, hiking, horseback riding, and backpacking in the U.S. and Puerto Rico.

Expanding Horizons
P.O. Box 3753
Arlington, VA 22203
(703) 525-4724

A women-owned outdoor adventure company specializing in outdoor programs for women. Offers trips in the Washington, DC area. Sign-language interpretation is available for all programs.

Forum for Women in Bridge
21755 S Tuller Ct.
Southfield, MI 48076
(313) 356-2246

An organization for women who play bridge. Works to educate women about bridge and organize bridge activities. Sponsors programs to teach children how to play bridge.

Hawk, I'm Your Sister
P.O. Box 9109
Santa Fe, NM 87504-9109
(505) 984-2268

Offers wilderness canoeing trips in the U.S., Canada, Russia, and Mexico. The program includes guided and fully outfitted river journeys, wilderness seminars, and writing retreats for women of all ages and abilities.

Heartland Women's Bicycle Tours
1 Orchard Cir.
Washington, IA 52353
(319) 653-2277

Offers tours that take place throughout the U.S. and the Caribbean.

Her Wild Song
Wilderness Journeys for Women
P.O. Box 515
Brunswick, ME 04011
(207) 721-9005

Provides wilderness retreats for women and combines natural history and ecology study with spiritual exploration and development of outdoor skills. Offerings include sea kayaking, canoeing, backpacking, cross-country skiing, and dogsledding at locations around the U.S.

International Association of Physical Education and Sport for Girls and Women
50 Skyline Dr.
Mankato, MN 56001
(507) 345-3665

A coalition of organizations worldwide interested in physical education for women and girls. Conducts research on women in sports and offers networking activities for people interested in promoting and supporting women athletes.

International Women's Fishing Association
P.O. Drawer 3125
Palm Beach, FL 33480

Sponsors competitions and fishing tournaments among women anglers. Stresses environmentalism and conservation. Also sponsors awards and scholarships.

Ladies Professional Bowlers Tour
7171 Cherryvale Blvd.
Rockford, IL 61112
(815) 332-5756;
Fax: (815) 332-9636

An organization for professional women bowlers. Conducts world-class tournaments, presents awards, and compiles statistics.

Ladies Professional Golf Association
2570 Vousia St., Ste. B
Daytona, FL 32114
(904) 254-8800;
Fax: (713) 980-4352

An association for professional women golfers and golf trainers. Provides a retirement program and maintains a hall of fame.

Lost Coast Llama Caravans
77321 Usal Rd.
Whitethorn, CA 95489

Runs llama-packing trips along Northern California's Lost Coast. Women-owned and operated. Many women-only trips.

Mariah Wilderness Expeditions
P.O. Box 248
Point Richard, CA 94807
(510) 233-2303, (800) 4-MARIAH

Offers hiking, white-water rafting, sea kayaking, and exploration trips in the U.S. and abroad.

National Association of Collegiate Women Athletic Administrators.
See Professional and Business Associations and Networks.

National Association for Girls and Women in Sport
1900 Association Dr.
Reston, VA 22091
(703) 476-3450;
Fax: (703) 476-9527

A membership organization comprised primarily of educators and coaches. Works to secure positions for women in coaching and leadership positions in sports and to increase the participation of females in athletics. See also Professional and Business Associations and Networks.

National Deaf Women's Bowling Association
33 August Rd.
Simsbury, CT 06070
(203) 651-8234

An organization of hearing-impaired bowlers. Promotes competition and improved playing conditions. See also Special Interests.

National Intercollegiate Women's Fencing Association
3 Derby Ln.
Dumont, NJ 07628
(201) 384-1722

A coalition of colleges and universities with varsity women's fencing teams. Promotes fencing for women, conducts fencing matches, workshops, and clinics, and maintains archives.

National Organization of Outdoor Women
P.O. Box 441134
Kennesaw, GA 30144
(800) 228-6669

A network of women who enjoy fishing, camping, boating, and other outdoor recreations.

National Recreation and Parks Association, Women and Minority Programs
3101 Park Center Dr., Ste. 1200
Alexandria, VA 22302
(703) 820-4940;
Fax: (703) 671-6772

Works to meet the needs of women and minorities through a variety of civic, professional, and technical projects. Also involved in research, education, policy, and program initiatives. See also Organizations Representing Women of Color.

National Senior Women's Tennis Association
1696 W Calimjrna, No. B
Fresno, CA 93711
(209) 432-3095

An organization of women over thirty interested in competitive tennis. Sponsors national events. See also Special Interests: Older Women's Services.

National Women's Martial Arts Federation
1377 Studer Ave.
Columbus, OH 43206
(614) 443-1025

An organization of female martial artists. Promotes excellence in martial arts, sponsors awards and competitions, and offers educational programs.

North American Network of Women Runners
P.O. Box 719
Bala-Cynwyd, PA 19004
(215) 668-9886

A network of women runners, marathoners, and others interested in health, fitness, and competition aspects of running. Sponsors women's workouts with child care in a number of community locations.

OceanWomyn Kayaking
620 11th Ave. E
Seattle, WA 98102
(206) 325-3970

Offers guided sea kayaking adventures for beginning and experienced sea kayaking women. Trips offered in Baja, California; British Columbia; the San Juan Islands; and Alaska.

Off the Beaten Path
Women's Sailing and Sea Kayaking
620 11th Ave. E
Seattle, WA 98102

Runs sailing trips in Baja, Mexico; California; the San Juan Islands, and elsewhere.

Outdoor Vacations for Women Over 40
P.O. Box 200
Groton, MA 01450
(508) 448-3331; Fax: (508) 448-3514

Offers outdoor adventure vacations for women over forty in the U.S. and abroad. Offerings include cross-country skiing, canoeing, whale watching, biking, swimming, snorkeling, rafting, hiking, and sailing. See also Special Interests.

Prairie Women Adventure and Retreat
P.O. Box 2
Matfield Green, KS 66862
(316) 753-3465

Provides women with an opportunity to spend time on a six-thousand-acre working ranch. The ranch, owned and operated by women, provides a setting for learning new skills, appreciating rural life, meeting other women, and relaxing.

Rock Woman Journeys Home
P.O. Box 6548
Denver, CO 80206
(800) 676-5404

A woman-owned and woman-run small business offering group experiences on the San Juan River in southeastern Utah. Trips open to all women, regardless of experience.

Run, Jane, Run
Women in Sports
P.O. Box 55108
Indianapolis, IN 46205-5108
(317) 571-0662

A woman's sports festival that is a fund-raiser for women-empowering *organizations. Also provides technical assistance for the implementation of local multisport festivals. See also* Art and Media; Foundations and Funding Sources.

Sea Sense: The Women's Sailing School
25 Thames St.
New London, CT 06320
(203) 444-1404, (800) 332-1404

Offers three-, five-, or seven-day sailing and power boating workshops to women. Classes are taught to all ability levels by women captains in New England, Florida, Lake Michigan, and the Caribbean.

Sheri Griffith Expeditions
P.O. Box 1324
Maob, UT 84532
(800) 332-2439;
Fax: (801) 259-2226

Offers one- to five-day river journeys in the U.S., Nepal, and Costa Rica. Combines rafting with horseback/horsepack and jeeping tours. Specialty trips include: Women Only, Expeditions in Luxury, Family Goes to Camp, Personal and Professional Developmental Seminars, and Politics and the Environment.

United States Women's Curling Association
4114 N 53rd St.
Omaha, NE 68104
(402) 453-6574

An organization of amateur women

curlers. Offers awards and maintains an archive of association competitions, awards, and records.

United States Women's Lacrosse Association
45 Maple Ave.
Hamilton, NY 13346
(315) 824-2480;
Fax: (315) 824-4533

An organization of women involved in or who support lacrosse. Trains umpires, conducts seminars and clinics, and sponsors tournaments.

Wander Women
136 N Grand Ave., #237
West Covina, CA 91791
(818) 966-8857

A travel and adventure organization for women over forty. Also publishes a quarterly newsletter. See also Special Interests.

Whelk Women
P.O. Box 1006A
Boca Grande, FL 33921
(813) 964-2027

Offers sailing journeys in the protected waters of Charlotte Harbor among uninhabited islands, tropical birds, and dolphins. Accommodations include outfitted camping in cabins, a remote inn, or bed and breakfast.

Wild Women Trips
P.O. Box 8222
Berkeley, CA 94707
(510) 524-3053

Offers a variety of outdoor adventures including backpacking, camping, and river trips.

Women Anglers of Minnesota

P.O. Box 580653
Minneapolis, MN 55458-0653
(612) 339-1322

An organization for women who fish. Provides opportunities to improve skills, offers information and educational programs, and promotes respect for fish and the environment. See also Special Interests.

Womanship, International

The Boat House
410 Severn Ave.
Annapolis, MD 21403
(410) 267-6661;
Fax: (410) 263-2036

Sponsors numerous sailing programs by and for women. The programs give women on-board learning experiences to provide skill and confidence in sailing. There are two- to ten-day courses and learning cruises offered at several locations nationwide, in addition to the San Juan Islands, the Virgin Islands, Greece, and New Zealand.

Woman Trek

1411 E Olive Way
Seattle, WA 98102
(206) 325-4772

Offers a variety of outdoor experiences and adventures including backpacking, mountain climbing, camping, and river trips.

Women Climbers Northwest

Box 20573
Seattle, WA 98102

A club for women who climb, hike, and snow ski. Networks women in these sports, encourages leadership and safety, and promotes environmentally sound practices in the wilderness.

Women for Fishing, Hunting, and Wildlife

P.O. Box 582342
Minneapolis, MN 55458-2342
(612) 333-4657

Works to educate women in the heritage of fishing, hunting, and wildlife conservation. Networks women, publishes a quarterly newsletter, and offers a resource bank for fishing, hunting, and education.

Women in the Wilderness

566 Ottawa Ave.
St. Paul, MN 55107
(612) 227-2284

Offers adventure vacations for women of all ages and experiences. Specializes in canoeing. Also features wilderness retreats and nature tours.

Women on Wheels

P.O. Box 5147
Topeka, KS 66605
(913) 267-3779, (800) 322-1969

An organization for women motor-

cyclists. Sponsors events and charity functions.

Women Outdoors
55 Talbot Ave.
Medford, MA 02155

A national network of women to help share information about sea kayaking, rock climbing, hiking, camping, bicycling, and other outdoor activities. Membership includes the Women Outdoors magazine and the opportunity to attend leadership development training workshops, local chapter events, and the ability to become eligible for scholarships.

Women's American Basketball Association
2713 Mt. Moriah
Memphis, TN 38115
(512) 523-7427

An organization of owners of professional women's basketball teams. Promotes and supports women's professional basketball.

Women's Distance Committee
306 River Isle Way
Sacramento, CA 95831
(916) 392-5111

Women and men who promote and support distance running for women. Sponsors women's running events, seminars and clinics, and meetings.

Women's International Bowling Congress
5301 S 76th St.
Greendale, WI 53129-1191
(414) 421-9000;
Fax: (414) 421-4420

Sanctions bowling for women and associations worldwide. Provides uniform regulations and qualifications to govern teams, leagues, and tournaments. Offers seminars and lane inspectors' workshops. Maintains hall of fame, museum, and archives.

Women's International Tennis Association
133 1st St. NE
St. Petersburg, FL 33701
(813) 895-5000;
Fax: (813) 894-1982

Professional women's tennis players. Represents members with regard to tournaments. Offers information and publications.

Women's International Tennis Council
100 Park Ave., 2nd Fl.
New York, NY 10017
(212) 878-2250

Sanctions, administers, and promotes women's tennis worldwide. Sponsors tournaments.

Women's Professional Racquetball Association
153 S 15th St.
Souderton, PA 18964
(215) 723-7356

Promotes the participation and appreciation of women in sports, especially racquetball. Conducts instructional seminars, sanctions tournaments, and provides information.

Women's Professional Rodeo Association
Rte. 5, Box 698
Blanchard, OK 73010
(405) 485-2277

Organizes rodeo and barrel-racing competitions. Conducts seminars and clinics on horsemanship and competition rules. Maintains a library and hall of fame.

Women's Self-Defense Alliance
614 Orange St.
New Haven, CT 06511
(203) 787-0031

Promotes women's involvement in the martial arts.

Women's Sports Foundation
Eisenhower Park
East Meadow, NY 11554

Goal is to improve the physical and mental well-being of women and girls through a participation in sports activities. Provides funding for travel and training, educational opportunities, and sports-related seminars. Maintains International Women's Sports Hall of Fame.

Women Together in Sports
Box 366
Hinsdale, IL 60522
(708) 323-8583

Primarily an information and referral service for lesbians. Directs lesbians and women to sport and recreational opportunities in the social climate provided in a lesbian and gay community. See also Lesbian and Gay Organizations.

Womyn on the Water
P.O. Box 502
Key West, FL 33041
(305) 294-0662

A sailboat charter for women. Offers five-hour sailing programs, snorkel trips, and two-hour sunset sailing trips.

Woodswomen
25 W Diamond Lake Rd.
Minneapolis, MN 55419-1926
(612) 822-3809;
Fax: (612) 822-3814

A large women's travel organization providing a variety of adventure travel programs. Activities include expeditions, leadership courses, guided canoe trips, outdoor programs for the economically disadvantaged, and educational service programs. Encourages women and children excursions. Publishes Woodswomen News.

❏ Religious and Spiritual Groups

American Atheist Women
7215 Cameron Rd.
Austin, TX 78752
(512) 458-1244;
Fax: (512) 467-9525

A group formed to liberate all women from the constraints of organized religion. Believes religion holds back women from achieving their full potential. Sponsors an annual convention, as well as monthly chapter meetings.

American Society of Church History
Women in Theology and Church History
Lutheran Theological Seminary
7301 Germantown Ave.
Philadelphia, PA 19119
(215) 248-4616;
Fax: (215) 248-4577

Offers support and guidance to women studying theology and church history. Promotes the teaching of these subjects. See also Women's History.

American Women's Clergy Association
The House of Imagene
214 P St. NW
Washington, DC 20001
(202) 797-7460

Promotes and encourages women clergy members. Operates shelters for homeless and battered women. Provides scholarships and sponsors awards and educational programs. See also Violence Against Women; Displaced Homemakers' Services.

Anna Howard Shaw Center
745 Commonwealth Ave., Box 81
Boston, MA 02215
(617) 353-3075;
Fax: (617) 353-3061

A center at the Boston University School of Theology that promotes, structures, and practices the necessity to empower women and honor diversity. Primary goals are research, education, support, and advocacy.

Beltane Papers.

See Newspapers, Newsletters, and Magazines.

Black Women in Church and Society
Interdenominational Theological Center
671 Beckwith St. SW
Atlanta, GA 30314
(404) 527-7740

Provides activities and support for African American women involved in church and community efforts. Conducts research, sponsors charitable activities, and offers information on liberation and African American theology, feminism, and African American women's history. See also Organizations Representing Women of Color.

Campus Ministry Women
802 Monroe
Ann Arbor, MI 48104
(313) 662-5189

A network of Protestant, Catholic, and Jewish women advocating for and supporting women ministers at colleges and universities. Networks women ministers and offers programs and resources.

Catholics for a Free Choice.

See Health Organizations: Family Planning and Reproductive Rights.

Center for Women and Religion
Graduate Theological Union
2400 Ridge Rd.
Berkeley, CA 94709
(510) 649-2490;
Fax: (510) 649-1417

Works to end sexism and promote justice for women in religious institutions. Provides feminist curriculum resources, publications, and programs on women's spirituality, experience, and culture. Publishes Journal of Women & Religion.

Center of WEB
P.O. Box 175
Marchaug, MA 01526
(508) 476-7081

Holds women's spirituality circles. Advocates the reverence for the earth and teaches herbal medicine.

Church Women United
475 Riverside Dr., Rm. 812
New York, NY 10115
(212) 870-2347

An ecumenical movement for Protestant, Catholic, and other Christian women. Supports peace, human rights, and women's rights activities. Sponsors World Day of Prayer and World Community Day. Publishes newsletter.

Coalition on Women and Religion
4759 15th Ave. NE
Seattle, WA 98105
(206) 525–1213

Helps women affirm and expand their spirituality regardless of their beliefs. Encourages women to increase their influence in organized religions and to become aware of new forms of feminist spirituality that are beginning to evolve.

Conference for Catholic Lesbians
P.O. Box 436, Planetarium Sta.
New York, NY 10024
(718) 921-0463

A national organization of lesbians that encourages members to expand their spirituality while affirming their lesbian identity. Sponsors lectures, retreats, and conferences. Publishes a newsletter.

Covenant of the Goddess
P.O. Box 1107
Los Alamos, NM 87544

Promotes goddess-centered religion that recognizes the interconnectedness of all living things in nature. Publishes a newsletter.

Creative Jewish Women's Alliance
4856 Fern Creek Dr.
Rolling Hills East, CA 90274
(310) 378-3707

A support group for Jewish women in the arts. Promotes the publication and sale of their work and encourages inclusion of Jewish cultural, ethnic, and religious content in their work. Sponsors annual conferences on poetry and the arts with Hebrew Union College in Los Angeles.

Daughters of Sarah.
See Newspapers, Newsletters, and Magazines.

Eagle Song Camps/Sky Lodge
P.O. Box 121
Ovando, MT 59854
(406) 793-5730

Offers women and men a wilderness retreat for spiritual renewal and self-transformation. Uses ancient tools and rituals, such as sweat lodges, ceremonial art, drumming, chanting, and dancing to promote growth and healing.

Earth Spirit Women's Vision Quests.
See Recreation, Fitness, and Sports Groups.

Episcopal Women's Caucus
P.O. Box 5172
Laurel, MD 20726

An organization of Episcopal women working toward the full ministry of women and minorities in the church. Publishes a quarterly newsletter.

Evangelical and Ecumenical Women's Caucus International
P.O. Box 209
Hadley, NY 12835
(518) 696-2406

An educational and support organization for women that promotes that the Bible supports equality of the sexes. Concerned and involved in most women's issues and problems.

Feminist Spiritual Community
Box 3771
Portland, ME 04104
(207) 797-9217

A group of women of diverse ages, backgrounds, and sexual orientation that gathers to affirm spirituality, mark life's passages, and build a community based on women's experiences.

Gaia Bookstore.
See Booksellers: Bookstores.

Gifts of the Goddess
973 Valencia
San Francisco, CA 94110
(415) 647-8406

Offers classes and workshops on spirituality and rents space for workshops. Sells books on women's spirituality.

Golden Isis.
See Newspapers, Newsletters, and Magazines.

Grace and Goddess Unlimited
P.O. Box 4367
Boulder, CO 80306

Offers books and tapes celebrating feminist spirituality, natural healing, and the earth. Offers information on earth-based religions.

Grace of God Movement for the Women of the World
c/o 3HO Found.
1620 Preuss Rd.
Los Angeles, CA 90035
(213) 552-3416

Provides women with holistic techniques to have well-balanced, healthy, and holy lives. Provides information on yoga exercises, recipes, feminine health, vegetarian cooking, parenting, and relationships. Conducts annual training camp.

The Grail
932 O'Bannonville Rd.
Loveland, OH 45140
(513) 683-0202

An international organization of women rooted in the Christian faith. Mission is to further women's rights and build a universal society of justice, peace, and love.

Heart of the Goddess Wholistic Center and Gallery
10 Leopard Rd.
Berwyn, PA 19312
(215) 695-9494;
Fax: (215) 993-3345

A wholistic learning center and gallery that offers educational programs and resources to enhance personal growth, empowerment, and balanced leadership. Works to help women restore self-esteem, affirm beauty, and trust their instincts.

Institute of Women Today
7315 S Yale
Chicago, IL 60621
(312) 651-8372

An interfaith organization of women who are Protestant, Jewish, and Catholic. Uses resources to empower women to fulfill their needs for shelter, income, education, and employment. Emphasizes the religious roots of women's liberation. Publishes a newsletter.

Kadima
2318 2nd Ave., Box 7
Seattle, WA 98121
(206) 523-4790

A progressive feminist Jewish organization dedicated to the union of Jewish heritage and activism for a just and peaceful society. Participates in political activism, celebration of Jewish culture, and social activities.

Leadership Conference of Women Religious of the U.S.A.
8808 Cameron St.
Silver Spring, MD 20910
(301) 588-4955;
Fax: (301) 587-4575

Links religious organizations throughout the U.S. Sponsors activities and seminars on religious women and leadership in religious orders. Provides information, references, and research studies.

Luna Press.
See Presses and Publishers.

Morning Glory Collective
P.O. Box 1631
Tallahassee, FL 32302
(904) 222-8115

Promotes nature-based Goddess-centered feminist spirituality. Publishes a lunar calendar.

National Assembly of Religious Women
529 S Wabash Ave., #404
Chicago, IL 60605
(312) 663-1980;
Fax: (312) 663-9161

A grass-roots feminist organization of women of faith. Works for justice in society, church, and the world. Offers programs to deal with racism, classism, and sexism.

National Black Sisters' Conference
1001 Lawrence St. NE, Ste. 102
Washington, DC 20017
(202) 529-9250

Organizes and supports religious efforts of African American women. Addresses racism in society and church. Offers retreats, consulting, leadership, and cultural activities.

Of A Like Mind.
See Newspapers, Newsletters, and Magazines.

Presbyterian Women
100 Witherspoon St., Rm. 4608A
Louisville, KY 40202
(502) 569-5385;
Fax: (502) 569-5018

An organization that is part of Women's Advocacy (formerly known as Justice for Women). Addresses issues of feminism as it relates to Presbyterian theology.

Priests for Equality
P.O. Box 5243
West Hyattsville, MD 20782
(301) 779-9298

An organization of Catholic priests promoting equality for women in the Catholic Church and in society. Sponsors sociological studies and surveys and conducts research. See also Research Centers and Organizations.

Rainbow City Express.

See Newspapers, Newsletters, and Magazines.

Reclaiming Collective: Center for Feminist Spirituality
P.O. Box 14404
San Francisco, CA 94114
(510) 236-4645 (Events line)

A collective of San Francisco Bay area women and men working to unify spirit and politics. Offers classes, workshops, and public rituals designed to train voices, bodies, energy, intuition, and minds.

Reformed Church Women
475 Riverside Dr., Rm. 1825
New York, NY 10027
(212) 870-2844

Promotes fellowship and spirituality among women. Sponsors theological programs and leadership seminars.

Re-formed Congregation of the Goddess
P.O. Box 6021
Madison, WI 53716
(608) 255-5092

An international women's religion that fosters positive spiritual growth and provides a spiritual, ethical, and social structure to validate women's experience.

Religious Network for Equality for Women.

See Women's Rights.

Resource Center for Women and Ministry in the South, Incorporated
331 W Main St., Ste. 608
Durham, NC 27701
(919) 687-0408

Offers resources and programs on feminism, religion, and spirituality.

Sage Woman.

See Newspapers, Newsletters, and Magazines.

Shekhinah
Box 2991
Santa Cruz, CA 95063
(408) 423-7639

Holds spiritual concerts, workshops, and rituals for women.

Sisters United
118 W Sparks St.
Galena, KS 66739

Researches and writes on the ques-

*tion of the New Testament. Sup-
ports homosexuality.*

**Task Force on Equality of
Women in Judaism**
838 5th Ave.
New York, NY 10021
(212) 249-0100

*Promotes religious equality for wom-
en within Reform Judaism. Works to
eliminate sexism in the liturgy and
educational curriculum. Conducts
seminars and training programs.*

**Unitarian Universalist Women's
Federation**
130 Prospect St.
Cambridge, MA 02139

*Federation of women's groups and
individual women in local Unitarian Universalist churches. Sponsors
activities and educational forums
on human rights, reproductive
rights, child care, and equality for
women in religion. Publishes a
newsletter.*

**United Methodist Church
General Board of Global
Ministries Women's Division**
475 Riverside Dr., 15th Fl.
New York, NY 10115
(212) 870-3752

*A national organization working on
issues of women's rights and the
rights of the socially and economically oppressed. Works for racial
justice, women's leadership, and
education. See also* Women's
Rights; Special Interests.

**United Methodist Church
General Commission on the
Status and Role of Women**
1200 Davis St.
Evanston, IL 60201
(708) 869-7330

*Fosters awareness of women's is-
sues throughout the church. Addresses sexism and inequity in personnel, policies, and publications.*

Venus Adventures
P.O. Box 167
Peaks Island, ME 04108
(207) 766-5655

*Offers Goddess tours to sacred
sites in England and Ireland and
mythical tours to Greece and Crete.
Journeys offer fun, inspiration, and
education.*

We'Moon
P.O. Box 1395
Estacada, OR 97023
(503) 630-7848

*A spiritual community of lesbians
dedicated to living and working in
a healing way. Publishes an astrological moon calendar and daily
diary for women, as well as art and
writing from women all over the
world.*

**Women and Spirituality
Conference**
Mankato State Univ.
MSU Box 300, P.O. Box 8400
Mankato, MN 56002-8400
(507) 389-2077;
Fax: (507) 389-6377

Provides a supportive and nurturing setting for a dialogue of caring and mutual respect among women from many spiritual religious traditions.

Women Church Convergence
590 E Lockwood Ave.
St. Louis, MO 63119
(314) 962-8112

A coalition of national Catholic organizations that deals with women's empowerment issues in society and the church. Deals especially with combatting racism, classism, sexism, and discrimination in the church.

Women in Constant Creative Action
P.O. Box 5080
Eugene, OR 97405
(503) 345-6381

A women's incorporated church working to empower women in their spiritual life. Holds open celebrations, rituals, retreats, and classes designed to help women get in touch with their own gifts and the goddess within. Publishes a newsletter.

Women of Matriarchal Beliefs on Sacred Land (WOMLAND)
P.O. Box 55
Troy, ME 04987

A feminist spiritual organization committed to creating balance on Earth. Preserves, protects, and acquires land to ensure access to it by current and future generations of women and children. Offers land to groups and individuals for ecological, low-impact use such as spiritual retreat centers, camping retreats or gatherings, educational workshops, or international peace centers. See also Land Trusts.

Women's Alliance for Theology, Ethics, and Ritual
8035 13th St., Ste. 3
Silver Spring, MD 20910
(301) 589-2509

An educational center and network of people working for theological, ethical, and liturgical development for and by women. Offers projects, publications, workshops, retreats, and liturgical planning. Publishes a newsletter.

Women's Mysteries
156 Hunter St.
Kingston, NY 12401
(914) 338-5984;
Fax: (914) 338-5986

A year-long spiritual healing and intuitive arts program for women. Led by an author/psychotherapist.

Women's Ordination Conference
P.O. Box 2693
9653 Lee Hwy., Ste. 11
Fairfax, VA 22031
(703) 352-1006;
Fax: (703) 352-5181

An international grass-roots movement committed to the ordination of Roman Catholic women to the *priesthood. Works to create solidarity. Conducts workshops, seminars, and conferences and offers research and information. Publishes newsletter.*

Women's Spirituality Forum
P.O. Box 11363
Oakland, CA 94611

Works to promote women's spirituality and feminist awareness. Conducts classes, workshops, and seminars on women's history, shamanism, and spirituality. Performs rituals, memorials, and blessings.

Women's Studies in Religion
Harvard Divinity School, Rm. 205
45 Francis Ave.
Cambridge, MA 02138
(617) 495-5761

Offers advisors to help students select courses in the women's studies programs that pertain to religion. Also chooses five scholars each year to teach a particular class in religion.

Women's Theological Center
P.O. Box 1200
Boston, MA 02117
(617) 536-8782

A women's organization committed to transforming oppressive religious and social structures. Offers alternative theological education for women of varying religious traditions and spiritual paths, in addition to offering anti-racism consultations, workshops, and retreats. See also Women's Rights.

❑ Research Centers and Organizations

Alan Guttmacher Institute
111 5th Ave.
New York, NY 10003
(212) 254-5656

Researches and offers information on health issues related to reproduction, family planning, and contraception. Offers numerous publications. See also Health Organizations.

Alverno College Research Center on Women
3401 S 39th St.
Milwaukee, WI 53215
(414) 382-6084

Researches women's changing role in society. Approaches research with political, cultural, and psychological emphasis. Offers library resources and sponsors women's conference.

Barnard Center for Research on Women
3009 Broadway
New York, NY 10027-6598
(212) 854-2067

Researches on gender issues, in-cluding women's culture, art, and policy affecting women. Provides resources and information to researchers, writers, and artists. Sponsors conferences, lectures, and luncheons.

Brigham Young University Women's Research Institute
945 SWKT
Provo, UT 84602
(801) 378-4609

Researches women's studies and gender issues. See also Educational Services and Organizations.

Brown University Pembroke Center for Teaching and Research on Women
Alumnae Hall, Box 1958
194 Meeting St.
Providence, RI 02912
(401) 863-2643

Researches historical, social, and cultural issues pertaining to women. Offers curriculum guidance. See also Educational Services and Organizations.

Business and Professional Women's Foundation
Rawalt Resource Center
2012 Massachusetts Ave. NW
Washington, DC 20036
(202) 293-1200

Researches women's economic issues, awards fellowships, and maintains a library. See also Educational Services and Organizations.

Case Western Reserve University Perinatal Clinical Research Center
3395 Scranton Rd.
Cleveland, OH 44109
(216) 459-4246

Conducts studies on pregnancy and conditions affecting newborns and fetuses. Researches the role of exercise and nutrition in successful pregnancies. Holds conferences and maintains a library.

Center for Reproductive Law and Policy
120 Wall St.
New York, NY 10005
(212) 514-5534;
Fax: (212) 514-5538

Addresses and researches federal law and policy as related to women's reproductive rights, abortion, and sexual education programs. Sponsors public education programs, seminars, and workshops. See also Health Organizations.

Center for the Study of Anorexia and Bulimia
1 W 91st St.
New York, NY 10024

Researches the condition and treatment of anorexia, bulimia, and other eating disorders. Offers information, publications, lectures, seminars, and meetings. Conducts programs for community organizations and schools. See also Health Organizations.

Center for Women Policy Studies
2000 P St. NW, Ste. 508
Washington, DC 20036
(202) 872-1770

A research center focusing on the social and political status and role of women. Designs model legislation, sponsors policy seminars, and recommends public policy. See also Legal Services; Women's Rights.

City University of New York Center for the Study of Women and Society
33 W 42nd St.
New York, NY 10036
(212) 642-2954

Researches problems and issues of women's health and working conditions. Offers publications, conducts seminars, and sponsors conferences.

College of St. Catherine Abigail Quigley McCarthy Center for Women
2004 Randolph Ave.
St. Paul, MN 55105
(612) 690-6783;
Fax: (612) 690-6024

Researches on women in the Cath-

olic tradition. Sponsors an awards program for new findings.

Columbia University Institute for Research on Women and Gender
763 Schermerhorn Ext.
New York, NY 10027
(212) 854-3277

Researches on gender issues. Focuses on issues of economically disadvantaged and minority women.

Duke-UNC Center for Research on Women
Univ. of North Carolina
Caldwell Hall
P.O. Box 90719
Durham, NC 27708-3135
(919) 684-6641

Researches women's issues. Uses findings to develop curricula and women's programs. Offers publications, seminars, and conferences.

Equity Policy Center
2000 P Street NW, #508
Washington, DC 20036
(202) 872-1770

Conducts research on how changing working conditions, labor issues, and home/work relationships affect men and women around the world.

Feminist Institute, Incorporated
P.O. Box 30563
Bethesda, MD 20824
(301) 951-9040

An organization promoting femi-nism worldwide through policymaking, education, research and social action. Projects focus on furthering women's equal treatment and autonomy in such areas as women's equal rights and violence prevention. Also seeks to retrieve women's history. Hosts a feminist walking tour of Capitol Hill.

Feminist Press at the City University of New York
311 E 94th St.
New York, NY 10128
(212) 360-5790

Researches women's education and equity issues. Conducts programs to examine the status and treatment of women in colleges and universities. Offers publications, sponsors programs, and maintains a library. See also Health Organizations.

George Washington University Women's Studies Program and Policy Center
Funger Hall 217
2201 G St. NW
Washington, DC 20052
(202) 994-6942

Researches public policy and its impact on women's issues. Addresses economic, educational, family, and social issues.

Hartford College for Women, Office of Women's Research
260 Girard Ave.
Hartford, CT 06105
(203) 236-1215

Studies gender and public policy.

Sponsors seminars and research forums.

Harvard University Women's Studies in Religion Program

Harvard Divinity School
45 Francis Ave.
Cambridge, MA 02138
(617) 495-5705

Studies gender issues in religious traditions. Assesses religious, social, and cultural issues of women. Publishes essays and offers seminars.

Humphrey Institute Center on Women and Public Policy

University of Minnesota
301 19th Ave. S
Minneapolis, MN 55455
(612) 625-4335;
Fax: (612) 625-6351

A teaching, research, and outreach center devoted to women's policy issues. Researches women's rights and issues worldwide. See also Global Feminism and World Peace; Women's Rights.

Institute for Feminist Studies

988 Market St., #609
San Francisco, CA 94102
(415) 922-3837

Provides assistance for research projects.

Institute for Women's Policy Research

1400 20th St. NW, Ste. 104
Washington, DC 20036
(202) 785-5100;
Fax: (202) 833-4362

Researches a wide range of women's issues as they affect policies about women. Through their work with legislators, women's groups, and historians, the institute provides findings that are sensitive to class, race, and ethnicity on topics such as family welfare, employment and careers, and women's health. These perspectives are implemented in national policy debates. Also holds forums to bring together activists, advocates, researchers, and policymakers to work on women's issues. IWPR is an independent, nonprofit organization funded through foundation grants and other contributions. See also Women's Rights.

International Center for Research on Women

1717 Massachusetts Ave. NW, 302
Washington, DC 20036
(202) 797-0007

Researches economic, political, and health concerns of women in developing countries. Studies centered on the environment, disease, nutrition, agriculture, family, and financial issues related to women. Offers publications, sponsors fellowships, and maintains a library. See also Global Feminism and World Peace.

Kent State University Project for the Study of Gender and Education

405 White Hall
Kent, OH 44242
(216) 672-2178

Researches the impact of gender on education.

League of Women Voters Education Fund
1730 M St. NW
Washington, DC 20036
(202) 429-1965

Researches political and governmental issues as they relate to women. Offers publications and sponsors meetings and leadership training. See also Political Groups.

Medical College of Pennsylvania Center for the Mature Woman
3300 Henry Ave.
Philadelphia, PA 19129
(215) 842-7180

Researches health issues concerning older women. See also Special Interests; Health Organizations.

Memphis State University Center for Research on Women
Clement Hall-339
Memphis, TN 38152
(901) 678-2770

Researches issues concerning Southern women and women of color in America. Examines roles of gender, class, and social inequity. Offers publications and sponsors workshops. See also Organizations Representing Women of Color.

Michigan State University Women and International Development Program
202 Center for International Programs
East Lansing, MI 48824
(517) 353-5040

Researches international women's issues. Focuses on the role of women in developing countries and issues of labor, politics, and economy as related to women. Offers publications, sponsors seminars and study groups, and holds conferences.

National Center on Women and Family Law
799 Broadway, Rm. 402
New York, NY 10003
(212) 674-8200

Researches family law, crime and violence, spouse abuse, battery, custody, child support, marital rape, and divorce. Offers publications and maintains a reference collection. See also Legal Services; Women's Rights; Violence Against Women.

National Council for Research on Women
The Sara Delano Roosevelt Memorial House
530 Broadway, 10th Fl.
New York, NY 10012
(212) 274-0730

A coalition of seventy centers and organizations that supports and researches feminist issues, public policies, and educational programs for women. Serves as a bridge connect-

ing scholarship and action. Publishes directories, makes referrals, and networks groups and individuals. See also Educational Services and Organizations; Presses and Publishers.

National Institute for Women of Color
624 9th St. NW
Washington, DC 20036
(202) 296-2661

Researches issues related to women of color, especially education, demographic trends, and gender. Publishes a resource packet on reproductive freedom for women of color. See also Organizations Representing Women of Color.

National Museum of Women in the Arts, Library and Research Center
1250 New York Ave. NW
Washington, DC 20005
(202) 783-5000

Conducts research on women in the arts. See also Art and Media.

National Women's Law Center The Women's Research and Education Institute
1616 P St. NW, #100
Washington, DC 20036
(202) 328-5150

An independent, national public policy research center concerned with issues affecting women. Provides policymakers with data, research, and policy analyses on key

issues for women. See also Women's Rights; Legal Services.

National Women's Studies Association
Univ. of Maryland
College Park, MD 20742-1325
(301) 405-5573

An organization that networks and promotes women's studies programs. Offers funding for research on women's issues. Holds conferences on curriculum development, trends in global feminism, and new research on race and gender issues. Offers scholarships and maintains a library.

Ohio State University Center for Women's Studies
207 Dulles Hall
230 W 17th Ave.
Columbus, OH 43210-1311
(614) 292-1021

Researches issues related to gender, culture, and history. Offers research grants and publications and sponsors lectures.

Radcliffe College Henry A. Murray Research Center
10 Garden St.
Cambridge, MA 02138
(617) 495-8140

Supports research on women. Offers publications and sponsors workshops and conferences.

Rocky Mountain Women's Institute
Foote Hall, Rm. 317
7150 Montview Blvd.
Denver, CO 80220
(303) 871-6923

Focuses on research dealing with women's art and humanities. Offers awards and education programs. Sponsors public lectures, seminars, and exhibits. See also Art and Media.

Russell Sage College Helen Upton Center for Women's Studies
90 1st St.
Troy, NY 12180
(518) 270-2306

Researches women and education. Offers publications, sponsors workshops, and maintains a library.

Rutgers University Center for the American Woman and Politics
Eagleton Institute of Politics
New Brunswick, NJ 08901
(908) 932-9384

Researches women's political participation and the impact of women in political office. Offers publications and maintains a library. See also Women's Rights.

Rutgers University Institute for Research on Women, Douglass College
27 Clifton Ave.
New Brunswick, NJ 08903
(908) 932-9072

Studies gender integration and curricular reform, reproductive laws, women and war and peace, feminist theory, and women's leadership. Offers publications and sponsors seminars.

Smith College Project on Women and Social Change
138 Elm St.
Northampton, MA 01063
(413) 585-3591

Studies women's health, political, and development issues. See also Global Feminism and World Peace; Science and Technology.

Spelman College Women's Research and Resource Center
Box 115
Atlanta, GA 30314
(404) 681-3643

Researches issues related to African American women. Focuses on humanities, education, and health. Offers publications and sponsors conferences, seminars, and workshops. See also Women's Rights; Organizations Representing Women of Color.

Stanford University Institute for Research on Women and Gender
Serra House
Serra St.
Stanford, CA 94305-8640
(415) 723-1994

Studies women and gender issues. Researches women's history, changing cultural significances of women's experiences, social standards for women, and women's health issues. Sponsors a lecture series, special seminars, and workshops and maintains a library collection. See also Women's Rights.

State University of New York at Albany Institute for Research on Women
Dept. of Sociology, SS 326
1400 Washington Ave.
Albany, NY 12222
(518) 442-4815

Researches women's issues. Sponsors international conferences and workshops. See also Global Feminism and World Peace.

Tulane University Newcomb College Center for Research on Women
1229 Broadway
New Orleans, LA 70118
(504) 865-5238

Researches Southern women's experiences and social impacts, as well as women's education.

University of Arizona Southwest Institute for Research on Women
102 Douglass Bldg.
Tucson, AZ 85721
(602) 621-7338

Researches women in the southwest United States, both past and present. Focuses on multicultural issues, education, and regional women's concerns. Offers publications and sponsors conferences.

University of California, Berkeley
Beatrice M. Bain Research Group
2539 Channing Way, Rm. 19
Berkeley, CA 94720
(415) 643-7172

Studies women and gender issues. Sponsors conferences, lectures, symposia, and colloquia.

University of California, Davis Women's Resources and Research Center
10 Lower Freeborn
Davis, CA 95616
(916) 752-3372

Studies women's issues. Offers publications and educational programs. See also Women's Rights.

University of California, Los Angeles Center for the Study of Women
236A Kinsey Hall
405 Hilgard Ave.
Los Angeles, CA 90024-1504

Studies women as related to health, violence, racism, history, arts, and education. Offers publications and holds seminars.

University of Cincinnati Women's Studies Research and Resources Institute
Center for Women's Studies
155 McMicken Hall
Cincinnati, OH 45221-0164
(513) 556-6654

Studies feminism and women's his-

tory. Gears projects toward cultural, political, and social impacts and achievements of women. Develops nonsexist, nonracist, and multicultural curricula for primary and secondary schools.

University of Connecticut Institute for the Study of Women and Gender
U-181
Stoors, CT 06268-1181
(203) 486-2186;
Fax: (503) 486-4789

Researches gender in education, technology, politics, and labor.

University of Minnesota Center for Advanced Feminist Studies
496 Ford Hall
224 Church St. SE
Minneapolis, MN 55455
(612) 624-6310

Studies gender roles and women's history. Offers publications and internships.

University of Minnesota Women, Public Policy, and Development Project
Humphrey Institute of
Public Affairs
301 19th Ave. S
Minneapolis, MN 55455
(612) 625-2505

A research policy center focusing on women's roles in society and education. Promotes women's equity and supports women's organiza-

tions. Sponsors meetings and maintains a library.

University of Mississippi Sarah Isom Center for Women's Studies
University, MS 38677
(601) 232-5916

Researches women and women's issues, with a focus on southern women.

University of Oregon Center for the Study of Women in Society
Eugene, OR 97403
(503) 346-5015

Studies women and gender issues. Offers publications, research support, and lectures that are open to the public.

University of Pennsylvania Alice Paul Research Center for the Study of Women
3440 Market, #590
Philadelphia, PA 19104
(215) 898-8740

Researches gender issues and women in the humanities.

University of Southern California Institute for the Study of Women and Men
734 W Adams Blvd., 208
Los Angeles, CA 90007
(213) 743-3683

Conducts gender studies in the areas of sexuality, society, and edu-

cation. Emphasizes feminine images in the media. See also Art and Media.

University of Texas at Arlington Women and Minority Work Research and Resource Center
Box 19129
Arlington, TX 76019
(817) 273-3131

Studies women and work, focusing on family issues, women entrepreneurs, child care, and sexism.

University of Tulsa Research in Women's Literature
600 S College
Tulsa, OK 74104
(918) 631-2503

Studies women's literature and history. Sponsors lectures and maintains a library. See also Women's History.

University of Washington Northwest Center for Research on Women
AJ-50
Seattle, WA 98195
(206) 543-9531

Researches women's issues in science, education, and society.

University of Wisconsin Women's Studies Research Center
209 N Brooks St.
Madison, WI 53715
(608) 263-2051

Studies feminist theory, public pol-

icy, women's mental and physical health, and women's history. Offers publications, holds lectures, sponsors grants, and maintains a library collection.

Utah State University Women and Gender Research Institute
Logan, UT 84322-3555
(801) 750-2376

Conducts research and prepares analysis on gender issues ranging from education and development to history and humanities.

Washington State University Women's Resource and Research Center
Pullman, WA 99164-7204
(509) 335-6830

Conducts gender studies and researches women's history and the feminist movement.

Wellesley College Center for Research on Women
828 Washington St.
Wellesley, MA 02181
(617) 431-1453

Researches women's issues as related to public policy, education, child care, science, and employment. Conducts seminars and colloquia.

Women's History Research Center
2325 Oak St.
Berkeley, CA 94708
(510) 524-1582

Maintains a microfilm library on marital and date rape, women and health, women and law, women's herstory, and more. Available for order by libraries and individuals.

Women's Institute for Freedom of the Press
3306 Ross Pl. NW
Washington, DC 20008
(202) 966-7783

Monitors and researches the role of women in the media, and the impact of media monopolies in limit-ing public discourse about women's issues and concerns.

Women's Research and Education Institute
1700 18th St. NW, Ste. 400
Washington, DC 20009
(202) 328-7070

Studies public policy as it relates to women. Links legislators and women's research and policy centers. Offers publications and conferences and maintains a clipping file on issues of interest to women. See also Women's Rights.

❏ Science and Technology

American Association for the Advancement of Science National Network of Women in Science
Office of Opportunities in Science
1333 H St. NW
Washington, DC 20005
(202) 326-6670

An education and advocacy organization working to promote women and minorities interested in science and engineering. Offers publications, information workshops, and career materials.

American Mathematical Society Joint Committee on Women in the Mathematical Sciences
Dept. of Mathematics,
Texas A&M Univ.
College Station, TX 77843
(409) 845-7531

Advocates full equality for women in the mathematical sciences. Identifies injustices and offers remedies. Studies and provides information on gender roles in mathematics and the history of women in mathematics. See also Women's History.

American Meteorological Society, Board on Women and Minorities
45 Beacon St.
Boston, MA 02108
(617) 227-2425;
Fax: (617) 742-8718

Offers information, education, and scholarships to women interested in meteorology.

Association for Women Geoscientists
10200 W 44th Ave., Ste. 304
Wheat Ridge, CO 80033
(303) 422-8527

An organization of women working or interested in geology or related fields. Encourages and promotes the participation of women in these fields. Conducts workshops and seminars on career development. See also Work, Union, and Career Services.

Association for Women in Science
1522 K Street NW, Ste. 820
Washington, DC 20005
(202) 408-0742;
Fax: (202) 408-8321

A membership organization seeking to encourage the participation of women and girls in all areas of science and to advance their educational and employment opportunities. Publishes newsletters, offers a guide to grants, and issues career guides and employment information. See also Newspapers, Newsletters, and Magazines.

Equals Project.

See Educational Services and Organizations.

Math/Science Interchange
c/o Department of Mathematics
Loyola Marymount Univ.
Los Angeles, CA 90045
(310) 338-2774

A volunteer organization dedicated to increasing the participation of women in math- and science-related fields. Works to increase awareness of young women about math and science in high school. Organizes an annual math and science career day for junior high school girls.

Math/Science Network
Preservation Park
678 13th St., Ste. 100
Oakland, CA 94612
(510) 893-6284

Works to further the education and career opportunities open to women in the fields of science and mathematics. Offers information

and materials on issues relating to women in math and science.

National Academy of Sciences, Committee on Women in Science and Engineering
2102 Constitution Ave. NW,
Rm. GR412
Washington, DC 20418
(202) 334-2709

Works to increase participation of women in the sciences and engineering.

National Network of Minority Women in Science
c/o American Association for the Advancement of Science
1333 H St. NW
Washington, DC 20005
(202) 326-6670

Seeks to increase the number and quality of minority women in science fields. Develops curriculum material to aid math and science education and career awareness. Offers networking opportunities, publications, conferences, seminars, and workshops.

National Science Foundation, Women's Programs Section
4201 Wilson Blvd.
Arlington, VA 22230
(703) 306-1637

Serves to enhance the participation of women in all areas of science and engineering. Supports careers and educational opportunities and disseminates information.

New York Academy of Science, Women in Science Committee
2 E 63rd St.
New York, NY 10021
(212) 838-0230
An organization concerned with the rights of women scientists. Offers workshops on various professional topics. See also Women's Rights.

Operation Smart
Girls Inc.
30 E 33rd St.
New York, NY 10016
(212) 683-1253
Encourages girls to pursue careers in math, science, and technology.

Women in Energy
555 N Kensington
La Grange Park, IL 70525
(708) 352-3746;
Fax: (708) 352-0499
An organization for women working in science, engineering, and related fields. Offers information, seminars, workshops, and exhibits, as well as tours of energy facilities.

Women in Science and Engineering Programs
School of Engineering and Computer Science
Cal State Univ.
Northridge, CA 91330
(818) 885-2146;
Fax: (818) 885-2140

A university-based program that sponsors activities designed to promote the recruitment and retention of women in science and engineering.

Women in Technology Project
Vermont Technical College
Randolph Center, VT 05061
(802) 728-3391;
Fax: (802) 728-3321

Encourages young women to choose careers in technology and to take the math and science courses in high school that are required for most technical degrees. Offers programs for school-age children.

Women's Technical Institute
1255 Boylston St.
Boston, MA 02215
(617) 266-2243

Offers hands-on programs in five different career paths, including electronics, computer repair, computer networking, biomedical, and drafting.

❏ Special Interests

ANIMAL RIGHTS GROUPS

Feminists for Animal Rights
P.O. Box 694 Cathedral Sta.
New York, NY 10025
(212) 866-6422

An organization working to raise the consciousness of the feminist community, the animal rights community, and the general public about the connections between the objectification, exploitation, and abuse of women and animals in patriarchal society.

Women for Animal Rights
Empowerment Vegetarian Activist
Collective
616 6th St., No. 2
Brooklyn, NY 11215
(718) 788-1362

An organization of individuals interested in the preservation and conservation of animals and the environment. Offers information and educational materials. Conducts research, maintains an archive of slides, and offers a student intern program.

ECONOMICALLY DISADVANTAGED SERVICES

**Arise for Social Justice,
Incorporated**
718 State St.
Springfield, MA 01013
(413) 788-6668;
Fax: (413) 781-3712

A low-income rights and advocacy membership organization. Works to educate low-income people about

their rights. See also Women's Rights.

**Bay Area Women's Resource
Center**
318 Leavenworth
San Francisco, CA 94102
(415) 474-2400;
Fax: (415) 474-5525

Conducts direct services, advocacy, and policy work on issues of low-income and homeless women, children, and families. See also Displaced Homemakers' Services.

National Center for Policy Alternatives Women's Economic Justice Center
1875 Connecticut Ave. NW, Ste. 710
Washington, DC 20009
(202) 387-6030;
Fax: (202) 986-2539

Conducts research and provides recommendations on public policy issues affecting disadvantaged women. Offers ideas to legislators and advocates on the state level, sponsors roundtable discussions, and creates a network whereby individuals can exchange ideas on topics ranging from abortion rights to economic self-sufficiency for women. See also Research Centers and Organizations.

Survival News
102 Anawan Ave.
W. Roxbury, MA 02132
(617) 327-4219

A newsletter advocating on the rights of the economically disadvantaged.

Welfare Warriors
4504 N 47
Milwaukee, WI 53218
(414) 444-0220

A multiracial group of local mothers. Has a mother's helpline and support groups for mothers and grandmothers who have had their children removed from their homes by child protective services. Publishes a quarterly bilingual journal for welfare mothers.

Women, Work, and Welfare Reform Coalition
3255 S Hennepin, #119
Minneapolis, MN 55408
(612) 822-6265;
Fax: (612) 827-6433

A welfare rights membership organization dedicated to organizing the economically disadvantaged in Minnesota, providing public education, and working toward building a diverse social movement toward political, economic, and social justice.

ENVIRONMENTAL GROUPS

EVE, Ecofeminists Emerging
402 W 46 St., #3W
New York, NY 10036
(212) 315-3107

Publishes a newsletter. Focuses on environmental concerns from a feminist perspective. Recognizes a connection between patriarchal dominance and control over the natural world and the male dominance over women.

Women in Touch
Box 3541
Nashua, NH 03061
(603) 883-9228

An environmental group for lesbians. Promotes networking activities and political events to work for a chemical-free environment.

Women's Council on Energy and the Environment
P.O. Box 33211
Washington, DC 20033
(202) 822-6755;
Fax: (202) 328-5002

Advocacy and education membership organization concerned with issues of energy and the environment. Sponsors programs, provides speakers, and promotes the professional development of women interested in energy and environmental issues.

Women's Environment and Development Organization
845 Third Ave., 15th Fl.
New York, NY 10022
(212) 759-7982;
Fax: (212) 759-8647

An international organization that works toward improving the environment, developing social justice, and advocating equality for women. The group monitors the implementation of international commitments to the environment, provides leadership and advocacy-training workshops, and offers information through publications, computer networking, and videos. See also Global Feminism and World Peace; Women's Rights.

World Women in the Environment
WorldWIDE Network
1331 H St. NW, #903
Washington, DC 20005
(202) 347-1514;
Fax: (202) 347-1524

An organization designed to help women share information and create solutions for environmental problems. Provides information to individuals, groups, and policymakers about the connection between women, natural resources, and sustainable development. Seeks to advance women's status in environ-

mental programs and law making. Publishes a directory and holds

a global assembly. See also Global Feminism and World Peace.

NETWORKING SERVICES

Greater Boston Women's Yellow Pages
P.O. Box 795
N. Scituate, MA 02060
(617) 545-9141

An annual directory of women's businesses and service organizations.

Greater Phoenix Women's Yellow Pages
4425 N Saddlebag Trail
Scottsdale, AZ 85251
(602) 945-5000

Lists and describes women's service organizations as well as businesses owned by women. Published annually.

Indiana Women's Yellow Pages
5241 Fountain Dr., #1
Crown Point, IN 46307
(219) 985-1120;
Fax: (219) 985-1121

A woman's business producing a monthly newspaper, yearly directory, and special events for women in Indiana and Illinois.

Louisiana Women's Yellow Pages
P.O. Box 4301
Lafayette, LA 70502
(318) 233-5075
Annual directory of women's orga-

nizations and businesses in the state.

National Council for Research on Women
Publications Division
530 Broadway, 10th Fl.
New York, NY 10012-3920
(212) 274-0730;
Fax: (212) 274-0821

Publishes several directories to enable networking. These include directories of national women's organizations and of women's media groups, as well as a directory of women's mailing lists.

Women in Business Yellow Pages of Metro Chicago
7358 N Lincoln, #150
Chicago, IL 60646
(708) 679-7800

An annual directory of business and professional women.

Women's Information Exchange National Women's Mailing List
P.O. Box 68
Jenner, CA 95450
(707) 632-5763;
Fax: (707) 632-5589

A computer database of feminists and feminist organizations. Provides tailored mailing lists to wom-

en's programs and progressive organizations. Allows grass-roots
feminist organizations to communicate by direct mail to thousands of
women who are interested in and
supportive of their work.

Women's Yellow Pages
Women's Business Network
P.O. Box 66093
Los Angeles, CA 90066
(213) 398-5761

Annual comprehensive directory of
women's businesses and service organizations in the greater Los Angeles area.

Women's Yellow Pages
1427 27th Ave.
Seattle, WA 98122
(206) 726-9687

An annual directory that allows
women to locate the women-owned
businesses and women's service organizations in the Seattle area.

**Women's Yellow Pages Directory
of Greater Kansas City**
10308 Metcalf, #178
Overland Park, KS 66212
(913) 341-4940

Lists women's businesses and professional women as well as organizations working on women's issues.

**Women's Yellow Pages of
Greater Atlanta**
P.O. Box 687
Alpharetta, GA 30239
(404) 772-0050;
Fax: (404) 442-8239

A directory of women's products
and services. Also sponsors EX-
CEL, a showcase for women in
business.

**Women's Yellow Pages of
Greater Cleveland**
983 Milridge Rd.
Highland Heights, OH 44143
(216) 449-1371

A directory of women's businesses,
professional women, and organizations.

**Women's Yellow Pages of
Greater Milwaukee**
P.O. Box 13827
Milwaukee, WI 53213
(414) 789-1346

Comprehensive directory, published
annually.

**Women's Yellow Pages of
Greater Mobile, Alabama**
P.O. Box 6021
Mobile, AL 36607
(205) 473-5320

Annual directory of organizations
serving women's interests and of
women-owned businesses in the
Mobile area.

**Women's Yellow Pages of
Greater Philadelphia**
P.O. Box 1002
Philadelphia, PA 19083
(215) 446-4747

A directory of women-owned businesses and services directed toward

women. Listings encompass the Delaware Valley.

Women's Yellow Pages of Maryland
2238 Bay Ridge Ave.
Annapolis, MD 21403
(410) 267-0886

Statewide directory of women's organizations and businesses.

Women's Yellow Pages of Oklahoma
P.O. Box 54475
Oklahoma City, OK 73154
(405) 524-7020;
Fax: (405) 524-9420

A directory of women-owned businesses and businesses that market to women. Also sponsors the Working Women's Fair, the largest women's networking event in Oklahoma. The directory's resource guide offers free listings to community organizations that provide free or sliding-scale services to women in need.

Women's Yellow Pages of Portland
1070 SW Portola Ave.
Portland, OR 97225

An annual directory of women's businesses and organizations.

OLDER WOMEN'S SERVICES

American Association of Retired Persons
Women's Activities
1909 K Street NW
Washington, DC 20049
(202) 434-2642

A group within the highly visible AARP that supports and lobbies for policies, programs, and legislation that provide increased benefits and opportunities for women entering midlife and beyond. Concerned with short and long-term health care issues, pension reform, social security, and employment practices.

Broomstick.
See Newspapers, Newsletters, and Magazines.

Crone Chronicles.
See Newspapers, Newsletters, and Magazines.

Forty Upward Network
16915 Detroit Ave.
Lakewood, OH 44107
(216) 521-8400

An organization of divorced, widowed, or never-married women. Provides support, affirmation, and reinforcement of the personal validity of single women. Offers education on financial and retirement planning and sponsors discussions, meetings, seminars, travel and social activities.

Grandmothers for Peace International.

See Global Feminism and World Peace.

Midlife Women's Network
5129 Logan Ave. S
Minneapolis, MN 55419
(612) 925-0020

Provides a range of services to midlife women in transition.

National Action Forum for Midlife and Older Women
Box 816
Stony Brook, NY 11790

Works to improve the quality of life for women over forty. Offers public education on older women's issues and provides national and international networking activities and central resource exchange for those with interests in issues affecting older women.

National Center for Women and Retirement Research
Long Island Univ.
Southampton Campus
Southampton, NY 11968
(800) 426-7386;
Fax: (516) 283-4678

Researches the way older women are affected by health, financial concerns, life after retirement, divorce, and other personal and relationship matters. Compiles books, provides videos and cassettes, and prepares materials for seminars. Publishes a quarterly newsletter.

See also Research Centers and Organizations.

Older Women's League
666 11th St. NW, #700
Washington, DC 20001
(202) 783-6686;
Fax: (202) 638-2356

A national membership organization whose sole mission is to advocate for the rights of midlife and older women. Focuses on economic and social equity for women as they age and often outlive family support systems and savings. Offers publications, education, and mutual support on health care, pensions, and social security. Has nearly 20,000 members in more than 120 chapters in 37 states.

Options for Women Over Forty
3543 18 St., Box 6
San Francisco, CA 94110
(415) 431-6405

Offers programs and services to older women, primarily in the area of employment.

Outdoor Vacations for Women Over 40.

See Recreation, Fitness, and Sports Groups.

Spinsterhaven, Incorporated
P.O. Box 718
Fayetteville, AR 72702

Creates and maintains community homes for aging women and women with disabilities.

Supportive Older Women's Network
2805 N 47th St.
Philadelphia, PA 19131
(215) 477-6000

Offers weekly support groups for women over age sixty in the Philadelphia area. These groups meet in a variety of community locations. Has also developed a manual for a model program that is being offered nationally.

Thanks Be to Grandmother Winifred Foundation.

See Foundations and Funding Sources.

U.S. House of Representatives Select Committee on Aging Task Force on Social Security and Women
Washington, DC 20515
(202) 225-5871

Concerned with retirement income as it relates to women.

Vintage '45 Press.

See Booksellers: Mail-Order Book Distributors.

We Are Visible
P.O. Box 1494
Mendocino, CA 95406
(707) 964-2756

A feminist publication for women fifty-five years and older. Includes news, editorials, reviews, and drawings on growing old.

Women's Needs Center
A Women's Midlife Resource Center
1825 Haight St.
San Francisco, CA 94117
(415) 487-5607

Offers health information and services to midlife women. Provides menopause information and support.

PHYSICALLY CHALLENGED SERVICES

Disabled Professional Woman of the Year
Pilot International
P.O. Box 4844
244 College St.
Macon, GA 31213
(912) 743-7403;
Fax: (912) 743-2173

Selects outstanding executive or professional women in the U.S. and Canada to recognize the achievements of physically challenged women.

Disabled Women's Theater Project.

See Art and Media: Film, Radio, and Television.

Dykes, Disability & Stuff.
See Newspapers, Newsletters, and Magazines.

Educational Equity Concepts.
See Educational Services and Organizations.

Hikane: The Capable Womon.
See Newspapers, Newsletters, and Magazines.

Kid's Project/Squeaky Wheels Anthology.
See Presses and Publishers.

National Clearinghouse on Women and Girls with Disabilities
Educational Equity Concepts
114 E 32nd St., Rm. 701
New York, NY 10016
(212) 725-1803

Offers information and materials dealing with issues and services for women with disabilities. Offers numerous publications.

National Deaf Women's Bowling Association.
See Recreation, Fitness, and Sports Groups.

Networking Project for Disabled Women and Girls
c/o YWCA of the City of New York
610 Lexington Ave.
New York, NY 10022
(212) 735-9767

Works to increase educational, social, and career opportunities of adolescent girls with disabilities by linking them to successful, disabled role models. Provides support groups, offers advocacy training, and mentoring.

Project on Women and Disability
1 Ashburton Pl., Rm. 1305
Boston, MA 02108
(617) 727-7440;
Fax: (617) 727-0965

A community organization serving women whose lives have been affected by disability. Works to eliminate sexism and disability bias and to promote women with disabilities as equal and active members of the community. Provides information and referrals, community building and training, and a quarterly journal.

Womyn's Braille Press
P.O. Box 8475
Minneapolis, MN 55408
(612) 872-4352

A publishing company that produces feminist and lesbian books and periodicals on tape and in Braille for readers who are blind or print-disabled. See also Presses and Publishers.

Wry Crips Disabled Women's Theater.
See Art and Media: Theater.

PRISONERS' SERVICES

Aid to Incarcerated Mothers
95 Berkeley St., Ste. 410
Boston, MA 02116
(617) 695-1588

*Offers a wide range of programs
and services to help women prisoners and their children.*

Genesis II for Women
3036 University Ave. SE
Minneapolis, MN 55414
(612) 348-2762;
Fax: (612) 348-6983

*Day treatment services for women
offenders and their children including therapy, parent education, child
care, education, and career development. All clients are referred
from family or criminal court.*

Institute of Women Today
7315 S Yale
Chicago, IL 60621
(312) 651-8372

*A service organization that pro-
vides legal services to incarcerated
women. Also runs two shelters for
homeless women and kids.*

**Legal Services for Women with
Children**
1535 Mission St., 2nd Fl.
San Francisco, CA 94103
(415) 255-7036

*Refers individuals to direct legal
services, provides information to
inmates, and works with policymakers.*

Program for Female Offenders
Penn/Library Pl.
520 Penn Ave.
Pittsburgh, PA 15222
(412) 642-7380;
Fax: (412) 642-9118

*Helps women who have been in-
volved in the criminal justice system or have substance abuse
problems. Provides residential and
community alternatives to incarceration by offering employment services and counseling and case
management. See also* Legal Services.

**Wish List: Samaritan Women
Prison Project**
730 Columbus Ave., #187
New York, NY 10025
(212) 865-7977;
Fax: (212) 865-0017

*Provides case management and
supportive services to incarcerated,
recently released, and paroled
women who are infected with the
HIV/AIDS virus. Services include
legal and housing advocacy, enti-
tlements and benefits, and support
and counseling services. See also*
Health Organizations.

**Women's Opportunity Resources
Center**
50 Clinton St., Ste. 100
Hempstead, NY 11550
(516) 483-0336;
Fax: (516) 483-4387

An educational and vocational skills program for female offenders. Requires a minimum of six months participation. Includes personal counseling as well as academic and job readiness training.

Women's Prison Association
110 Second Ave.
New York, NY 10003
(212) 674-1163; Fax: (212) 677-1981

Assists women in making the transition from incarceration to independent living in the community.

REFUGEES AND FOREIGN-BORN WOMEN SERVICES

See also Global Feminism and World Peace.

Advocates for Immigrant Women.

See Violence Against Women.

Cosmopolitan Associates
P.O. Box 1491
West Caldwell, NJ 07007
(201) 992-2232

An association of foreign-born women living in the U.S. Serves as a support and social network for its members. Helps women maintain ties with their countries of birth.

Refugee Women in Development, Incorporated
810 First St. NW, Ste. 300
Washington, DC 20002
(202) 289-1104

Helps meet the economic, social, and cultural needs of third-world women who have immigrated to the U.S. Serves to settle women in their new environment, find employment, and feel secure. Addresses eco-nomic self-sufficiency, health, child care, and domestic violence, and tries to recognize and develop leadership in refugee communities through education.

Refugee Women's Alliance
3004 S Alaska St.
Seattle, WA 98108
(206) 721-6243;
Fax: (206) 721-6282

A nonprofit multiservice agency that helps refugee women achieve self-sufficiency in America. Provides educational and support services and networking opportunities.

Refugee Women's Association of Metro Atlanta
149 Peachtree Cir., #1
Atlanta, GA 30309
(404) 875-3862

Serves as an education advocacy organization. Programs include language partnership mentorship, economic improvement, and public relations.

SOCIAL AND VOLUNTEER CLUBS

Women's clubs engage in volunteer services and social activities. Women in these clubs sponsor charitable activities, competitions, or bestow awards, projects to beautify the community, support the arts, etc. The following is a list of the national associations.

Association of Junior Leagues International
1319 F Street NW, Ste. 604
Washington, DC 20004
(202) 393-3364;
Fax: (202) 393-4517

Main headquarters of this well-known women's organization that is dedicated to serving and improving local communities. It promotes the spirit of volunteerism and advocates training people to serve as volunteers to achieve results. Programs focus on teenage pregnancy prevention, improvements in education, and general child welfare issues. Other programs address child care, family and medical leave, and domestic violence. Local chapters can be found in every state.

Drifters.

See Organizations Representing Women of Color.

General Federation of Women's Clubs
1734 N Street NW
Washington, DC 20036-2990
(202) 347-3168;
Fax: (202) 835-0246

Members are women's clubs across the country and around the world. Regional clubs help to promote education, preserve natural resources, stress good citizenship, contribute to world peace, and participate in the arts through volunteer services. See also Global Feminism and World Peace.

Soroptomist International
1616 Walnut St., Ste. 700
Philadelphia, PA 19103
(215) 732-0572

A large service organization whose membership generally consists of professional women. Actively involved in community service and fund-raising. Chapters are located throughout the U.S.

□ Violence Against Women

ANTI-PORNOGRAPHY GROUPS

D.C. Feminists Against Pornography
2147 O St. NW, #305
Washington, DC 20037

A consciousness-raising group that advocates the elimination of pornography. Seeks to affect public policy.

Feminists Fighting Pornography
P.O. Box 6731, Yorkville Sta.
New York, NY 10128
(212) 410-5182

Works to combat pornography by lobbying the federal government. Maintains a speakers' bureau and conducts slide shows.

International Feminists Against Traffic in Women
777 United Nations Pl.
New York, NY 10017
(212) 756-3500

A governmental agency working to end pornography.

Organizing Against Pornography
310 E 38th St., No. 109
Minneapolis, MN 55409
(612) 822-1476

Distributes feminist anti-pornography material. Offers newsletters, information packets, and audiocassettes.

Pornography Awareness
411 Morris St., #200
Durham, NC 27701

Seeks to educate the public about how pornography cripples women's status in society. Offers informational and educational materials.

Twin Cities Women for Take Back the Night
P.O. Box 8974
Minneapolis, MN 55408

Group that works to end pornography.

Women Against Pornography
P.O. Box 845, Times Square Sta.
New York, NY 10036-0845
(212) 307-5055

Provides public education on the damage pornography does to women, especially regarding their basic safety and status. Conducts slide shows, demonstrations, and offers publications.

Women's Alliance Against Pornography
Box 382027
Cambridge, MA 02238
(617) 630-1506

A feminist organization that aims at educating the public about pornography and how its production and use abridge women's and children's civil rights.

ANTI-VIOLENCE COALITIONS, ASSOCIATIONS, AND SPECIAL SERVICES

There are over 1,200 battered women's organizations serving victims of domestic violence. The following is a list of the state and national coalitions and organizations that can refer you to local programs. Also included are organizations serving special populations. These are marked by an asterisk (*).

Action Ohio, Coalition for Battered Women
P.O. Box 15673
Columbus, OH 43215
(614) 221-1255

A statewide coalition of almost one hundred battered women's shelters.

Advocates for Immigrant Women
3094 Kaloaluiki St.
Honolulu, HI 96822
(808) 988-6026

Works to improve the condition of victims of domestic violence, especially immigrants from Asian regions.

* American Indian Women's Circle Against Domestic Abuse
1929 S 5 St.
Minneapolis, MN 55454
(612) 340-0470

Advocates for an end to domestic violence within the Native American community.

* Asian Task Force Against Domestic Violence
P.O. Box 73
Boston, MA 02120
(617) 739-6696;
Fax: (617) 277-1326

A coalition of individuals working

to eliminate domestic violence in Asian communities. Organizes to create bilingual and culturally appropriate services, advocates for accessibility to resources and services, and provides education and training about domestic violence.

Center for Prevention of Sexual and Domestic Violence
1914 N 34th, Ste. 105
Seattle, WA 98103
(206) 634-1903;
Fax: (206) 634-0115

Offers training workshops geared toward religious leaders in order to prevent violence against women. Also offers professional consultation, speakers, a resource library, videos, publications, and a quarterly newsletter. Works interdenominationally. See also Religious and Spiritual Groups.

Central Minnesota Task Force on Battered Women
Box 195
St. Cloud, MN 56301
(610) 253-6900

In addition to providing shelter and advocacy services, the Task Force is a coalition of six programs providing information and assistance to criminal justice agencies in policy development and implementation.

Clearinghouse on Femicide
P.O. Box 12342
Berkeley, CA 94701-3342
(510) 845-7005

A nonprofit research service and archive. Provides information and resource materials to stop the murder of women. See also Research Centers and Organizations.

Clothesline Project
Box 727
East Dennis, MA 02641
(508) 385-7004;
Fax: (508) 385-7011

A grass-roots network of local projects that works to fight violence against women. Survivors of violence and friends of survivors decorate shirts that are color-coded for murder, rape, assault, incest, abuse, and lesbian-bashing and hung as a visual statement of these crimes.

Colorado Domestic Violence Coalition
P.O. Box 18902
Denver, CO 80218
(303) 573-9018;
Fax: (303) 573-9023

An organization of people involved in issues related to battered women and their families. Represents both rural and urban areas throughout the state. Provides support, education, and training to all Colorado residents working to eliminate violence in families and communities.

Council on Domestic Violence and Sexual Assault
Box 111200
Juneau, AK 99811-1200
(907) 465-4356;
Fax: (907) 465-3627

A state agency that administers grants to shelter programs across Alaska. Also maintains an information system on services provided to victims and monitors and supports legislation of concern to victims of domestic violence and sexual assault.

Domestic Violence Association of Central Kansas
1700 E Iron
Salina, KS 67401
(913) 827-5862

An organization that oversees domestic violence services in thirteen countries. Offers guidance and technical assistance. Also operates a shelter for women and children.

Domestic Violence Institute
50 S Steale St., #850
Denver, CO 80209
(303) 322-1831

Provides information, training, and workshops for professionals in the field. Also coordinates the training of small groups that work with battered women.

Family Violence Prevention Fund
Bldg. 1, Ste. 200
San Francisco, CA 94110
(415) 821-4553

An organization dedicated to prevent all forms of domestic violence. Works with institutions, law enforcers, judges and medical personnel.

Provides educational materials and training. Recently released a public opinion poll on family violence.

Florida Coalition Against Domestic Violence
P.O. Box 1201
Winter Park, FL 32790
(407) 628-3885

A coalition for the thirty-five shelters located in Florida. Provides networking opportunities, training, and technical assistance. Conducts workshops and seminars.

Illinois Coalition Against Domestic Violence
937 S Fourth St.
Springfield, IL 62703
(217) 789-2830

A state agency for all the direct service programs for battered women and children. Provides referrals. Also offers guidance, support, and technical assistance to member programs.

Institute on Black Chemical Abuse.

See Health Organizations: Substance Abuse Services.

Kansas Coalition Against Sexual and Domestic Violence
Box 1341
Pittsburg, KS 66762
(316) 232-2757

A network of programs reaching across Kansas to help end battering and sexual assault. Provides support and programs to the victims of these crimes.

National Assault Prevention Center
606 Delsea Drive
Sewell, NJ 08080
(908) 369-8972

Offers educational materials and workshops to prevent domestic violence.

National Battered Women's Law Project
799 Broadway, #402
New York, NY 10003
(212) 674-8200

Provides legal assistance to attorneys and battered women's advocates.

National Clearinghouse for the Defense of Battered Women
125 S 9th St., Ste. 302
Philadelphia, PA 19107
(215) 351-0010;
Fax: (215) 351-0779

Provides assistance and consultation to attorneys, battered women advocates, and expert witnesses on issues affecting battered women who have killed or assaulted their abusers while attempting to protect themselves against brutal and life-threatening violence. Provides direct support to battered women in prison. See also Legal Services; Special Interests.

National Coalition Against Domestic Violence
Box 34103
Washington, DC 20043
(202) 638-6388

A national network of women's shelters and direct service programs for battered women and children located around the country. Supports service of these programs, disseminates information, and operates a speaker's bureau.

New Hampshire Coalition Against Domestic and Sexual Violence
P.O. Box 353
Concord, NH 03302-0353
(603) 224-8893

A statewide network of programs that provides services to victims of domestic violence and sexual assault. Coordinates services, manages state and federal funding programs, and provides legislative and social service systems advocacy to benefit victims.

New Jersey Coalition for Battered Women
2620 Whitehorse-Hamilton Square Rd.
Trenton, NJ 08690
(609) 584-8107

A statewide coalition of twenty-three domestic violence service programs and concerned individuals. The coalition advocates for *battered women with state-level governmental and private organizations to support legislation and policies that will benefit victims of domestic violence. It serves as the state clearinghouse for information on domestic violence. Publishes a newsletter.*

New York Asian Women's Center
39 Bowery, Box 375
New York, NY 10002
(212) 732-5230

Provides numerous services for battered Asian women, including crisis intervention, counseling, and legal service referrals.

North Carolina Coalition Against Domestic Violence
P.O. Box 51875
Durham, NC 27717
(919) 490-1467

A membership organization representing sixty-five programs in North Carolina working to end domestic violence. Works to provide technical assistance and information to programs while coordinating statewide public policy, public awareness, and training activities.

Pennsylvania Coalition Against Domestic Violence
6400 Flank Dr.
Harrisburg, PA 17112
(717) 545-6400

State headquarters of member programs that refer women to local

shelters for support, legal advice, and safety.

* Sakhi for South Asian Women
P.O. Box 1428 Cathedral Sta.
New York, NY 10025
(212) 866-6591;
Fax: (212) 714-9153

Helps Asian Indian, Bangladeshi, Nepali, Pakistani, and Sri Lankan communities in New York resist domestic violence. Offers emotional support and referrals for shelters, legal issues, health, housing, and social services.

Southern California Coalition on Battered Women
P.O. Box 5036
Santa Monica, CA 90405
(213) 655-6098

Agency committed to supporting and educating women who are battered or sexually assaulted. Refers victims to local shelters. Provides public information as well as training and technical assistance to direct service providers.

USCCCN National Crime Division
Women's Issues Div.
P.O. Box 1092
South Orange, NJ 07079
(908) 549-2599;
Fax: (908) 549-2599

Provides programs, publications, and training related to safety and security, sexual assault, child abuse, fraud and scam prevention, and domestic abuse. Services deal with awareness, training, intervention, and prevention. See also Special Interests.

Violence Against Women Coalition
3033 Excelsior Blvd., Ste. 190
Minneapolis, MN 55416
(612) 920-4642

A coalition consisting of thirty member organizations that seeks to break the cycle of sexual violence by exploring societal attitudes and encouraging change through education and awareness. Its ultimate goal is to stop all forms of violence against women. Maintains an advertising campaign and a speaker's bureau.

Virginians Against Domestic Violence
2850 Sandy Bay Rd., Ste. 101
Williamsburg, VA 23185
(804) 221-0990

A statewide coalition of all the shelters in Virginia. Coordinates conferences and provides technical assistance. Also lobbies for legislation benefitting victims of violence. Sponsors a toll-free hotline for those who need help.

* White Buffalo Calf Women's Society and Shelter
P.O. Box 277
Mission, SD 57555

Provides shelter and support services to Native American women.

YWCA Battered Women's Programs

Consult your local phone book for the YWCA nearest you. Most offer a range of services, including shelters for battered women, and women in crisis.

INCEST GROUPS

Adults Recovering from Incest Anonymous
P.O. Box 24692
Minneapolis, MN 55424

A support group for adult victims of incest. Offers comfort, guidance, and understanding.

Center for Abuse Recovery
6200 North Central Expwy., #209
Dallas, TX 75206
(214) 373-6607

Provides individual and group therapy to help incest survivors.

Incest Recources, Incorporated
c/o Cambridge Women's Center
46 Pleasant St.
Cambridge, MA 02139

Nonprofit organization of survival therapists. Provides tapes, hardbooks, and other educational materials to survivors of incest.

Incest Survivor Information Exchange
P.O. Box 3399
New Haven, CT 06515

A clearinghouse of educational information that benefits survivors of incest.

Incest Survivors Education Project
United Ministries of Higher Education
1118 S Harrison Rd.
East Lansing, MI 48823
(517) 332-2338

Provides educational materials and support to incest survivors.

Incest Survivors Resource Network International, Incorporated
P.O. Box 7375
Las Cruces, NM 88006
(505) 521-4260

An educational resource for incest survivors. Operates a helpline answered by incest survivors and offers education and information.

National Center for Redress of Incest and Sexual Abuse
1858 Park Rd. NW
Washington, DC 20010
(202) 667-1160

A nonprofit organization dedicated to advancing the legal rights of survivors and victims of childhood sexual victimization. Publishes a monthly legislative update.

New Hampshire Incest Center
P.O. Box 547
Concord, NH 03301
(603) 746-5233

A self-help, volunteer, nonprofit group that provides information and referrals about services, research, and assistance. Fosters public education through a newsletter, speaker's bureau, and workshops.

SELF-DEFENSE SERVICES

DC Self-Defense Karate Association
701 Richmond Ave.
Silver Spring, MD 20910
(301) 589-1349

Offers a variety of self-defense programs for women, including a four-week course that teaches verbal skills and defense techniques and a twenty-five-hour, full-contact training course called D.C. Impact. Also offers a number of workshops.

Feminists in Self-Defense Training
P.O. Box 1883
Olympia, WA 98507
(206) 438-0288

FIST provides assault prevention information and skills training to women and teen girls. Its goal is to empower women. Offers self-defense workshops of one hour to one day, or ongoing training. Publishes a newsletter.

Feminist Karate Union
5429 Russell Ave. NW
Seattle, WA 98107
(206) 789-4561

Teaches self-defense and self-protection, and karate to women, children, senior citizens, and physically and/or mentally disabled persons, and battered wives. Offers demonstrations, workshops, seminars, and training to community and educational groups.

Fighting Woman News Magazine.

See Newspapers, Newsletters, and Magazines.

Karate School for Women
149 Bleecker St.
New York, NY 10002
(212) 982-4739

Offers karate and yoga classes to all adults and children.

Seven Star Women's Kung Fu
703 East Pike St.
Seattle, WA 98122

Offers classes that teach kung fu to women and girls.

Triangle Women's Martial Arts Center
P.O. Box 61643
Durham, NC 27715

Teaches karate to women and girls age six and older. Classes vary, so contact the center for specific information.

Women's Self-Defense Alliance
614 Orange St.
New Haven, CT 06511
(203) 787-0031

Provides workshops and classes on self-defense for women and girls. Also hosts speakers, offers company employee education programs for women in high-risk careers, and sponsors a child assault prevention program.

SEXUAL ASSAULT AND HARASSMENT SERVICES

American Rape Prevention Association
50 Muth Dr.
Orinda, CA 94563
(415) 254-0963

A coalition of individuals and organizations working to prevent rape, incest, domestic violence, rape, and sexual harassment.

Migima Designs
P.O. Box 5582
Eugene, OR 97405
(503) 343-3440;
Fax: (503) 683-3821

Offers books, tapes films and anatomical dolls regarding sexual assault prevention and investigation. Also provides consulting, expert testimony, and training seminars.

Ohio Coalition on Sexual Assault
65 S 4th St.
Columbus, OH 43215
(614) 469-0011

Provides education, advocacy, and networking to agencies and individuals in Ohio working to provide sexual assault crisis intervention and prevention services.

Violence Against Women Coalition
3033 Excelsior Blvd., #190
Minneapolis, MN 55416
(612) 920-4642;
Fax: (612) 920-5923

Seeks to break the cycle of sexual violence by exploring societal attitudes and encouraging change through education. Works in the areas of public relations, grant-seeking, conference workshops, and community outreach.

Washington Coalition of Sexual Assault Programs
110 E 5th Ave., #214
Olympia, WA 98501
(206) 754-7583

A statewide coalition of sexual assault programs. Provides technical assistance to programs, sponsors educational trainings, maintains a resource library, and lobbies for effective state public policy regarding sexual assault issues. Also publishes and distributes material on sexual assault prevention and education.

Wisconsin Coalition Against Sexual Assault
1051 Williamson St., #2
Madison, WI 53703
(608) 257-1516

A statewide organization dedicated to ending sexual violence in Wisconsin through education and advocacy.

Women's Transit Authority
306 N Brooks St.
Madison, WI 53715
(608) 256-3710

A nighttime rape prevention ride service run by women for women and their children. Provides free door-to-door rides for any woman in the city of Madison within a four-mile radius of the capitol.

WRATH: Women Refusing to Accept Tenant Harassment
607 Elmira Rd., #299
Vacaville, CA 95687
(707) 449-1122;
Fax: (707) 449-1122

Provides information, resources, and referrals to tenants who are experiencing sexual harassment by a landlord or property management employee. Assists with options and strategy planning at no cost to tenants through an intervention program.

**National Clearinghouse on
Marital/Date Rape**
2325 Oak St.
Berkeley, CA 94708
(510) 524-1582

*Offers information and actively
seeks to educate the public on marital and date rape. Also provides
data for research projects, consultation, and speakers' bureau.*

❑ Women's Centers

*I*n general, women's centers offer support and educational groups, discussion forums to exchange ideas, and resources and referrals. Some also offer crisis intervention services. Since most are multipurpose centers, be sure to check chapters such as Health Organizations and Violence Against Women for additional local listings.

Alaska Women's Resource Center
111 E 9th St.
Anchorage, AK 99501
(907) 276-0528;
Fax: (907) 278-8944

Provides counseling services for domestic violence, prematernal health, employment, and substance abuse. Operates a halfway house for women recovering from substance abuse and their children. Operates an information and referral service.

Bexar County Women's Center
1401 N Main
San Antonio, TX 78212
(210) 978-8800;
Fax: (210) 978-8824

Helps women, children, and men through employment information and education, self-esteem and assertiveness workshops, referrals, and counseling services.

Chrysalis Center for Women
2650 Nicollet Ave. S
Minneapolis, MN 55408
(612) 871-0118;
Fax: (612) 871-1814

A multipurpose women's center serving women and their families. Services offered include a mental health clinic, chemical dependency services, support groups, legal assistance, and an information and referral/crisis line.

Dolores Mission Women's Cooperative
171 S Gless St.
Los Angeles, CA 90033
(213) 268-9880;
Fax: (213) 268-7228

Offers services to single mothers and young women. Services include a child care center, leadership programs, a thrift store, and job training.

Everywoman's Center
Univ. of Massachusetts
Amherst, MA 01002
(413) 545-0883

Established in 1972, this organization provides a number of direct service programs for women, including rape crisis services, peer and general counseling, and referrals to local health care centers. Also has a women of color program.

Focus: A Women's Resource Center
1508 Grady Ave.
Charlottesville, VA 22903
(804) 293-2222

A United Way member agency that assists women in obtaining education, employment, and empowerment for themselves, their families, and their communities.

Fort Wayne Women's Bureau
303 E Washington Blvd.
Fort Wayne, IN 46802
(219) 424-7977;
Fax: (219) 426-7576

Offers programs that promote equity and create opportunities for women and their families. Programs, services, and support groups work to enhance personal growth for women.

Hispanic Women's Resource Center
2700 Westfield Ave.
Camden, NJ 08105
(609) 365-7393

Dedicated to assisting low-income Latina women in job placement and training. Offers educational programs that teach English as a second language, life-coping skills, literacy, and others. Also sponsors a day-care program for school-age children. Part of the Hispanic Family Center of Southern New Jersey.

Kinheart
2214 Ridge Ave.
Evanston, IL 60201
(708) 918-9001

A feminist center that provides a place for women to discuss and explore women's issues, including sexual orientation. Offers education on numerous women's issues.

Leominster Women's Center
26 Main St.
Leominster, MA 01453
(508) 537-7395

Holds educational programs and support groups for women who have had breast cancer and for female survivors of sexual abuse. Publishes a newsletter and sponsors a women's history essay contest for children.

**Lesbian Resource Project
Women's Center**
P. O. Box 26031
Tempe, AZ 85282
(602) 966-6152

See also Lesbian and Gay Organizations.

National Association of Women's Centers
Miami University Women's Center
Oxford, OH 45056
(513) 529-1510;
Fax: (513) 529-3841

Provides an array of services to women's centers around the nation. Helps new centers with their start-up activities, challenges policymakers to formulate legislation sympathetic to women's rights, and encourages women's organizations to strengthen their activities.

New Haven Women's Center
614 Orange St.
New Haven, CT 06511
(203) 776-2658

Offers support and referrals for women. Responds to women's needs through community organizing, information sharing, and advocacy.

Northeast Women's Center
673 E 38 Ave.
Denver, CO 80207
(303) 355-3486

Produces resources and referrals, offers a job readiness program, and has a teen center.

Orange County Women's Center
210 Henderson St.
Chapel Hill, NC 27514
(919) 968-4610

Provides ongoing services, programs, and support to encourage and enhance self-esteem and self-sufficiency in women. Offers financial, legal, career, and personal counseling, as well as a variety of workshops and classes on writing, self-esteem, relationships, and feminism.

Our Own Place
1411 Watts St.
Durham, NC 27701
(919) 688-0223

Sponsors feminist and lesbian activities in the Durham area. Offers support groups for women, sponsors events, and has a newsletter that can be ordered.

Sacramento Women's Center, Incorporated
2306 J St., Ste. 200
Sacramento, CA 95816
(916) 441-4209

Promotes the economic development of women and their families through job placement services, networking, and personal support.

Siuslaw Area Women's Center
P. O. Box 2144
Florence, OR 97439
(503) 997-2816

Provides support services to women and their families. Offers temporary housing, crisis intervention, phone counseling, and assistance in attaining restraining orders. See also Violence Against Women.

Umbrella
1 Prospect Ave.
St. Johnsbury, VT 05819
(802) 748-8645

Offers women in northern Vermont a rape and battering hotline, a women's issues resource center, parenting and childcare support and information, and referrals.

Union Center for Women
8101 Ridge Blvd.
Brooklyn, NY 11209
(718) 748-7708

Offers support groups, workshops, and special programs for women.

West Side Women's Center
4209 Lorain Ave.
Cleveland, OH 44113
(216) 651-1450

Provides short-term drug and alcohol rehabilitation program support groups for women who are HIV positive, teenage mothers, battered women, etc., as well as practical education for parenting.

Woman Centered
5 School Ave.
Montpelier, VT 05602
(802) 229-6202

Provides women with empowerment through workshops, support groups, referrals, public forums on women's issues, peer counseling, and advocacy for women's issues.

A Woman's Place
440 S 44th St.
Lincoln, NE 68510
(402) 477-5666

Provides space for group meetings, centralized information and referrals, performance arts, arts and crafts classes, a bookstore, workshops, classes, speakers, and media production for women.

The Woman's Place
YWCA
15 N Naches Ave.
Yakima, WA 98901
(509) 248-7796;
Fax: (509) 575-5398

Works to be a force within the community that is responsive to women's needs. Offers services for battered women, sex education classes, information, and workshops.

Women Helping Women Services
543 N Fairfax Ave.
Los Angeles, CA 90036
(213) 655-3807

A community service offering a telephone talkline, workshops, support groups, and volunteer opportunities. Addresses issues of sexual harassment, divorce, life transition, suicide, depression, loss, and career change.

The Women's Building
79 Central Ave.
Albany, NY 12206
(518) 465-1597;
Fax: (518) 465-1597

The Women's Community Center of the Greater Capital Region. Houses a variety of women's organizations and sponsors its own programs, which range from legal clinics to fitness classes and cultural events.

The Women's Building of the Bay Area
3543 18th St.
San Francisco, CA 94110
(415) 431-1180;
Fax: (415) 861-8969

Provides low-cost office space for women's organizations. Offers programs to assist women, children, and other oppressed people in their struggles.

The Women's Center
424 Pine St., #102
Ft. Collins, CO 80524
(303) 484-1902

Offers services to enhance the status of women and their families. Services include employment and career counseling, health care for low-income women, child care resources and referrals, and educational workshops.

The Women's Center
46 Pleasant St.
Cambridge, MA 02139
(617) 354-8807

Provides free self-help support groups on many issues, including incest, battering, homosexuality, aging, disabilities, eating disorders, and cancer. Offers information and resources such as housing listings, job listings, therapists, groups, and health care providers.

Women's Center
128 E Hargett St., Ste. 10
Raleigh, NC 27601
(919) 829-3711;
Fax: (919) 829-9960

A multiservice counseling and resource center. Promotes the growth, productiveness, and well-being of women through a variety of counseling and educational programs.

The Women's Center
P. O. Box 354
Binghamton, NY 13902
(607) 724-3462;
Fax: (607) 770-8585

A forum for feminist concerns. Sponsors committees on women's issues.

The Women's Center
133 Park St. NE
Vienna, VA 22180
(703) 281-2657;
Fax: (703) 242-1454

A nonprofit community organization that provides immediate and affordable individual and group counseling to women and their families. Also provides workshops and educational programs address-

ing the psychological, legal, financial, and professional concerns of women.

The Women's Center of Central Kentucky
178 N Martin Luther King Blvd.
Lexington, KY 40507
(606) 254-9319;
Fax: (606) 233-0257

Offers crisis counseling, social work services, community outreach programs, job training programs, and substance abuse prevention education.

The Women's Center of Tarrant County, Incorporated
1723 Hemphill St.
Fort Worth, TX 76110
(817) 927-4006;
Fax: (817) 924-2562

Offers job search training and placement, a welfare-to-work program, rape crisis intervention, crisis intervention, and short-term counseling.

The Women's Community Building
100 W Seneca St.
Ithaca, NY 14850
(607) 272-1247

Offers continuing education classes to women, men, and children, transitional housing for women, a women's information network, a job search support group and listing, and meeting room rentals.

Women's Information Center
601 Allen St.
Syracuse, NY 13210
(315) 478-4636

A group of volunteers that provides information on health, careers, support, families, and so on.

Women's Resource Center
252 State St. SE
Grand Rapids, MI 49503
(616) 458-5443;
Fax: (616) 458-5445

Offers career counseling, employment services, volunteer and peer support programs, and advocacy on social issues of importance to women.

Women's Resource Center
304 N 8th
St. Joseph, MO 64501
(816) 232-4481

Provides a variety of services for women. Works to create opportunities that encourage growth and enhance the self-esteem of women.

Women's Resource Center
P. O. Box 888
Dillon, MT 59725
(406) 683-6106;
Fax: (406) 683-2411

Facilitates, advocates, and supports women's active participation in decisions affecting their physical, emotional, and spiritual health. Programs address domestic abuse, parenting, self-esteem building, prevocational training, and com-

puter training. The center also has a library with books and tapes about issues concerning women, families, and personal growth.

Women's Resource Center
P. O. Box 309
Wayne, PA 19087
(215) 687-6391

Offers women in the Delaware Valley support groups, educational workshops, counseling, legal information, and referrals.

Women's Resource Center
4621 Ross Ave.
Dallas, TX 75204
(214) 821-9595;
Fax: (214) 826-4548

A social-services branch of the YWCA. Develops programs to meet the needs of women and works to empower them to fill their potential in work, at home, and in society.

Women's Rights Information Center
108 W Palisade Ave.
Englewood, NJ 07631
(201) 568-1166;
Fax: (201) 568-0762

Provides information, drop-in and phone counseling, and educational programs to women.

Women's Survival Center
167 W Pike St.
Pontiac, MI 48341
(313) 335-2685

Works to empower women by offering education, child care, and transitional housing. Also sponsors numerous public education programs regarding women's issues.

Young Women's Christian Association of the U. S. A. (YWCA)
726 Broadway
New York, NY 10003
(212) 614-2700

A national women's association with over four thousand locations nationwide. Offers support groups as well as an assortment of programs covering peer counseling, teen pregnancy prevention, breast cancer, career counseling, victims of domestic abuse, young mothers, health care, and child care. Call or write for the location of the center nearest you.

❑ Women's History

American History Association
Committee on Women Historians
400 A St. SE
Washington, DC 20003
(202) 544-2422

Promotes and supports women historians and the study of women's history. Sponsors and funds research projects.

Archives and Special Collections on Women in Medicine
Medical College of Pennsylvania
3300 Henry Ave.
Philadelphia, PA 19129
(215) 842-7124

Collects and makes available to qualified researchers materials relating to the history of women in medicine. Collections include college history from 1850 to present, women's professional medical organizations, personal papers, and books.

Arkansas Women's History Institute
P.O. Box 77
Little Rock, AR 72217
(501) 623-7396

Offers publications on Arkansas women's history. Holds conferences on women's history and sponsors research.

Association of Black Women Historians
c/o Jacqueline Rouse
Dept. of History
Georgia State Univ.
Atlanta, GA 30303

Promotes and supports black women historians. Provides information about black women in history. Location of office changes every two years. See also Professional and Business Associations and Networks.

Berkshire Conference of Women Historians
Women's Studies Program
Univ. of North Carolina, CB #3135
207 Caldwell Hall
Chapel Hill, NC 27599-3135
(919) 962-3908

Holds one of the major conferences on women's history and supports the efforts of those in the profession. See also Professional and Business Associations and Networks.

Bethune Museum and Archives National Archives for Black Women's History
1318 Vermont Ave. NW
Washington, DC 20005
(202) 332-1233

A museum and archives focusing on African American women's history. The museum offers tours, lectures, and presentations. Publishes a quarterly newsletter.

Coalition for Western Women's History
Washington State Univ.
History Dept.
Pullman, WA 99164
(509) 335-1560

Offers networking opportunities and information about research in Western women's history.

Elizabeth Cady Stanton Foundation
P.O. Box 603
Seneca Falls, NY 13148

Publicizes and offers the feminist insights of Elizabeth Cady Stanton. Supports the development of women's history projects.

History of Science Society
Women's Committee
35 Dean St.
Worcester, MA 01609
(508) 831-5712;
Fax: (508) 831-5483

Encourages and promotes women historians in the fields of science, technology, and medicine. Con-

ducts an annual job survey and offers career information. See also Science and Technology.

Lesbian Herstory Archives.
See Lesbian and Gay Organizations.

Michigan Women's Historical Center and Hall of Fame
213 W Main St.
Lansing, MI 48933
(517) 484-1880

Offers exhibits, a museum shop, an art gallery, a Hall of Fame, and a botanical garden celebrating Michigan women's history.

Midlands Ad-Hoc Committee for Women's History
c/o YWCA of the Midlands
1505 Blanding St.
Columbia, SC 29201
(803) 252-2151

Works to educate students and teachers on women's history. Offers activities, programs, exhibits, curriculum information, and speakers.

Minnesota Historical Society Women's History Project
345 Kellogg Blvd.
St. Paul, MN 55102
(612) 296-6126

Sponsors a woman's history month honoring the achievements of Minnesota women. Exhibitions usually include papers, photographs, artistic works, and artifacts.

Montana Women's History Project
Univ. of Montana
Mansfield Library
Missoula, MT 59812
(406) 243-4153

Maintains a library containing books and materials on women's history in Montana. Also offers a women's history month, usually in February, featuring the achievements of women.

National Coordinating Committee for the Promotion of History—Women's History Project
400 A St. SE
Washington, DC 20003
(301) 544-2422

An advocacy office for women historians. Conducts lobbying efforts and promotes women's history and women's history projects. See also Women's Rights.

National Women's Hall of Fame
76 Fall St.
P.O. Box 335
Seneca Falls, NY 13148
(315) 568-8060

Honors extraordinary American women and their achievements.

National Women's History Project
7738 Bell Rd.
Windsor, CA 95492
(707) 838-6000;
Fax: (707) 838-0478

Seeks to advance the study of women's history in schools and universities as well as among the general public. Calls for a multicultural approach to history emphasizing women's changing roles and contributions. Accomplishes these goals by selling curriculum materials, books, videos, etc. to educators. Also conducts teacher training seminars. Write for extensive catalog.

Pioneer Woman Museum
701 Monument
Ponca City, OK 74604
(405) 765-6108

Exhibits women's memorabilia from pioneer homes. Offers educational programs and events.

Schlesinger Library
Radcliffe College
3 James St.
Cambridge, MA 02138
(617) 495-8647

A research library on the history of women in the U.S. Open to the public. Materials do not circulate. See also Research Centers and Organizations.

Smithsonian Institution Museum of American History
National Women's History Collection
Washington, DC 20560
(202) 357-2008

Holds materials from the National American Woman Suffrage Associa-

tion and collections on women in politics and society. Also offers information on women's history repositories and materials throughout the U.S. See also Educational Services and Organizations.

Sophia Smith Collection
Smith College
Northampton, MA 01063
(413) 585-2970;
Fax: (413) 585-2904

A repository for primary sources in women's history. Holdings document the historical experience of women in the U.S. Collection includes documents on birth control, women's rights, reform, international work, journalism, arts, professions, and middle-class life in nineteenth century New England.

Southern Association for Women Historians
COE College
Dept. of History
Cedar Rapids, IA 52402
(319) 399-8619

Works to advance the status of women historians in the South. Conducts activities to increase interest in Southern history and women's history.

Susan B. Anthony House
17 Madison St.
Rochester, NY 14608
(716) 235-6124

Displays Susan B. Anthony's and

other suffragettes' furniture, mementos, and artifacts.

United Federation of Teachers Women's Rights Committee
260 Park Ave. S
New York, NY 10010
(212) 598-6879;
Fax: (212) 533-2704

Offers teachers information on how to integrate women's history into school curriculums.

Upper Midwest Women's History Center for Teachers
Central Community Center
6300 Walker St.
St. Louis Park, MN 55416
(612) 928-6750

Develops curriculum programs for teaching women's history and culture. Offers books, audio-visual materials, and workshops for educators.

Women in the Military Service for America Memorial Foundation
Dept. 560
Washington, DC 20042-0560
(800) 222-2294;
Fax: (703) 931-4208

Raises funds to erect a memorial to America's servicewomen. The purpose of the memorial is to honor servicewomen, to educate the public about their achievements, to make their contributions a visible part of American history, and to il-

*lustrate their partnership with men
in defending the nation.*

Women's Heritage Museum
1509 Portola Ave.
Palo Alto, CA 94306
(415) 321-5260

*Preserves, documents, interprets,
exhibits, and researches women's
history. Sponsors public education
programs.*

Women's Heritage Museum
Univ. of Kentucky
404 King Library S
Lexington, KY 40506-0391

*Offers traveling exhibits, a wom-
en's hall of fame, and a history museum. Sponsors a public education
series on women's history.*

Women's History Library and Research Center
2325 Oak St.
Berkeley, CA 94708
(510) 524-1582

*Holds documents recording wom-
en's history. Strengths are in
women and law and women and
health.*

Women's History Museum
Box 209
West Liberty, WV 26074
(304) 335-7159

*A mobile museum that features ex-
hibits on seven women from U.S.
history. Conducts costumed performances about the life of each
woman.*

Women's Rights National Historical Park
P.O. Box 70
Seneca Falls, NY 13148
(315) 568-2991;
Fax: (315) 568-2141

*Consists of the Wesleyan Methodist
Chapel site of the first women's
rights convention, the home of Elizabeth Cady Stanton, the Mary Ann
M'Clintock house, and a visitor
center that tells the story of the
first convention.*

❑ Women's Rights

Affirmative Action Coordinating Center
443 W 50th St.
New York, NY 10019
(212) 688-5177

A network of women's organizations working to implement affirmative action programs and overcome oppression and racial inequity. Offers information, resources, research, and referrals. See also Special Interests.

American Civil Liberties Union, Women's Rights Project
132 W 43rd St.
New York, NY 10036
(212) 944-9800;
Fax: (212) 921-7916

Dedicated to achieving full equality for women under the law. It has focused on hundreds of discrimination cases in the past twenty years from pay and promotion equality to sexual harassment to unequal treatment in the military. In many ways, it has been considered the legal arm of the women's movement. Many offices are located throughout the United States. See also Legal Services.

Amnesty International USA Women and Human Rights Project
322 Eighth Ave.
New York, NY 10001
(212) 775-5161

Works to educate women and men on human rights abuses against women around the world. Through seminars, petitions, and mailings, it provides information so people can find a way to eliminate these abuses.

Center for Constitutional Rights, Women's Rights Program
666 Broadway, 7th Fl.
New York, NY 10012
(212) 614-6464

Fights for women's equality and justice through civil rights litigation.

Challenging Media Images of Women
P.O. Box 902
Framingham, MA 01701
(508) 879–8504

A feminist activist organization that protests sexism in the media and works to uphold women's rights. Produces a quarterly newsletter.

Clearinghouse on Women's Issues
P.O. Box 70603
Friendship Heights, MD 20813
(301) 871-6106

Collects and disseminates articles and information on numerous women's issues.

Congressional Caucus for Women's Issues
2471 Rayburn House Office Bldg.
Washington, DC 20515
(202) 225-6740

Works to improve the status of women and eliminate discrimination, especially through legislation. See also Political Groups.

Equal Rights Advocates
1663 Mission St., Ste. 550
San Francisco, CA 94103
(415) 621-0672;
Fax: (415) 621-6744

A feminist and multicultural public interest law center. Offers legal advice and counsel in cases regarding sex discrimination. Provides services to individuals and organizations bringing suit on issues such as sexual harassment, discrimination based on pregnancy or gender, and sexual issues as related to employment. Sponsors a lecture series and public education programs. See also Legal Services.

Equal Rights Congress
4167 S Normandy Ave.
Los Angeles, CA 90037
(213) 291-1092

A coalition of national organizations for minorities. Works to end prejudice, fight discrimination, and protect human rights. Conducts educational programs, provides training, and sponsors competitions.

Equity Policy Center
2000 P St. NW, #508
Washington, DC 20036
(202) 872-1770

Conducts research and provides information on areas in national and international development programs where women's interests have been neglected. Suggests policy and program improvements. Offers seminars, speakers, and internships. See also Global Feminism and World Peace; Research Centers and Organizations.

Federal Council on Women
63 Monte Vista
Novato, CA 94947
(415) 897-4694;
Fax: (415) 897-4694 (call first)

Seeks wider representation of women's views in local, state, and national governments. Works to lobby for legislation to these ends. See also Political Groups.

**Feminist Institute and
Clearinghouse**
P.O. Box 30563
Bethesda, MD 20824
(301) 951-9040

*A nonprofit organization dedicated
to promoting a feminist future.
Serves as a clearinghouse for information.*

Feminist Majority Foundation
P.O. Box 6412
San Rafael, CA 94903
(415) 883-1233;
Fax: (415) 883-1966

*A feminist organization that con-
ducts research on women and the
social and political inequities they
face. Campaigns on contraceptive
research and abortion rights. Offers publications and videos.*

**Feminists Concerned for Better
Feminist Leadership**
P.O. Box 1348 Madison Square Sta.
New York, NY 10159
(718) 796-1467

*An organization of feminists con-
cerned for better feminist leadership to represent nationalist
feminism and women's rights. Distributes feminist educational material.*

**Foundation for Women's
Resources**
Leadership America
700 N Fairfax St., #302
Alexandria, VA 22314
(703) 549-1102

*Has created a national model lead-
ership training program for women
that is held three times a year.
These programs seek to develop
greater skills for women in positions of leadership.*

Fund for the Feminist Majority
1600 Wilson Blvd., Ste. 704
Arlington, VA 22209
(703) 522-2214;
Fax: (703) 522-2219

*A women's rights, abortion rights,
advocacy, and research group that
works for the general empowerment of women. Offers conferences
and publications.*

**International Women's Rights
Action Watch.**

See Global Feminism and World
Peace.

KNOW, Inc.
P.O. Box 86031
Pittsburgh, PA 15221
(412) 241-4844

*An organization dedicated to
spreading the meaning of feminism.
Publishes articles on human rights
and researches women's changing
roles in society. Offers a library,
books, newspapers, and periodicals.*

**National Association of
Commissions for Women**
624 9th St. NW, Ste. M-10
Washington, DC 20001
(202) 628-5030

A government-created organization consisting of county, state, and regional commissions that work to end discrimination and improve the status of all women. Works with national women's organizations to share information, plan, and act on women's issues.

National Commission for Women's Equality
c/o American Jewish Congress
15 E 84th St.
New York, NY 10028
(212) 879-4500;
Fax: (212) 249-3672

Dedicated to networking individuals and organizations in order to better fight for women's equality. Offers information, programs, and events on issues such as reproductive freedom, economic equity, child care, equality in religious life, and the politics of feminism.

National Council on Women of the USA, Incorporated
777 United Nations Pl., 12th Fl.
New York, NY 10017
(212) 697-1278

A nonprofit, completely volunteer organization working for the full equality of women. Offers programs, workshops, seminars, and international alliances.

National Organization for Women
1000 16th St. NW, #700
Washington, DC 20036
(202) 331-0066;
Fax: (202) 785-8576

A large multifaceted organization that is the voice of all women. Its mission is to end inequality, prejudice, and discrimination in all aspects of American life. Over 530 state and local chapters are established nationwide.

National Women's Conference Center
16100 Golf Club Rd., #201
Fort Lauderdale, FL 33326
(305) 389-1879

Helps the National Women's Conference Committee attain its National Plan of Action for women's rights. It accomplishes this by providing information. Also publishes materials on the national plan to educate the public and conducts professional seminars and workshops.

National Women's Conference Committee
P.O. Box 65605
Washington, DC 20035-5605
(715) 836-5717;
Fax: (715) 834-5922

Goal is to implement the National Plan of Action for women's rights adopted at the 1977 National Women's Conference. Locates supporters for the action and provides consulting and training conferences. See also Political Groups.

National Women's Rights Organizing Coalition
P.O. Box 1092
Trolley Sta.
Detroit, MI 48231
(313) 730-3577

A coalition of women's organizations dedicated to advancing women's rights.

National Women's Strike Day
2650 Table Mesa Dr.
Boulder, CO 80303
(800) 262-6973

Organized by women who want to channel the impatience women feel about inequities in the workplace and the continued devaluation of women's work. See also Work, Union, and Career Services.

Network Exchange of the National Women's Conference Center
P.O. Box 455
Beaver Dam, WI 53916
(414) 887-1078;
Fax: (414) 887-2876

Provides public information and educational services to implement policy that combats all forms of discrimination against women.

North Carolina Equity
505 Oberlin Rd., #100
Raleigh, NC 27605
(919) 833-4055;
Fax: (919) 833-2907

A private, nonprofit public policy, education, and advocacy organization. Works to advance the well-being of North Carolina women and their families with emphasis on those of low and moderate income.

Oklahoma Women's Network
P.O. Box 14339
Tulsa, OK 74159
(918) 493-1994;
Fax: (918) 494-2900

Promotes educational, economic, social, and legislative activities toward the goal of full development of women. Offers information on women's issues, seminars, workshops, study groups, and public education. See also Educational Services and Organizations.

Redstockings of the Women's Liberation Movement
P.O. Box 744
Stuyvesant Sta.
New York, NY 10001
(212) 777-9241

A think tank comprised of feminists, scholars, and political activists, among others. Dedicated to upholding women's rights. Conducts research, offers information and speakers and develops consciousness-raising groups. See also Research Centers and Organizations.

Religious Network for Equality for Women
475 Riverside Dr., Rm. 812-A
New York, NY 10115
(212) 870-2995;
Fax: (212) 870-2338

A coalition of groups from a variety of religions committed to full legal and economic equality for women. Sponsors education and advocacy programs calling for better medical and family leave benefits, economic equity, and an end to discrimination. Lobbies for national legislation. See also Religious and Spiritual Groups.

Union Institute Center for Women
1731 Connecticut Ave. NW
Washington, DC 20009
(202) 667-1313;
Fax: (202) 265-0492

Works on projects addressing the needs of women, including employment issues, violence, racism, health care, and sexual harassment. Serves as a clearinghouse for women's issues, supports women's studies programs, and offers resources.

Washington Women United
P.O. Box 2174
Olympia, WA 98507
(206) 754-9880

Lobbies the Washington state legislature on issues concerning women and women's rights. An annual membership pool is used to determine legislative positions and priorities. Also offers education and networking opportunities.

Women for Racial and Economic Equality
198 Broadway, Ste. 606
New York, NY 10038
(212) 385-1103

Promotes women's rights in racial equality, child care, health, employment, and global peace. Goal is to implement the Women's Bill of Rights. Sponsors awards and an annual holiday bazaar.

Women's Action Alliance, Incorporated
370 Lexington Ave., Ste. 603
New York, NY 10017
(212) 532-8330;
Fax: (212) 779-2846

A national organization working for full equality for all women. Provides educational information on women's issues, offers networking and job opportunities, and develops programs such as a women's alcohol and drug education project, computer equity projects, and a book about children of single parents and their schools.

Women's Advocacy
100 Witherspoon St.,
Rm. 4608A
Louisville, KY 40202
(502) 569-5385;
Fax: (502) 569-5018

Formerly known as Justice for Women, this is a women's rights organization advocating full equality and addressing inclusive language and reproductive rights.

Women's Economic Agenda Project
518 17th St., Ste. 200
Oakland, CA 94612
(510) 451-7379;
Fax: (510) 763-4327

Works toward ensuring women's economic rights. Provides leadership development, advocacy, and support to empower women to speak out and act on economic, political, and social issues that impact women. See also Health Organizations; Political Groups.

Women's Economic Rights Project
99 Hudson St., 12th Fl.
New York, NY 10013
(212) 925-6635;
Fax: (212) 226-1066

Works for women's equity in career, education, and society. Conducts public educational programs and offers publications.

Women's Equity Action League and Minnesota Coalition for Sex Equality
1711 Laurel Ave.
St. Paul, MN 55104
(612) 644-2739

A membership organization that seeks to achieve economic and educational equity for women.

Women's Equity Program
Nelson House
Univ. of Massachusetts
Amherst, MA 01003
(413) 545-1558

Researches women's issues and women's rights. Provides nonsexist and nonracist teacher training for women.

Women's Legal Defense Fund.
See Legal Services.

Women's Network of the Red River Valley
116 S 12th St.
Moorhead, MN 56560
(218) 236-0483

An association of individuals and organizations committed to feminist goals and women's rights. Provides networking opportunities, a resource center, and education activities. See also Women's Centers.

Women's Rights Committee
c/o Human Rights Dept.
American Federation of Teachers
555 New Jersey Ave. NW
Washington, DC 20001
(202) 879-4400

Works to implement policy resolutions regarding women's rights, gender equity, and empowerment of women as mandated by the American Federation of Teachers. Funds research projects, holds educational programs, and sponsors public education seminars. See also Special Interests.

Women's Rights Law Reporter.
See Newspapers, Newsletters, and Magazines.

Women's Technical Assistance Project
733 15 St. NW, #510
Washington, DC 20005
(202) 638-0449

Provides community-based grass-roots women's groups with training geared at strengthening them organizationally and thereby making them more effective in advancing feminist goals.

❏ Work, Union, and Career Services

Alumnae Resources
120 Montgomery, #1080
San Francisco, CA 94104
(415) 274-4700

A nonprofit career development organization designed to provide career planning assistance and job search support, especially to college-educated women.

Apprenticeship and Non-Traditional Employment for Women
P.O. Box 2490
Renton, WA 98056
(206) 235-2212;
Fax: (206) 235-7864

Links education, labor, industry, and the community to create the conditions essential for women's successful entry and progression in blue-collar jobs. Offers management consulting, recruitment, training, and placement services.

California Feminist Credit Union
P.O. Box 16587
San Diego, CA 92176
(619) 280-1922

Offers savings accounts, consumer loans, and financial education by phone and mail. Loans include car loans and special, automatically approved loans to help establish or reestablish credit.

Center for Women's Development
1650 Bedford Ave.
Brooklyn, NY 11225
(718) 270-5020

Offers a full range of vocational services, counseling, workshops, and support.

Center for Women's Economic Alternatives
P.O. Box 1033
Ahoskie, NC 27910
(919) 332-4179

Provides career counseling and support services for working women.

Chicago Women in the Trades
37 S Ashland Ave.
Chicago, IL 60607
(312) 942-1444;
Fax: (312) 942-0802

A support and advocacy group for women. Operates a pre-apprentice tutorial program to increase the number of tradeswomen and offers a leadership development program.

Coalition of Labor Union Women
15 Union Square W
New York, NY 10003
(212) 242-0700;
Fax: (212) 255-7230

Works to promote affirmative action in the workplace, stimulate political action and legislation on women's issues, and increase the participation of women in their unions. Publishes a newsletter. Chapters exist in many cities.

Federally Employed Women
1400 Eye St. NW, Ste. 425
Washington, DC 20005
(202) 898-0994

An international nonprofit membership organization for civilian and military women employed by the federal government. Holds national training programs and works in coalition with other federal and women's organizations to foster full potential for working women. Publishes a newsletter.

Foundation for Women's Resources
Leadership America
700 N Fairfax St., #302
Alexandria, VA 22314
(703) 549-1102;
Fax: (703) 836-9205

Offers executive leadership development for accomplished women. Members are diverse in their ethnic, professional, and geographic backgrounds.

Fuerza Unido
1305 N Flores
San Antonio, TX 78212
(210) 229-1318;
Fax: (210) 229-1318

An organization of women of color displaced from their jobs when Levi Strauss & Co. moved operations to Costa Rica. Organized to fight against American plants moving abroad and leaving injured workers without regard to the trauma caused. See also Organizations Representing Women of Color.

Garment Workers' Justice Center
110 E 15th St.
Los Angeles, CA 90015
(213) 746-4971

Works to improve conditions for workers in garment industry.

Hacer: Hispanic Women's Center
545 Fifth Ave., 11th Fl.
New York, NY 10018

Provides vocational services to Hispanic women, including workshops, information and referral.

Institute for Women and Work
Cornell Univ.
15 E 26th St., 4th Fl.
New York, NY 10010
(212) 340-2800

Holds conferences and seminars dealing with issues pertaining to women and work.

Institute on Women and Work in Washington
Mt. Vernon College
2100 Foxhall Rd.
Washington, DC 20007
(202) 625-4506;
Fax: (202) 298-6616

Addresses issues and concerns affecting women and work across the nation and in Washington, DC. Collects and shares information.

International Network for Women in Enterprise and Trade.
See Professional and Business Associations and Networks.

La Mujer Obrera
Centro Obrero, Inc.
2900 Cypress Street
El Paso, TX 79905
(915) 533-9710

Provides job training, counseling, and aid to economically disadvantaged Hispanic women.

National Association of M.B.A. Women.
See Professional and Business Associations and Networks.

National Committee on Pay Equity
1126 16th St. NW, Rm. 422
Washington, DC 20036
(202) 331-7343;
Fax: (202) 331-7406

A national coalition of numerous groups dedicated to achieving equal pay regardless of age, race, or gender. Disseminates information, creates public education, campaigns on local and national levels, and has a speaker's bureau. See also Women's Rights.

National Women's Economic Alliance Foundation
1440 New York Ave. NW, Ste. 300
Washington, DC 20005
(202) 393-5257;
Fax: (202) 639-8685

Advances women's opportunities in business, particularly in obtaining senior-level positions on corporate boards. Develops and offers leadership seminars. Members are corporate and business executives.

New Ways to Work
149 9th St.
San Francisco, CA 94103
(415) 552-1000

Provides research, information, and advocacy for women who want to work part time or job share. Offers seminars, public education, and publications. See also Research Centers and Organizations.

9 to 5 National Association of Working Women
614 Superior Ave. NW, Rm. 852
Cleveland, OH 44113
(216) 566-9308, (800) 245-9865
(Job Survival Hotline);
Fax: (216) 566-0192

A large, active membership organization of office workers. Advocates women's rights in the workplace on such issues as equal pay, pregnancy discrimination, sexual harassment, health and family leave, child care, etc. Provides job training, offers a job survival hotline, and publishes a newsletter. Chapters exist in many cities.

Non-Traditional Employment for Women
243 W 20th St.
New York, NY 10011
(212) 627-6252;
Fax: (212) 255-8021

A training and placement organization that helps women achieve positions in a variety of blue-collar jobs. Offers training, technical assistance, and information with regard to jobs in nontraditional employment.

Northern New England Tradeswomen
1 Prospect Ave.
St. Johnsbury, VT 05819
(802) 748-3308;
Fax: (802) 748-1768

A nonprofit organization providing advocacy and training for women wishing to enter nontraditional trades programs. Services include a thirteen-week training program called STEP UP and a job bank for women and minorities looking to enter highway construction.

Orientation to Non-Traditional Occupations
North Education Center, Columbus Public Schools
100 Arcadia Ave.
Columbus, OH 43202
(614) 365-6000;
Fax: (614) 365-6458

Provides women with entry-level skills required to enter occupations that have less than twenty-five percent women in the fields. Focuses on math, mechanical, and spatial aptitudes, self-esteem, interviewing, resume writing, job hunting, physical fitness, and affirmative action law. See also Special Interests.

PRIDE—From Prostitution to Independence, Dignity, & Equality
3125 E Lake St.
Minneapolis, MN 55406
(612) 729-0340

Aids sex workers in making the transition out of prostitution. Provides support groups and other services.

Tradeswomen
P.O. Box 40664B
San Francisco, CA 94140
(415) 821-7334

A nonprofit organization dedicated to increasing the number of women in blue-collar work. Provides support and advocacy. Publishes a national newsletter.

Tradeswomen of Philadelphia
Women in Non-Traditional Work
3001 Dickinson St.
Philadelphia, PA 19146
(215) 551-1808;
Fax: (215) 551-1246

Provides referrals, job information, support groups, speakers, training programs, and a bimonthly news-letter.

Trade Women of African Heritage
P.O. Box 1033 Cooper Sta.
New York, NY 10003
(212) 655-1657;
Fax: (212) 547-5696

Helps African American women in the labor movement deal with problems pertaining to discrimination, work, family, health, education, and self-awareness.

Wages for Housework Campaign
P.O. Box 86681
Los Angeles, CA 90086-0681
(213) 221-1698;
Fax: (213) 227-9353

An international organization that seeks compensation for the unpaid work women do. The campaign targets women from every sector— women of color, prostitutes, disabled women, and mainstream wage earners—to receive additional benefits as well as wages for unwaged work. These additional monies are to be added to every country's gross national product. Also seeks to increase public awareness of the exhausting employment/family obligations women face every day. Provides speakers, publications, and conferences to meet objectives. See also Global Feminism and World Peace.

WERC—Women's Employment Resources Corporation
3362 Adeline
Berkeley, CA 94703
(510) 652-5484

Provides career counseling services, workshops, networking information, and referrals.

Wider Opportunities for Women
1325 G Street NW
Lower Level
Washington, DC 20005
(202) 638-3143;
Fax: (202) 638-4885

An established national organization dedicated to promoting economic independence and job equality for women and girls. Provides job skill training, career development seminars, and technical assistance. Nationally, WOW seeks to influence policymakers to support programs for women in the workplace.

WISE—Women's Institute for Self-Employment
P.O. Box 192145
San Francisco, CA 94119
(415) 624-3351

Offers workshops and information

that aid women in starting their own business.

Womanswork
P.O. Box 543
York, ME 03909
(207) 363-0804;
Fax: (207) 363-0805

A mail-order business designed to sell work tools such as gloves, tools, and apparel made especially for women.

Women Employed Institute
22 W Monroe St., Ste. 1400
Chicago, IL 60603
(312) 782-3902

Develops programs that aid women in the work force such as training programs for the economically disadvantaged or readiness programs for women reentering the job market. Works at the local, state, and federal levels to create policies that provide equal opportunities and equal access to job training and education. See also Special Interests.

Women Empowering Women
P.O. Box 6506
Albany, CA 94706
(510) 525-7645

Provides construction skills training for women. Programs include summer building camps, weekend workshops, and training and support groups.

Women for Justice for Homecare Workers
310 W 43rd St.
New York, NY 10036
(212) 582-1890

An advocacy group working to improve the economic conditions of homecare workers.

Women in Community Service
1900 N Beauregard St., Ste. 14
Alexandria, VA 22311
(703) 671-0500;
Fax: (703) 671-4489

A large volunteer organization dedicated to helping people, both young and old, to find employment opportunities. Offers training, education, and counseling.

Women in the Building Trades
555 Amory St.
Jamaica Plains, MA 02130
(617) 524-3010;
Fax: (617) 524-3508

Assists women in entering the building trades and other blue-collar, nontraditional jobs.

Women in the Trades
550 Rice St.
St. Paul, MN 55103
(612) 228-9955;
Fax: (612) 292-9417

Helps women find and keep well-paying jobs in nontraditional employment. Offers a job hotline, employment referral service, information and guidance, a mentor program, support groups, and monthly social meetings.

Women Involved in Farm Economics

Box 191
Hingham, MT 59528

A nonprofit organization whose mission is to increase profits in agriculture by lobbying congress and sponsoring public education in schools. Also researches rural issues as they relate to women.

Women's Alliance for Job Equity

1422 Chestnut St., Ste. 1100
Philadelphia, PA 19102
(215) 561-1873;
Fax: (215) 561-7112

A nonprofit organization dedicated to improving economic and workplace conditions for women. Provides direct services, public education, peer support, and advocacy on behalf of women working in nonmanagement jobs.

Women's Bureau

U.S. Dept. of Labor
200 Constitution Ave. NW
Washington, DC 20210
(202) 523-6611

Advocates policies, develops programs, provides technical assistance, publications, information, and referral on women's employment issues. See also Rights of Women.

Women's Business Development Center

205 Gurley Hall
Russel Sage College
Troy, NY 12180
(518) 270-2302;
Fax: (518) 271-4545

Works to help women increase business skills and business ownership. Offers resources to help in businesses.

Women's Educational and Industrial Union

356 Boylston St.
Boston, MA 02116
(617) 536-5651;
Fax: (617) 247-8826

A nonprofit social service organization that promotes the social, educational, and industrial advancement of women. Assists women looking for a job or changing careers, elderly and disabled women, teen mothers, homeless women, and battered women with children. See also Special Interests.

Women's Family and Work Coalition

901 H St., Ste. 310
Sacramento, CA 95814
(916) 444-7486

A group of state, regional, and local organizations and individuals presenting a legislative package that addresses the economic concerns of low- and middle-income women and their families. See also Special Interests.

Working Opportunities for Women
2700 University Ave. W, #120
St. Paul, MN 55114
(612) 647-9961;
Fax: (612) 647-1424

A nonprofit agency offering ser-vices to women entering the job market, considering a career change, or seeking advancement within their present career. Prepares women to secure better-paying employment and overcome barriers to rewarding work.

MILITARY SERVICES

Minerva Center, Incorporated
20 Granada Rd.
Pasadena, MD 21122-2708
(410) 437-5379;
Fax: (410) 437-5379

A nonprofit educational foundation that provides information and support on subjects relating to women and the military. Publishes a journal, an international news magazine, and a science fiction novel.

Pallas Athena
Network for Women Veterans
P.O. Box 1171
New Market, VA 22844
(703) 349-2593

Provides women veterans with opportunities to socialize and network without regard to their geographic location.

Vietnam Women's Memorial Project
2001 S St. NW, #710
Washington, DC 20009
(202) 328-7253;
Fax: (202) 986-3636

Placed the first memorial honoring women's military service in Washington, DC. Offers education on women's role in the Vietnam War. Networks women veterans.

Women in Military Service Memorial Foundation
5510 Columbia Pike, Ste. 302
Arlington, VA 22204
(800) 222-2294

A nonprofit organization involved in raising funds to erect a memorial in Arlington cemetery honoring all women who have served in the military.

Index

What Is the Women's Information Exchange?

1280 Newsletters	We connect individuals with the women's and progressive organizations that serve their interests. We don't send out information directly, we use computer database technology to create the National Women's Mailing List, specialized mailing lists which allow individuals and groups to network with each other.
225 Bookstores	
670 Women's Centers	
480 Women's Studies	

Groups Mail To Individuals

180 Publishers

You register YOUR interests with us. Later, when a women's group wants to do a mailing we supply a mailing list of individuals who are interested in the group's work.

850 Health Groups

500 Art & Media

You hear from a group only once—they are not allowed to put you on their mailing list—and you'll only hear from them if it's the type of mail you've selected on your registration form.

645 Professional

760 Activist Groups

For example, you may only want to hear about women's books, or workshops. Perhaps you only want to receive political action alerts in specific areas. Or do you only want sports mail?

445 Work & Career

575 Women of Color

285 Sports Groups

Mailing To Groups

580 Lesbian Groups

This book represents a sampling of our list of over 10,000 women's organizations. You may request mailing labels of women's organizations tailored to your needs—special types of groups, specific states or regions, or exactly what is in this book.

1425 Anti-Violence

480 Spiritual Groups

260 Legal Groups

To Find Out More ...

Conferences

Send a self-addressed stamped envelope to the address listed below. Write **REGISTRATION FORM** on the front if you want to sign up to receive mail, and **ORDER FORM** if you're planning on doing a mailing. If you're an organization that wants to be included in our resource lists or in the next edition of this book, send us a short description of your services.

Festivals

Workshops

Cruises

ON LABELS, IN ZIP CODE ORDER, READY FOR MAILING

Women's Information Exchange
PO Box 68   (707) 632-5763
Jenner, CA 95450   FAX: (707) 632-5589